Ready®
Florida LAFS

4 | **English Language Arts** INSTRUCTION

D1367066

Ashton

Vice President of Product Development: Adam Berkin
Editorial Director: Katherine Rossetti
Executive Editor: William Kelleher
Project Manager: Audra Bailey
Editors: Melissa Brown, Anne Cullen, John Ham, Rob Hill, Susan James
Cover Design: Matt Pollock
Cover Illustrator: O'Lamar Gibson
Design/Production: William Gillis, Mark Nodland, Lisa Rawlinson, Jennifer Sorenson, Jeremy Spiegel

ISBN 978-1-4957-0559-5

BTS19

Table of Contents continued

*Standards in **boldface** are the focus standards that address major lesson content.*

*Standards in **boldface** are the focus standards that address major lesson content.*

Table of Contents

*Standards in **boldface** are the focus standards that address major lesson content.*

Acknowledgments

Elana Kopel, "Flying with a Tiger," Copyright © 2011 by Highlights for Children, Inc., Columbus, OH.

"Fulton's Success" by Lois Miner Huey, *Cobblestone*, July/August 2009. All Cricket Media material is copyrighted by Carus Publishing Company, d/b/a Cricket Media, and/or various authors and illustrators. Any commercial use or distribution of material without permission is strictly prohibited.

Steven Dowshen, MD, "Minerals" adapted from *Kids' Health Online*. Copyright © 1995-2012 by The Nemours Foundation/KidsHealth®. Reprinted with permission.

"It All Began with *Spacewar!*" by Peter Roop, *Cobblestone*, June 1984. All Cricket Media material is copyrighted by Carus Publishing Company, d/b/a Cricket Media, and/or various authors and illustrators. Any commercial use or distribution of material without permission is strictly prohibited.

"Why Salt? Valuable Little Cubes" by Leigh Anderson and David Chandler, *Appleseeds*, March 2007. All Cricket Media material is copyrighted by Carus Publishing Company, d/b/a Cricket Media, and/or various authors and illustrators. Any commercial use or distribution of material without permission is strictly prohibited.

"And Away We Go: Rockets" from Kids Discover, March 2012, Vol. 22, Issue 3. Copyright © 2012 Kids Discover. Used by permission. All rights reserved.

E. Nesbit after William Shakespeare, "King Lear" from *Beautiful Stories from Shakespeare*, published by D. E. Cunningham & Co. (1907).

Maude L. Radford, "Sir Irvaine" from *King Arthur and His Knights*, published by Rand McNally & Company (1903).

Rachel Field, "Roads" from *Favorite Poems, Old and New: Selected Poems for Boys and Girls*.

Sam Walter Foss, "The House by the Side of the Road" from *Dreams in Homespun*, published by Lee & Shepard (1897).

"The Path That Leads to Home" from *A Heap o' Livin'* by Edgar A. Guest, Chicago: Reilly & Britton Co., 1916.

"The Blind Men and the Elephant" from CHILDREN'S CLASSICS IN DRAMATIC FORM, BOOK 2 by Augusta Stevenson, published by Houghton Mifflin (1909).

"The Two Frogs" from *The Violet Fairy Book*, edited by Andrew Lang, published by Longmans, Green & Company (1901).

From *The Moffats* by Eleanor Estes. Copyright 1941 by Eleanor Estes. Copyright © renewed 1969 by Eleanor Estes. Reprinted by permission of Harcourt Children's Books, an imprint of Houghton Mifflin Harcourt Publishing Company.

Reprinted from *The History of Movie Making*. Copyright © 1995 by Gallimard Jeunesse, SA. Reprinted by permission of Scholastic, Inc.

Tenzing Norgay, excerpt from *Tiger of the Snows*.

Sinking of the Titanic and Great Sea Disasters, edited by Logan Marshall, published by L. T. Myers (1912).

From *To Space and Back* by Sally Ride with Susan Okie. Copyright © 1986 by Sally Ride and Susan Okie. Used by permission of HarperCollins Publishers.

"Ferris's Grand Idea" by Marcia Amidon Lusted, *Cobblestone*, February 2009. All Cricket Media material is copyrighted by Carus Publishing Company, d/b/a Cricket Media, and/or various authors and illustrators. Any commercial use or distribution of material without permission is strictly prohibited.

Denton J. Snider, "The Ferris Wheel" from *World's Fair Studies*, published by Sigma Publishing Company (1893).

Oliver Herford, "The Catfish" from *The Book of Humorous Verse*, compiled by Carolyn Wells, published by George H. Doran Company (1920).

W. M. Thackeray, "A Tragic Story" from *The Book of Humorous Verse*, compiled by Carolyn Wells, published by George H. Doran Company (1920).

"How Doth the Little Crocodile" from *Alice's Adventures in Wonderland* by Lewis Carroll, Boston: Lothrop Publishing Company, 1898.

"The Endless Tale" from CHILDREN'S CLASSICS IN DRAMATIC FORM, BOOK 2 by Augusta Stevenson, published by Houghton Mifflin (1909).

"The Sound of Money" retold by D.L. Ashliman from http://www.pitt.edu/~dash/hodja.html#foodsmell. Used by permission.

Edward Richard Shaw, "Henry Hudson" from *Explorers and Discoverers*, published by American Book Publishers (1900).

John Bach McMaster, "The Coming of the Dutch" from *A Brief History of the United States*, published by American Book Company (1907).

"Air Works for Me" from *The Courage to Soar* by National Aeronautics and Space Administration, Marshall Space Flight Center Exploration Systems Mission Directorate: Ares Projects. Courtesy of NASA.

Count Lev. N. Tolstoy, "The Peasant and the Cucumbers" from *Fables for Children*, trans. and ed. by Leo Wiener, published by J. M. Dent and Company (1904).

"The Two-Headed Weaver" retold by D.L. Ashliman from http://www.pitt.edu/~dash/hodja.html#foodsmell. Used by permission.

Charles Perrault, "The Ridiculous Wishes" from *Old-Time Stories Told by Master* Charles Perrault, translated by A. E. Johnson, published by Dodd Mead and Company (1921).

F. Anton Schiefner, "The Monkeys and the Moon" from *Tibetan Tales Derived from Indian Sources*, translated by W. R. S. Ralston, published by Kegan Paul, Trench, Trubner, and Company (1906).

Mary Hoffman, "The King's Fire Dog" from *Sun, Moon, and Stars*. Copyright © 1998 by Mary Hoffman. Reproduced with permission of the author c/o Rogers, Coleridge & White Ltd., 20 Powis Mews, London W11 1JN.

"How Maui Snared the Sun" from *Hawaiian Folk Tales: A Collection of Native Legends*, compiled by Thos. G. Thrum, published A.C. McClurg & Company (1907).

Common Core State Standards © Copyright 2010. National Governors Association Center for Best Practices and Council of Chief State School Officers. All rights reserved.

Language Arts Florida Standards (LAFS) © 2014. Florida Department of Education.

Language Handbook

Conventions of Standard English

Lesson

Knowledge of Language

Lesson

Vocabulary Acquisition and Use

Lesson

UNIT 1
Key Ideas and Details in Informational Text

How are readers like detectives? For starters, both readers and detectives are curious. Just as a detective asks questions and hunts for clues, a good reader looks for **key ideas** and **details** in a text.

Being detective-like is important when reading history, science, technical and other informational texts. Sometimes, the answers to questions about key ideas and details will be as clear as footprints in the sand. They can lead a detective right to a solution. Other times, you'll need to read between the lines (or footprints!) to find an answer not directly stated in the text.

In this unit, you'll learn to recognize how one event leads to another and how one thing can cause another to happen. You'll also practice putting together what you read with what you know to come up with new ideas. With these reading skills, you'll be on your way to solving the mystery of the main idea: what a text is all about. So read like a detective. Pick up your magnifying glass—or, rather, your book—and start reading!

✓ Self Check

Before starting this unit, check off the skills you know below. As you complete each lesson, see how many more skills you can check off!

I can:	Before this unit	After this unit
find the main idea of an informational text.	☐	☐
explain how key details support the main idea of an informational text.	☐	☐
explain what happened and why based on information presented in historical, technical, and scientific texts.	☐	☐
summarize an informational text.	☐	☐
refer to details and examples when explaining and inferring what a text says.	☐	☐

page 19

page 32

page 61

page 48

page 68

page 74

page 89

page 90

👥 **Introduction**

LAFS.4.RI.1.2 Determine the main idea of a text and explain how it is supported by key details. . . .

Lesson 1
Finding Main Ideas and Details

Learning Target

Identifying the biggest, most important idea about a topic and the details that tell more about that idea will help you understand an informational text.

▶ **Read** As you read an informational text, figure out the point, or what the author wants you to understand about the topic. The **main idea**—the most important idea—is what the text mostly tells about a topic. **Key details** support the main idea by giving important facts, examples, and other information that explain more about it.

In an informational text, an author often states the main idea early in a paragraph or passage. Key details that say more about the main idea usually follow right after it.

Read the passage below. Underline the main idea. What key details support the main idea?

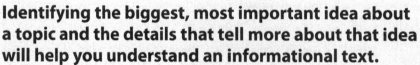

Lewis and Clark's Faithful Companion

When Lewis and Clark explored the western United States, a dog named Seaman protected them. One night, a large buffalo came near their tent. Seaman chased the buffalo away. Another night, a grizzly bear entered their camp. Seaman barked and barked at the bear. He barked until the bear ran away. Seaman also protected Lewis and Clark by making sure they had food. Every day, Seaman hunted squirrels for the men to eat.

▶ **Think** Use what you've learned about reading informational texts to identify two key details that support the main idea of the passage. Complete the chart by adding two more key details.

Main Idea

Lewis and Clark's dog, Seaman, protected the explorers.

Key Detail	**Key Detail**	**Key Detail**
Seaman chased away a buffalo.		

▶ **Talk** Share the key details you added with a partner.

- Did you and your partner agree?
- How do the key details support the main idea?

> **Academic Talk**
> Use these words to talk about the text.
> - **main idea**
> - **key detail**

▶ **Read**

The Snake

AND THE CHARMER

BY SYLVESTER CAPELLO

1   You have probably viewed the following scene in a movie or on TV: A snake charmer sits in front of a straw basket and plays a flute-like instrument. Suddenly, from inside the basket, a long, hooded cobra rises up. As the snake charmer plays the music, the cobra sways back and forth. It does not try to attack the snake charmer. Instead, the snake appears to be swaying in rhythm to the music.

2   In reality, nothing could be further from the truth. The cobra is quite deaf. It has no ears and can only sense vibrations in the ground. What the cobra sways to is not the music. It sways to the motion of the flute that the snake charmer moves back and forth as he plays. The cobra is trying to get into position to strike at the flute. However, as long as the snake charmer keeps the flute in motion, the snake cannot attack.

3   The Indian cobra is a favorite of snake charmers because daylight interferes with the snake's ability to strike. At night, however, the Indian cobra is extremely dangerous and more accurate. Cobras don't normally attack people, however. Instead, they go after frogs, fish, birds, and small mammals.

> **Close Reader Habits**
>
> Think about the main idea of the passage, or what it mostly tells about. Then **underline** key details that support the main idea.

Explore

What is the main idea of the science article, and how is it supported by key details about the cobra?

▶ **Think**

> Look for key details that give you information about the cobra's actions.

1 Complete the chart below with information that shows that the cobra is not really "charmed" by the snake charmer.

Main Idea

↓ ↓ ↓

Key Detail	**Key Detail**	**Key Detail**
		The cobra sways to the motion of the flute as the snake charmer moves back and forth.

▶ **Talk**

2 Discuss how snake charmers use their knowledge of cobras to "charm" the snakes. Then make a list of important details about the trick.

 ▶ **Write**

3 **Short Response** Explain how the key details about cobras help you understand the snake charmer's trick. Include details from your chart and your discussion in your answer. Use the space provided on page 16 to write your response.

> **HINT** Think about how to tell details about the cobra in an order that makes sense.

Lending an Ear))

by Michael Simon

1   Mitzi, a Labrador retriever, is always by her owner Leah's side. This isn't just because Mitzi and Leah like each other. Mitzi is Leah's hearing dog. Leah is mostly deaf, and Mitzi's job is to alert Leah to sounds she cannot hear. Mitzi is happy as a constant, helpful companion for Leah.

2   Hearing dogs listen for sounds that people with hearing loss cannot hear. These dogs alert their owners to sounds by touching them with their nose or paw. After giving the alert, hearing dogs lead their owners to the source of the sound. For example, hearing dogs can be trained to recognize many household sounds. These sounds include doorbells, telephones, oven timers, alarm clocks, and fire and smoke alarms. Hearing dogs keep their deaf or partly deaf partners both active and safe by alerting them to such important noises.

3   Hearing dogs don't just help around the home. They also help their partners live and thrive in the world outside. People who can't hear sometimes feel lonely and isolated from other people. Hearing dogs can help their partners feel comfortable in public by making them aware of sounds. A hearing dog must wear an orange coat when in public. This tells other people that the dog's owner has some degree of hearing loss. Those other people can then adjust their own behavior when it is necessary.

4   Living and working side-by-side every day, hearing dogs and their partners become a special team—just like Mitzi and Leah.

Close Reader Habits

How do hearing dogs help their owners? Reread the article. **Underline** the key details that explain what hearing dogs do.

▶ **Think** Use what you learned from reading the magazine article to answer the following questions.

1 This question has two parts. Answer Part A. Then answer Part B.

Part A

Which statement below **best** describes the main idea in paragraph 2?

   A Hearing dogs are trained to recognize the sounds of telephones and smoke alarms.

   B Hearing dogs alert their owners to sounds the owners cannot hear themselves.

   C Hearing dogs wear orange vests in public to tell people their owners have a hearing loss.

   D Hearing dogs are happy, constant companions.

Part B

Which **two** key details **best** support your answer to Part A?

   A Hearing dogs recognize many household sounds.

   B Hearing dogs touch their owners with a paw or their noses to alert them to sounds.

   C Hearing dogs help their owners feel comfortable in public.

   D Hearing dogs lead their owners to the source of a sound.

   E Hearing dogs are always at their owners' sides.

   F Hearing dogs' orange vests make them stand out to others.

> Each paragraph may give a main idea about the topic. Together, these ideas help develop the main idea of the passage.

▶ **Talk**

2 Explain how hearing dogs help their owners at home and outside the home. Use the chart on page 17 to organize your thoughts.

▶ **Write**

3 **Short Response** Use the information in your chart to explain how hearing dogs help their owners. Tell why people and their dogs are a special team. Use at least **two** details from the passage in your answer. Use the space provided on page 17 to write your response.

> **HINT** Think about how the dog's behavior helps its partner at home and in the world.

Write Use the space below to write your answer to the question on page 13.

The Snake
AND THE CHARMER

3 **Short Response** Explain how the key details about cobras help you understand the snake charmer's trick. Include details from your chart and your discussion in your answer.

> **HINT** Think about how to tell details about the cobra in an order that makes sense.

_____

_____

_____

_____

_____

_____

_____

Check Your Writing

Don't forget to check your writing.

☐ Did you read the prompt carefully?

☐ Did you put the prompt in your own words?

☐ Did you use the best evidence from the text to support your ideas?

☐ Are your ideas clearly organized?

☐ Did you write in clear and complete sentences?

☐ Did you check your spelling and punctuation?

Lending an Ear

2 **Use the chart below to organize your ideas.**

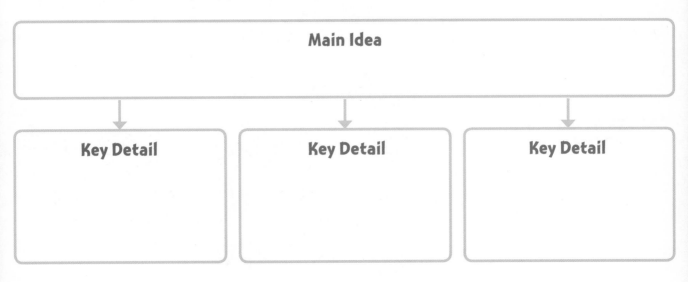

Write **Use the space below to write your answer to the question on page 15.**

3 **Short Response** Use the information in your chart to explain how hearing dogs help their owners. Tell why people and their dogs are a special team. Include at least two details from the passage in your answer.

> **HINT** Think about how the dog's behavior helps its partner at home and in the world.

_____

_____

_____

_____

_____

_____

_____

Flying with a Tiger

by Elana Kopel, *Highlights*

1   I am a zookeeper at the Dallas Zoo in Texas. One of my jobs is to care for Sumatran tigers.

2   These tigers live in the wild on the island of Sumatra and in some other parts of Asia. They are endangered, and their numbers are declining. But zoos around the world keep a few of the big cats to teach people about tigers and to let the tigers have cubs.

3   When a zoo wants a new tiger, it tries to get one from another zoo. That way, more tigers can stay in the wild. Some animals travel from zoo to zoo by truck, and some go by airplane. When we moved one of our tigers, a female named Skylar, to the San Francisco Zoo in California, she went by plane. I went along to help keep her safe.

Skylar in the Sky

4   Skylar spent the first two years of her life wrestling with her sister and stalking and pouncing on her brother. This is how tigers learn to hunt. By the age of three, Skylar was old enough to leave her siblings and start her own family. That's what she would have done in the wild.

5   Before Skylar could take to the skies, we needed to prepare her for the journey. We trained her to go into a shipping crate and let us close the door behind her. When she cooperated, we gave her an uncooked meatball, her favorite treat. . . .

Meatballs Galore

6   When moving day arrived, we put lots of meatballs inside Skylar's crate. Once Skylar was inside, the crate was loaded into the back of a truck. Skylar turned around in the crate to see what was happening, but she was quiet and calm the whole way to the airport.

7   Skylar and I flew on an airplane that carries packages, not people. Skylar's crate was loaded on with other large packages. . . . The plane left at midnight, and we stopped in Indiana to change aircraft. While we waited at the Indiana airport, I peeked into Skylar's crate. I was happy to see her sleeping peacefully.

8   Our second plane landed in San Francisco at eight o'clock in the morning. A zookeeper from the San Francisco Zoo met us and took us to Skylar's new home. . . . I knew Skylar was nervous. She did not come out of the crate as quickly as she had gone in. She growled at her new zookeepers. We left her alone to calm down.

9   Skylar's new keepers took me to see the tiger exhibit where Skylar would be living. I told them that Skylar liked to take a dip in her swimming pool and to play with plastic barrels, giant plastic balls, empty plastic flowerpots, perfume-scented logs, and ice. . . . By the next day, Skylar had calmed down a little.

10   After my last visit with Skylar, I returned to Dallas on a regular airplane. I knew I would miss Skylar, but I hoped that she would like her new zoo and teach the people of San Francisco about the wildlife of Asia. I hoped she would start a new family, too.

More Tigers in the World

11   Months later, Skylar gave birth to three male cubs. She is a good mom, and she has brought more Sumatran tigers into the world. Maybe one day her cubs will be dads and there will be even more of these beautiful creatures.

▶ **Think** Use what you have learned from reading the science article to respond to the following questions.

1 Read the following sentence from the passage.

Before Skylar could take to the skies, we needed to <u>prepare</u> her for the journey.

Which dictionary entry **best** defines <u>prepare</u>?

A get ready

B make a meal

C deal with

D turn down

2 The main idea of paragraphs 2 and 3 is that zoos help protect wildlife and teach people about wild animals such as Sumatran tigers. Draw Xs next to the **two** key details in the chart that **best** support the main idea of those paragraphs.

Detail from the Article	Supports the Main Idea
"Some animals travel from zoo to zoo by truck, and some go by airplane."	
"When a zoo wants a new tiger, it tries to get one from another zoo. That way, more tigers can stay in the wild."	
"These tigers live in the wild on the island of Sumatra and in some other parts of Asia. They are endangered, ..."	
"But zoos around the world keep a few of the big cats to teach people about the tigers. . . . ."	

3 This question has two parts. First, answer Part A. Then answer Part B.

Part A

Which sentence **best** explains the main idea of the passage?

A Zoos often help increase the number of wild animals by raising and setting free animals that were born in a zoo.

B Transporting animals from zoo to zoo must be done carefully so that the animals are kept healthy and safe.

C The number of Sumatran tigers has been declining quickly.

D Skylar's keeper hopes that Skylar will start a new family.

Part B

Pick the **three** details from the passage that **best** support your answer in Part A.

A "They are endangered, and their numbers are declining."

B "When we moved one of our tigers, a female named Skylar, to the San Francisco Zoo in California. . . . I went along to help keep her safe."

C "By the age of three, Skylar was old enough to leave her siblings and start her own family."

D "We trained her to go into a shipping crate and let us close the door behind her."

E "While we waited at the Indiana airport, I peeked into Skylar's crate. I was happy to see her sleeping peacefully."

F "She growled at her new zookeepers. We left her alone to calm down."

G "I knew I would miss Skylar, but I hoped that she would like her new zoo and teach the people of San Francisco about the wildlife of Asia."

4 Which sentence **best** explains why Skylar's keeper gave her raw meatballs?

A Skylar liked to eat human food more than food meant for tigers.

B Skylar's keeper wanted to travel with Skylar to San Francisco.

C It is the only food Skylar would eat when she was traveling.

D Skylar's keeper wanted to reward her for going in the crate.

Write

5 **Short Response** The author states in paragraph 3, "When a zoo wants a new tiger, it tries to get one from another zoo." Reread paragraphs 2 and 3. Then explain how this statement supports the main idea of the text. Use details from the text in your answer.

_____

_____

_____

_____

_____

_____

_____

 Learning Target

You've learned how to identify the main idea and key details about a topic. Explain how this can help you develop a deeper understanding of informational text.

_____

_____

_____

_____

👥 **Introduction**

LAFS.4.RI.1.3 Explain events [and] ideas . . . in a historical . . . text, including what happened and why, based on specific information in the text.

Lesson 2
Understanding Historical Texts

Learning Target

Explaining information in historical texts, including what happened and why, can help you understand the connections among various events and ideas in the text.

▶ **Read** Writers of **historical texts** often organize **information** to answer the questions "What happened?" and "Why did it happen?" This is sometimes called **cause and effect**. Cause and effect is a relationship in which one thing brings about, or causes, something else to occur. Historical texts don't just describe several events or ideas. The texts also explain why they happened and why they matter.

Look at the illustrations below. One shows an event that happened. The other shows why it happened. Think about which event is which.

▶ **Think**   Consider what you've learned about causes and effects and why writers use them to organize their writing. Remember, understanding what happened and why helps you understand what happens around you every day.

In the chart below, describe what happened in the first illustration. Then explain why the event happened.

What Happened?		Why?
The boy had a flat tire.	→	The boy ran over a nail.

▶ **Talk**   Share your chart with a partner.

- Based on the events in the illustrations, what do you think the boy will do next?

- Explain why the boy will do that next.

◎ **Academic Talk**
Use these words and phrases to talk about the text.
- **cause and effect**   - **information**   - **historical text**

The Model T

 by **Thomas A. Moore**

1   When the first cars were produced, only wealthy people could afford them. Henry Ford wanted to build a car that the average working person could afford. In 1908, the Ford Motor Company introduced a new, low-cost car. It was called the Model T and sold for $825. Although the car was reasonably priced, Ford kept thinking of ways to make it even cheaper. He knew that the lower the price, the more customers he would gain and the more money he would make.

2   Ford's early cars were all handcrafted. This meant that each automobile was slightly different from the next. It also meant that each took a long time to make. Ford decided his cars would no longer be handcrafted. They would be put together in exactly the same way, saving time and money. In 1913, Ford began producing cars with the help of a moving assembly line.

3   The moving assembly line achieved Ford's goal of turning out a car faster and for increasingly lower prices. In time, Ford's factory was turning out one automobile every 90 minutes. By 1915, the Ford Motor Company was earning record profits. And by 1918, half of all cars in the United States were Model Ts. Almost overnight, the United States became a nation on wheels.

Close Reader Habits

Underline words and phrases that help you figure out why more people began owning cars.

How did the production of Henry Ford's Model T lead to more people owning cars?

▶ **Think**

Look for details that answer the questions "What happened?" and "Why?"

1 What did the Ford Motor Company do in 1908 and 1913? Why did these events occur? Write the details in the chart.

What Happened?		**Why?**
1908 ford motor company introduced a new, low-cost car for $825.	→	So they can get more money and consumers.
1913 ford began producing cars with the help of a moving assembly line	→	

▶ **Talk**

2 In 1913, Henry Ford decided his cars would no longer be handcrafted. Discuss how this decision led to a new way of making cars. Write down an idea you talked about with your partner.

HINT One thing can cause another thing to happen.

 ▶ **Write**

3 **Short Response** Explain why half of all cars in the United States were Model T's by 1918. Include text details telling what happened and why. Use the space provided on page 30 to write your response.

The Bicycle's First Century

by J. Soo

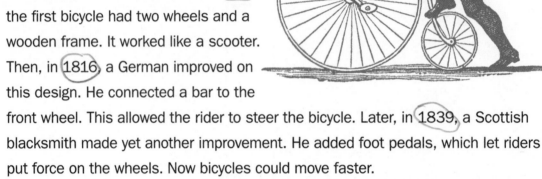

1   Two centuries ago, bicycles did not look like the bikes you know today. Invented by a Frenchman around 1790, the first bicycle had two wheels and a wooden frame. It worked like a scooter. Then, in 1816, a German improved on this design. He connected a bar to the front wheel. This allowed the rider to steer the bicycle. Later, in 1839, a Scottish blacksmith made yet another improvement. He added foot pedals, which let riders put force on the wheels. Now bicycles could move faster.

2   In the 1870s, the "high-wheel" bicycle appeared. It was called this because the front wheel was far larger than the rear wheel. The pedals turned the front wheel only, but the size of that wheel meant that each turn of the pedals took the rider a greater distance than before. On the high-wheel bicycle, the rider sat up high, over the front wheel. Consequently, when the large front wheel struck a rut or rock in the road, the rider could be pitched head-first over the front of the bicycle! The high-wheel bicycle wasn't very safe.

3   In 1885, an Englishman made the first "safety" bicycle. The bicycle was now beginning to look more like the modern one you see every day. Its front and rear wheels were the same size, and sprockets and chains linked the pedals and the rear wheel. In the 1890s, inventors added air-filled rubber tires. Then came a coaster brake and adjustable handlebars. The first hundred years of the bicycle—from 1790 to the 1890s—brought many changes, and the next century would bring even more improvements.

Close Reader Habits

How does each bicycle model improve upon the model before it? Reread the article. **Underline** details that tell *why* each model was an improvement.

▶ **Think** Use what you learned from reading the article to respond to the following questions.

> History texts often tell how one event caused several other events to occur. This is called a series of events.

1 Reread paragraph 1. Choose the **two** statements that **best** tell why the bicycle was a better machine by 1839.

    A A bar allowed the rider to steer.

    B A wooden frame meant that the bicycle was lighter.

    C Foot pedals meant that bicycles could move faster.

    D The first bicycles could move like a scooter.

    E The front wheel was larger than the rear wheel.

2 This question has two parts. Answer Part A. Then answer Part B.

Part A
What conclusion can you draw about what happened to many riders of the bicycles described in paragraph 2?

    A They would be able to see over other bicycle riders.

    B They were likely to get hurt if they hit a rock.

    C They could not go as fast using the larger wheels.

    D They found ways to link the large and small wheels together.

Part B
Which **two** sentences in paragraph 2 **best** support the answer to Part A? **Circle** them in the passage.

▶ **Talk**

3 Based on information in the text, what changes to bicycle designs came about in the 1800s? What can you conclude about why the designs kept changing?

▶ **Write**

4 **Short Response** Explain how the design of the bicycle was improved in the 1800s and why the changes were necessary. Use details from the text to support your answer. Use the space provided on page 31 to write your answer.

> **HINT** Be sure to use words that show why the changes were made, such as *because* and *since*.

▶ 📝 **Write** **Use the space below to write your answer to the question on page 27.**

The
Model **T**

3 **Short Response** Explain why half of all cars in the United States were Model T's by 1918. Include text details telling what happened and why.

half of all of the cars were model T's because,

Don't forget to check your writing.

Write Use the space below to write your answer to the question on page 29.

The Bicycle's First Century

4 **Short Response** Explain how the design of the bicycle was improved in the 1800s and why the changes were necessary. Use details from the text to support your answer.

HINT Be sure to use words that show why the changes were made, such as *because* and *since*.

_____

_____

_____

_____

_____

_____

_____

_____

Check Your Writing

☐ Did you read the prompt carefully?

☐ Can you put the prompt in your own words?

☐ Did you use the best evidence from the text to support your ideas?

☐ Are your ideas clearly organized?

☐ Did you write in clear and complete sentences?

☐ Did you check your spelling and punctuation?

Read

from
FULTON'S SUCCESS
by Lois Miner Huey, *Cobblestone*

Robert Fulton was the inventor of the steamboat.

1   "Fulton's Folly," people jeered as they passed Browne's Shipyard in New York City. It was 1807. Browne's was the site where inventor Robert Fulton and his partner, Robert R. Livingston, Jr., were building a very strange boat. The two men knew that putting a steam engine onboard a vessel was still new and dangerous. But they ignored the taunts. They were convinced that Fulton's steamboat ideas, combined with Livingston's financial backing, would revolutionize transportation in America. And they were right.

2   On August 17, after devoting about five months to its construction, Fulton launched a vessel that measured 150 feet long, 13 feet wide, and 9 feet deep.

3   Fulton and a group of invited guests prepared to steam up the Hudson River from New York City to Albany. Albany is the state capital. The guests had to put up with primitive conditions. There were no cabins, no beds, and a roaring, uncovered steam engine mounted in the center of the boat. There was also the fear of the engine's exploding!

4   They cast off at 1 P.M. The vessel puffed away from the dock and stalled. The passengers' whispering turned into loud mumbles, which eventually gave way to shouts of dismay. Sensing their fear, Fulton promised to return to the dock if he could not fix the problem.

5   After a short time, there was a huge blast of smoke. Once again, the boat churned upriver. It was described as looking like a giant teakettle. The vessel's engine let off steam and rained down sparks that sizzled in the water. The noise was deafening, but the boat was moving. The passengers cheered. The boat chugged upstream against the tide at a fast four to five miles per hour. It easily passed sailing ships and fishing craft.

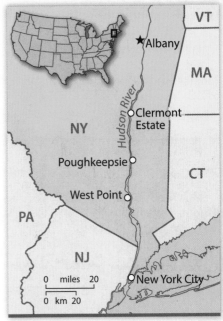

Fulton's route up the Hudson River from New York City to Albany

This steam yacht is similar to the first steamboat built by Robert Fulton in 1807.

A replica of Robert
Fulton's steamboat sails
the Hudson River in 1909.

6   In its wake, the boat's two side paddlewheels left waves of foamy water and lots of terrified onlookers. Nothing like it ever had been seen before. Darkness fell, but the boat continued its journey. With a full moon and warm breezes, the passengers stayed up all night singing songs by candlelight. They had mostly forgotten their fears.

7   The next day, the boat docked at Livingston's estate, called Clermont. After spending the night, it continued steaming to Albany the following morning. It pulled into that city at 5 P.M. on August 19. The boat had made the 150-mile trip in 32 hours of travel time. Crowds cheered its arrival. No longer a joke, "Fulton's Folly" had become the first successful steamboat in America.

▶ Think

Use what you learned from reading the history article to respond to the following questions.

1 Which sentence from the article tells why Fulton and Livingston kept working on their boat even though others thought they were being foolish?

A "The two men knew that putting a steam engine onboard a vessel was still new and dangerous."

B "They were convinced that Fulton's steamboat ideas . . . would revolutionize transportation in America."

C "Fulton and a group of invited guests prepared to steam up the Hudson River from New York City to Albany."

D "The boat had made the 150-mile trip in 32 hours of travel time."

2 This question has two parts. First, answer Part A. Then answer Part B.

Part A
Read the sentence from paragraph 3 of "Fulton's Success."

The guests had to put up with <u>primitive</u> conditions.

What does the word <u>primitive</u> mean as it is used in the sentence?

A original and unusual

B restful and cozy

C natural and ancient

D rough and uncomfortable

Part B
Which detail from the article **best** supports your answer to Part A?

A "The vessel puffed away from the dock and stalled."

B "Fulton launched a vessel.that measured 150 feet long, 13 feet wide, and 9 feet deep."

C ". . . no cabins, no beds, and a roaring, uncovered steam engine . . ."

D ". . . also the fear of the engine's exploding!"

3 This question has two parts. First, answer Part A. Then answer Part B.

Part A

Which statement **best** explains why some people who saw Fulton's boat steaming up the Hudson River were terrified?

    A They were excited about Fulton's strange new invention.

    B The new steamboat looked and sounded dangerous.

    C The people were upset that they were not allowed to ride on the steamboat.

    (D) The steamboat was oddly shaped and easily passed the other boats on the river.

Part B

Underline **three** sentences from paragraph 5 that **best** support your answer in Part A.

> After a short time, there was a huge blast of smoke. Once again, the boat churned upriver. It was described as looking like a giant teakettle. The vessel's engine let off steam and rained down sparks that sizzled in the water. The noise was deafening, but the boat was moving. The passengers cheered. The boat chugged upstream against the tide at a fast four to five miles per hour. It easily passed sailing ships and fishing craft.

 Write

What conclusion can be drawn about why the steamboat was known as "Fulton's Folly" and how it became "Fulton's Success"? Reread the text. **Underline** details that show the reasons the steamboat was a success.

4 **Plan Your Response** First, identify why the steamboat was originally called "Fulton's Folly." Then identify what turned it into a success. Use a chart to help organize your thoughts by explaining "What happened?" and "Why?"

5 **Write an Extended Response** Use evidence from the text and the information in your chart to describe why the steamboat was called "Fulton's Folly" and how it eventually became "Fulton's Success."

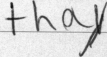

thay

_____
_____
_____
_____
_____
_____
_____
_____
_____
_____
_____
_____

 Learning Target

In this lesson, you learned different ways that historical texts may answer the questions "What happened?" and "Why?" Now explain how this understanding about causes and effects can help you as you read other historical texts.

_____
_____
_____

 **Introduction**

LAFS.4.RI.1.3 Explain . . . procedures, ideas, or concepts in a . . . technical text, including what happened and why, based on specific information in the text.

Lesson 3
Understanding Technical Texts

 **Learning Target**

Understanding the order of steps to take to complete a process will help you understand what is important in technical texts you read.

▶ **Read** When you read **technical texts**, you learn important information about **procedures**. A procedure is a **sequence** of steps followed in order. Some technical texts describe procedures, or steps, and tell you why to follow them. Other times you must figure out why the steps are given in a certain order. As you read a technical text, keep in mind not just *what* it tells you to do but also the reason *why*.

At some point, you've probably followed directions for putting together a toy or making food. If so, you were using a technical text, or a text that explains how to do a task.

Read the list below of the ingredients you need to make a recipe.

How to Make Smashamole

What You Need

- 2 avocados
- 8 cherry tomatoes
- 1 tablespoon onion powder
- 1 tablespoon lime juice
- 2 plastic zipper-seal bags
- 1 unopened can of food

Next, you must put everything together. What steps should you follow?

▶ **Think**   You've learned you need to follow steps in technical texts and figure out why. Below are the steps to make the Smashamole recipe, but they are out of order. First, read the steps and think about which step should be done first, second, and so on. Write that order in the column "Step Number." Then explain why you need to complete each step.

Steps for Making Smashamole

Step Number	What You Do	Why You Do It
Fourth	Roll the can over the bags until the food is mashed and mixed.	
	Put the first bag into the second bag. Zip the second bag closed.	Using a second bag keeps the food safe in case rolling the can on it breaks the first bag.
	When everything is smashed, open the bags. Put the Smashamole in a bowl. Use as a dip for chips.	
	Peel the avocados and remove the pits. Wash the cherry tomatoes.	
Second	Put the first four ingredients on the list into a bag. Zip the bag. Squeeze out the air.	

▶ **Talk**   Share your *Sequence Chart* with a partner. Did you list the steps in the same order? Did you agree on why you had to follow certain steps? Why must the steps in recipes follow a certain order?

 Academic Talk
Use these words to talk about the text.
- **technical text**   - **procedures**   - **sequence**

©Curriculum Associates, LLC   Copying is not permitted.   **Lesson 3** Understanding Technical Texts   **39**

> **Read**

Finding Your Pulse Rate

by
Maria Arroyo

1   Everyone has a pulse. As the heart pumps blood through our bodies, the pumping makes a rhythm you can measure. This rhythm is your pulse.

2   The **pulse rate** is a measure of the number of times the heart beats each minute. To find your pulse rate, follow these steps. First, place your index and middle fingers on the thumb side of your wrist, slightly below the base of your thumb joint. Then press gently until you feel the beat of your pulse.

3   After you find your pulse, use a watch to count the number of beats that occurs in 15 seconds. Then multiply this number by 4 to find the number of beats that occurs in one minute. Next, write the number on a piece of paper. The result is your pulse rate.

4   If you were not exercising just before taking your pulse, then this is your **resting pulse rate**. To find your **exercising pulse rate**, run in place for 60 seconds or do 10 jumping jacks. After that, check your pulse rate and record it on a piece of paper. Most likely, your resting and exercising rates will differ. What do you think causes this difference?

5   There are many reasons to find and check your pulse rate. Your pulse rate can tell a doctor how well your heart is working. It can also give important information about your overall health and fitness.

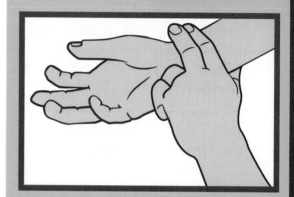

15 seconds

Close Reader Habits

As you read, **circle** words, such as *then* and *after*, that show the order of steps in finding a pulse rate.

Explore   How do the details about taking a pulse add to your understanding of why your pulse rate is important?

> Keep in mind what you must do for each step, and think about why you are doing it.

▶ Think

1 Complete the Sequence Chart below by writing the first two steps you must follow to find your pulse rate. Then explain why you need to complete the steps in this order.

Step Number	What You Do	Why You Do It
1		
2		

▶ Talk

2 Take turns finding your resting and exercising pulse rates. Then discuss what a pulse rate is and why the two rates are different.

▶ Write

3 **Short Response** Explain why it's important to know how to find and check your pulse rate. Use the space provided on page 44 to write your response.

> **HINT** Before you begin, **underline** two reasons in the text for checking your pulse rate.

▶ **Read**

Making a
Rhino Bank
by Matt Kincaid

1   Lots of people have piggy banks. Here's how to make something different—a rhino bank. You will need:

- a round balloon
- newspaper torn into strips
- a large bowl of papier-mâché (PAY per meh SHAY) paste
- cardboard tubes from paper towels or toilet paper
- masking tape

2   **Part 1:** Blow up the balloon and tie a knot. Cut the cardboard tube into four short lengths and tape them to the balloon as "legs." Roll some newspaper into the shape of a cone and tape it to the front of the balloon, as a horn. Make sure the form looks like a rhino (not a pig). This is, after all, a rhino bank.

3   **Part 2:** Dip one strip of newspaper into the papier-mâché paste. Use your fingers to squeeze extra paste back into the bowl. Then stick the pasted strip over the balloon and smooth it down. Continue dipping and placing strips, one at a time, until you have completely covered your creation. Do not use any more paste than is necessary. If there is too much paste, the strips will not lie flat and might not stick to each other.

4   **Part 3:** After 24 hours, the paste will be dry and the shape will harden. Have an adult cut a coin slot in the top with a knife. The balloon will pop. You can paint and decorate your rhino bank if you want. A rhino bank is much better than a piggy bank!

Close Reader Habits

Why must you follow the steps in each part? Reread the text. **Underline** the details that tell *why* you must follow a step.

▶ **Think** Use what you learned from reading the technical text to respond to the following questions.

1 This question has two parts. Answer Part A. Then answer Part B.

> Read through all the directions to understand what you're making or doing. Then reread step by step and picture what to do at each step.

Part A
Which statement **best** explains why you need to use a balloon?

   A The balloon holds the rhino shape while the pasted pieces dry.

   B The pasted newspaper will only stick to a balloon.

   C The balloon makes the bank look like a rhino and not like a pig.

   D The balloon will keep the newspaper strips from getting too much paste on them.

Part B
Underline **one** sentence from Part 3 that **best** supports your answer to Part A.

> **Part 3:** After 24 hours, the paste will be dry and the shape will harden. Have an adult cut a coin slot in the top with a knife. The balloon will pop. You can paint and decorate your rhino bank if you want. A rhino bank is much better than a piggy bank!

▶ **Talk**

2 Explain why you need newspaper and papier-mâché and what you must do with them. Use the Sequence Chart on page 45 to organize your thoughts. Discuss why the steps in Part 2 are important to the whole process of making the rhino bank.

▶ **Write**

3 **Short Response** Use the information in your Sequence Chart to explain the purpose of Part 2. Why is Part 2 important to the procedure? Use at least **two** details from the passage to support your response. Use the space provided on page 45 to write your response.

> **HINT** Think about what the bank will look like at the end of Part 1.

Write Use the space below to write your answer to the question on page 41.

Finding Your Pulse Rate

> **HINT** Before your begin, **underline** two reasons in the text for checking your pulse rate.

3 **Short Response** Explain why it's important to know how to find and check your pulse rate.

_____

_____

_____

_____

_____

_____

_____

_____

> Don't forget to check your writing.

Check Your Writing

☐ Did you read the prompt carefully?

☐ Did you put the prompt in your own words?

☐ Did you use the best evidence from the text to support your ideas?

☐ Are your ideas clearly organized?

☐ Did you write in clear and complete sentences?

☐ Did you check your spelling and punctuation?

Making a Rhino Bank

2 **Use the Sequence Chart below to organize your ideas.**

Steps for Making a Rhino Bank

Step Number	What You Do	Why You Do It

Write **Use the space below to write your answer to the question on page 43.**

3 **Short Response** Use the information in your Sequence Chart to explain the purpose of Part 2. Why is Part 2 important to the procedure? Use at least **two** details from the passage to support your response.

> **HINT** Think about what the bank will look like at the end of Part 1.

_____

_____

_____

_____

_____

_____

_____

▶ **Read**

Floating 💧 or Sinking LIQUIDS

WORDS TO KNOW
As you read, look inside, around, and beyond these words to figure out what they mean.

- **dissolved**
- **particle**

1   Many liquids mix easily with water. But some float on top of it. Others sink below it. That's because each liquid is different in many ways.

2   One difference is that each liquid has its own density. The more dense or "heavy" a liquid is, the more easily things will float on it. To find out about the density of liquids, you can make a tool called a hydrometer. Then use it to perform a fun experiment.

MAKE THREE HYDROMETERS

You will need:

- 1 plastic drinking straw with stripes
- scissors
- 1 small lump of clay, divided into 3 equal pieces
- 3 clear glasses or plastic cups of the same size
- ½ cup tap water
- ½ cup vegetable oil
- ½ cup maple syrup

1 Cut the drinking straw into three equal pieces.

2 Form 3 small clay balls. Make them larger than the hole in the straw. Be sure the balls are equal in size.

3 Insert one end of each straw into a ball of clay. Be sure to center the straws and push them into the clay to the same depth. The three hydrometers should look the same.

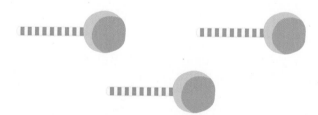

TESTING FOR DENSITY

4 Label each cup. Write "Water," "Oil," or "Syrup" on the container.

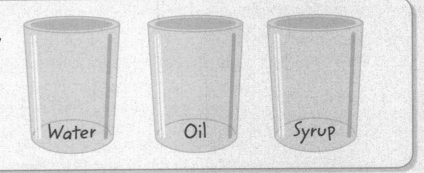

5 Fill each container with one liquid. Be sure the containers have equal amounts of the water, oil, and syrup.

6 Carefully place a hydrometer into each liquid so it stands as straight up and down as possible. Also make sure no liquid gets into the straw.

7 Observe what happens to each hydrometer. Compare the different levels at which the hydrometers float. You will see that the hydrometer in the oil sinks the lowest. The hydrometer in the syrup floats the highest.

Time to Think

Add 2 tablespoons of salt to the container of water. Stir until most of the salt is dissolved. You've packed more particles into the water, so now it's denser. What effect will this change have on the hydrometer?

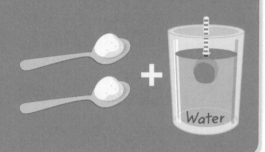

HOW DENSITY WORKS

3   Your hydrometers float at different levels because the water, oil, and syrup have different densities. The density of each liquid is determined by (1) the size and weight of its particles and (2) how closely its particles are packed together. The heavier and more closely packed the particles are, the more dense the liquid.

4   When a hydrometer is placed in a dense liquid, the packed, heavy particles will "push" harder on the hydrometer. As a result, the hydrometer floats higher than it would in a less dense liquid.

5   Weight plays a key part in density. For example, imagine one container filled with foam balls and one filled with metal balls of the same size. Both containers are packed with the same number and size of "particles." But the one with metal balls would be much heavier, or more dense. Lift each container to see which one is heaviest. It will also have the densest materials.

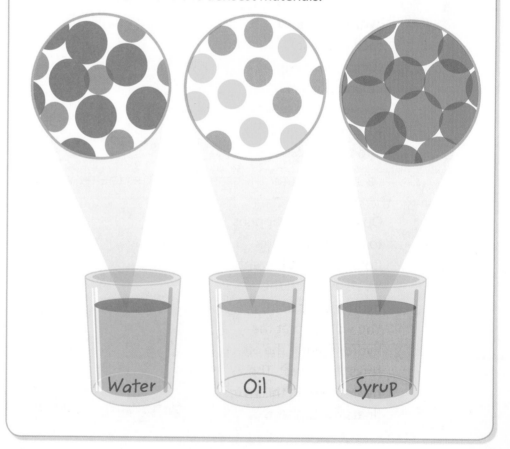

▶ **Think** Use what you learned from the experiment to respond to the following questions.

1 What is the meaning of the word <u>perform</u> as it is used in paragraph 2?

    A   to do or carry out

    B   to entertain an audience

    C   to participate in a tradition

    D   to use a special skill

2 This question has two parts. First, answer Part A. Then answer Part B.

Part A

How do the clay balls keep liquid from getting into the straw during Step 6?

    A   They cause the straws to sink.

    B   They help the straw stand up straight.

    C   They cover the hole at the bottom of the straw.

    D   They make the liquid denser.

Part B

What evidence from the text **best** supports the answer to Part A?

    A   "Form 3 small clay balls."

    B   "Make them larger than the hole in the straw."

    C   "Be sure the balls are equal in size."

    D   "Be sure to center the straws and push them into the clay to the same depth."

3 Why is it important to make all the hydrometers the same?

    A   to keep them from sinking too low

    B   to get results that are accurate

    C   to show how different liquids move the clay balls

    D   to make it easier to handle the hydrometers

4 What do the actions of the hydrometers in Step 7 help you understand about the density of the three liquids?

    A Syrup is the densest liquid.

    B Each liquid has the same density.

    C Oil is denser than water or syrup.

    D Water is the liquid that is least dense.

5 The box below contains details from the experiment.

What the Hydrometer Does	Reason
• Sinks less than one but more than the other • Sinks the least • Sinks the most	• It has loosely packed particles. • It has tightly packed particles. • Its particles are packed tighter than one liquid but not as tight as the other.

Use details from the box above to fill in the "What the Hydrometer Does" and "Reason" columns in the table below.

	What the Hydrometer Does	Reason
Oil		
Water		
Syrup		

Write

6 **Short Response** Explain why the hydrometers float at different levels on the water, oil, and syrup. Use details from the text to support your response.

_____

_____

_____

_____

_____

_____

_____

 Learning Target

In this lesson, you learned about the importance of steps and why you should follow them in order. Explain how this helps you better understand technical texts.

_____

_____

_____

_____

LAFS.4.RI.1.3 Explain events, . . . ideas, or concepts in a scientific . . . text, including what happened and why, based on specific information in the text.

Lesson 4
Understanding Scientific Texts

Thinking carefully about information in science texts will help you understand what happens in the natural world and why or how it happens.

▶ **Read** A good **scientific text** is like having a science expert at your side explaining the **causes** and **effects** of everything that goes on around you. It tells *what* happens during a set of **events** in nature. It also answers important questions by explaining *how* the event happens and *why* it happens. These answers help you understand the world you live in.

Look at the cartoon below. Think about *what* events are happening. Also think about *how* and *why* they are happening.

A fish dies and sinks to the ocean bottom. It is buried in mud, which may harden.

2,000,000 years ago

Slowly, the fish bones dissolve and are replaced by other minerals. They become a fossil.

The ocean drains away, and erosion uncovers the fossil.

today

▶ **Think**   Consider everything you've learned so far about reading scientific texts. Use information in the cartoon and the *How and Why* column to add the events to the *What Happened* column of the chart. List the events in the order they occur in nature. These events answer the question: "What happened?"

What Happened	**How and Why**
Events That Created a Fossil	**How and Why a Fossil Is Created**
	Over millions of years, the fish skeleton dissolves and is replaced by other minerals. They harden in the shape of the skeleton. This creates a fossil. Later, erosion wears away the rock and soil to uncover the fossil.

▶ **Talk**   Share the events you added to the chart with a partner.

- Did you agree on the events and their order?
- How did the details in the chart help you understand more about the causes and effects of the events being shown?

Academic Talk
Use these words and phrases to talk about the text.
- **scientific text**   • **causes**   • **effects**
- **events**

▶ **Read**

A POWERFUL ROCK

by Patrick Pierce

1   Coal may look like an ordinary black rock. But inside, it contains powerful energy that can be used for heat and electricity. Coal is made from plant matter that was buried far below the Earth's surface for millions of years. Being buried so deeply and for so long put the plant matter under intense heat and pressure. The heat and pressure caused the chemical and physical characteristics of the plant matter to change. Eventually, the plant matter turned into coal.

2   Coal must be mined, or dug up from below the ground. After it is mined, the coal travels to a machine that cleans it. This process removes dirt, rocks, and other unwanted materials. Next, heavy machines crush the coal until it becomes a fine powder. Finally, the coal is burned to make steam. Special machines called turbines use this steam to create electricity.

3   Today, generators fueled by coal supply much of the world's energy. But the processes used to mine coal and convert it into fuel can pollute our air, land, and water. When coal is burned, harmful chemicals are released into the air. These chemicals get carried through the air by the wind and fall in the raindrops. This is called acid rain. It can make plants and animals very sick.

4   Engineers are developing new technologies to reduce the potential air pollution from coal. These promising solutions may help us get the most from this powerful rock while protecting our precious planet.

Close Reader Habits

As you read, **circle** details that describe how coal forms. Then **underline** details that explain its uses.

Explore **What information in "A Powerful Rock" helps you understand how coal is formed and how it is used today?**

▶ Think

> Look for the parts of the text that answer *what*, *how*, and *why* questions.

1 Complete the chart below by adding the descriptions of what happens. Then explain how or why it happens.

What Happens	How and Why It Happens
How Coal Is Formed	
Plant matter from millions of years ago is changed into coal.	
How Coal Is Used	
	Coal is used to produce energy that creates electricity.
Using coal harms the environment.	

▶ Talk

2 Explain why the author describes coal as a "powerful rock." Describe **two** benefits and **two** problems created by people's use of coal.

▶ Write

3 **Short Response** Explain how people process and use this "powerful rock." Include at least **one** benefit and **one** problem caused by people's use of coal. Include details to support your response. Use the space provided on page 58 to write your answer.

> **HINT** Find details about benefits and problems, such as "supply energy" and "harmful chemicals."

Gold

by Carl Gelb

1   People have valued gold for thousands of years. Because of the metal's durability, gold ornaments, statues, and jewelry look as brilliant today as when the artists of ancient Egypt and other cultures crafted them thousands of years ago. Gold is one of nature's true wonders.

2   **Properties:** Gold is an element. It cannot be broken down into simpler substances. Gold is also very malleable, which means it is easily flattened into a thin sheet. Gold is also ductile, which means it can be pulled into a wire. For these reasons, gold is useful in making jewelry. One ounce of gold can become 187 square feet of gold leaf or one mile of gold wire. Gold also conducts heat and electricity very well.

3   **Alloys:** Pure gold is very soft. Because it's so soft, gold is often mixed with other metals to make a mixture, or alloy, that is stronger than gold alone. Adding silver, copper, and zinc to gold produces the color we associate with jewelry.

4   **Today's Uses:** In the past, gold was mainly used for jewelry, statues, and other decorations. But today we use gold for more than just its beauty. It is an excellent conductor of electricity. This means that electricity flows through it easily. As a conductor, gold coats electrical parts inside our cell phones and computers. It helps speed the flow of electricity. Thin films of gold also reflect radiation on satellites, the sun visors of space suits, and the windows of skyscrapers. Gold's uses are many and important!

Computer Microchips ▶

Close Reader Habits

What was gold used for in the past, and what is it used for today? Reread the article. **Underline** details that tell how people have used gold in the past and the present.

Think Use what you learned from reading "Gold" to respond to the following questions.

1 The following question has two parts. First, answer Part A. Then answer Part B.

> In science texts, the cause of what happens often appears near words such as *because* and *reasons*.

Part A
Which statement **best** explains why gold is used for making jewelry?

   A Gold cannot be broken down into a simpler substance.

   B Gold can be made into a mile of gold wire.

   C Gold is durable and easily flattened, stretched, and shaped.

   D Gold is a good conductor of heat and electricity.

Part B
Read paragraph 2. Underline **two** sentences that **best** support your answer to Part A.

> Properties: Gold is an element. It cannot be broken down into simpler substances. Gold is also very malleable, which means it is easily flattened into a thin sheet. Gold is also ductile, which means it can be pulled into a wire. For these reasons, gold is useful in making jewelry. One ounce of gold can become 187 square feet of gold leaf or one mile of gold wire. Gold also conducts heat and electricity very well.

Talk

2 Explain why people have valued gold for thousands of years. Use the chart on page 59 to organize your thoughts about people's use of gold in the past and the present.

 Write

3 **Short Response** Use the information in your chart to explain what makes gold useful and why people valued gold in the past and today. Include at least **two** details from the passage to support your answer. Use the space provided on page 59 to write your response.

> **HINT** Think about how people's use of gold today is similar to and different from its use in the past.

Write Use the space below to write your answer to the question on page 55.

A POWERFUL ROCK

3 **Short Response** Explain how people process and use this "powerful rock." Include at least **one** benefit and **one** problem caused by people's use of coal. Include details to support your response.

> **HINT** Find details about benefits and problems, such as "supply energy" and "harmful chemicals."

_____

_____

_____

_____

_____

_____

Check Your Writing

☐ Did you read the prompt carefully?

☐ Did you put the prompt in your own words?

☐ Did you use the best evidence from the text to support your ideas?

☐ Are your ideas clearly organized?

☐ Did you write in clear and complete sentences?

☐ Did you check your spelling and punctuation?

Don't forget to check your writing.

Talk **2** Use the chart below to organize your ideas.

What Happens	How and Why It Happens

Write Use the space below to write your answer to the question on page 57.

HINT Think about how people's use of gold today is similar to and different from its use in the past.

3 **Short Response** Use the information in your chart to explain what makes gold useful and why people valued gold in the past and today. Include at least **two** details from the passage to support your answer.

_____

_____

_____

_____

_____

_____

▶ **Read**

Minerals

by Steven Dowshen, MD, *Kids' Health Online*

WORDS TO KNOW
As you read, look inside, around, and beyond these words to figure out what they mean.
- **immune**
- **supplements**
- **function**

1   Did you ever notice how TV commercials for breakfast cereal always mention vitamins and minerals? But when you think of minerals, food isn't the first thing that comes to mind. Aren't minerals something you find in the earth, like iron and quartz?

2   Well, yes, but small amounts of some minerals are also in foods—for instance, red meat, such as beef, is a good source of iron.

3   Just like vitamins, minerals help your body grow, develop, and stay healthy. The body uses minerals to perform many different functions— from building strong bones to transmitting nerve impulses. Some minerals are even used to make hormones or maintain a normal heartbeat.

MACRO and TRACE

4   The two kinds of minerals are: macrominerals and trace minerals. *Macro* means "large" in Greek (and your body needs larger amounts of macrominerals than trace minerals). The macromineral group is made up of calcium, phosphorus, magnesium, sodium, potassium, chloride, and sulfur.

5   A *trace* of something means that there is only a little of it. So even though your body needs trace minerals, it needs just a tiny bit of each one. Scientists aren't even sure how much of these minerals you need each day. Trace minerals include iron, manganese, copper, iodine, zinc, cobalt, fluoride, and selenium.

6   Let's take a closer look at some of the minerals you get from food.

CALCIUM

7   Calcium is the top macromineral when it comes to your bones. This mineral helps build strong bones so you can do everything from standing up straight to scoring that winning goal. It also helps build strong, healthy teeth for chomping on tasty food.

CALCIUM
milk, cheese, yogurt, broccoli

IRON
beef, tuna, eggs, beans

POTASSIUM
bananas, broccoli, tomatoes, potatoes

ZINC
beef, pork, lamb, legumes

IRON

8   The body needs iron to transport oxygen from your lungs to the rest of your body. Your entire body needs oxygen to stay healthy and alive. Iron helps because it's important in the formation of hemoglobin (say: HEE-muh-glo-bun), which is the part of your red blood cells that carries oxygen throughout the body.

POTASSIUM

9   Potassium (say: puh-TAH-see-um) keeps your muscles and nervous system working properly. Did you know your blood and body tissues, such as muscles, contain water? They do, and potassium helps make sure the amount of water is just right.

ZINC

10   Zinc helps your immune system, which is your body's system for fighting off illnesses and infections. It also helps with cell growth and helps heal wounds, such as cuts.

11   When people don't get enough of these important minerals, they can have health problems. For instance, too little calcium—especially when you're a kid—can lead to weaker bones. Some kids may take mineral supplements, but most kids don't need them if they eat a nutritious diet. So eat foods with those minerals and stay healthy!

Think Use what you learned from reading the science article to respond to the following questions.

1 The box below lists four benefits to your body from minerals in food.

> builds strong bones and teeth
> helps muscles and the nervous system work properly
> transports oxygen from the lungs to the rest of the body
> helps the immune system

Complete the table below by writing each benefit in the correct box.

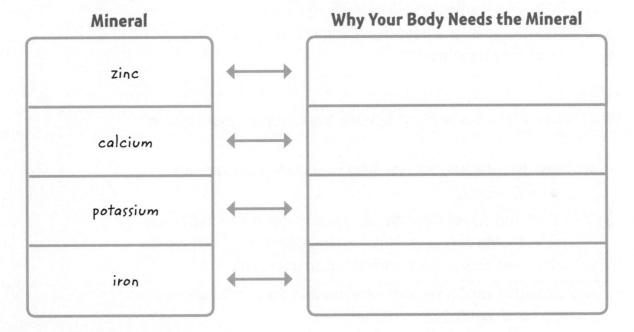

Mineral		Why Your Body Needs the Mineral
zinc	⟷	
calcium	⟷	
potassium	⟷	
iron	⟷	

2 Read the sentence from the passage.

The body needs iron to <u>transport</u> oxygen from your lungs to the rest of your body.

What does the root *trans* mean in the word <u>transport</u>?

  A many

  B all

  C across

  D against

3 The following question has two parts. First, answer Part A. Then answer Part B.

Part A
What conclusion about macrominerals and trace minerals is supported by the passage?

A Macrominerals are more important because they exist in larger quantities than trace minerals.

B Macrominerals and trace minerals are needed for a healthy heart, blood and tissues, and immune system.

C Trace minerals like iron are more important for keeping your bones healthy than macrominerals are.

D Macrominerals and trace minerals must come from food and also from supplements.

Part B
Which **three** sentences from the passage **best** support your answer in Part A?

A "Just like vitamins, minerals help your body grow, develop, and stay healthy."

B "The two kinds of minerals are: macrominerals and trace minerals. Macro means "large" in Greek (and your body needs larger amounts of macrominerals than trace minerals)."

C "Scientists aren't even sure how much of these minerals you need each day."

D "Calcium is the top macromineral when it comes to your bones."

E "The body needs iron to transport oxygen from your lungs to the rest of your body."

F "They do, and potassium helps make sure the amount of water is just right."

 **Write**

4 **Short Response** What are the two main types of minerals? Identify examples of each type, and explain how our bodies get them. Use details from the article and the food chart in your response.

_____

_____

_____

_____

_____

_____

_____

Learning Target

You've learned how to think carefully about information that answers _what_, _how_, and _why_ questions in science texts. Explain how this can help you develop a deeper understanding of a text and the world around you.

_____

_____

_____

_____

Lesson 5
Summarizing Informational Texts

Learning Target

Summarizing a text by briefly restating the main idea and key details will deepen your understanding of the information you read.

▶ **Read** Writers of informational texts organize their information around main ideas and key details about a topic.

To **summarize** a text, briefly restate the **main idea** and **key details** about the topic. Only include details that are important—details that answer questions about the main idea. Put your information in an order that makes sense, and be sure to use your own words.

Read the text below. How would you summarize it in a sentence or two?

Even the Toothbrush Has a History

The toothbrush has a history dating back thousands of years. Ancient Egyptians used toothbrushes made from the frayed ends of twigs. In the 1400s, the Chinese invented the first bristle toothbrush. The bristles were made from pig hairs attached to a bamboo handle. In 1938, the invention of nylon led to a modern toothbrush made of soft bristles. These improvements led to today's toothbrush, which comes in all shapes and sizes. But the basic job of the tool has not changed much. The toothbrush is still used to keep our teeth healthy and clean.

▶ **Think**   Use what you've learned so far about summarizing informational texts. First, complete the chart below by identifying three key details that support the main idea of the text. Then use the information in your chart to write a **summary** of the article.

Main Idea

The materials used to make toothbrushes have changed over thousands of years.

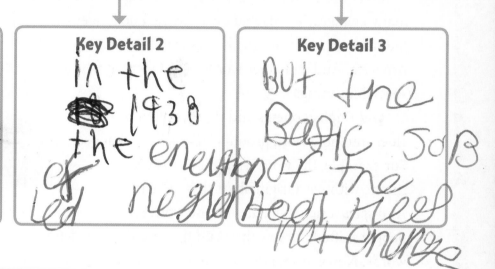

Key Detail 1

they hoft to be eqol

Key Detail 2

In the 1938 the eneuton led neglented

Key Detail 3

But the Basic Job of the Heel not enange

Summary: _____

_____

_____

_____

▶ **Talk**   Share your summary with a partner.

• Did you agree on the main idea and key details in your charts?

• How did the text organization of a main idea and key details help you create your summary?

Academic Talk

Use these words and phrases to talk about the text.

• **summarize**   • **main idea**
• **key details**   • **summary**

> **Read**

New Ways with Words

by S. L. Hughes

1   Over the centuries, the English language has undergone many changes. Words that once rhymed no longer sound the same. Others have their origins in lands far from America. And still other words have taken on new and special meanings.

2   Old English poems and rhymes often provide clues into how word pronunciations have changed. For example, the word *sea* did not always rhyme with *see*. Originally, it rhymed with *say*. And *speak* once rhymed with the word *brake*. Sometime after the 1600s, people shifted the way they said the sound for the letters *ea* in many words. Now *sea* sounds like *tea* or *pea*, and *speak* rhymes with *beak*, not *break*. No wonder spelling can be confusing!

3   Today we think of everyday words like *shirt*, *zero*, and *dollar* as part of our vocabulary. But they were "borrowed" from other languages long ago. *Average*, *check*, and *scarlet* are just a few words that came from the Arab world. The Vikings, old Germans, and Romans loaned us words like *glitter*, *weird*, and *soldier*. We also borrowed words such as *prairie* and *mesa* from the French and Spanish. And we needed to name food such as *chocolate*, *ketchup*, *oranges*, *pickles*, and *pretzels*, so we've added those words to our vocabulary, too.

4   Even now, English continues to change. Consider how new technology has given familiar words like *mouse* or *menu* new meanings. Now you can *surf the Web* without getting wet or tangling with a spider. And you can catch a *bug* or a *virus*, but so can your computer. Certainly, these surprising changes to English make talking and writing a real adventure.

Close Reader Habits

As you read, **underline** key details that explain three main ways that words have changed over time.

Explore **How and why have words in the English language changed over time?**

Think

As you read, sum up the main idea in each paragraph. They can become the key details to include in your summary.

1️⃣ Complete the chart below by adding three key details. Then explain why you chose to include each key detail.

Main Idea
The English language has undergone many changes over the years.

Key Detail 1	Key Detail 2	Key Detail 3
Why did you include this detail?	Why did you include this detail?	Why did you include this detail?

Talk

2️⃣ Explain why words in the English language have changed over time. To support your explanation, provide text evidence.

 ## Write

3️⃣ **Short Response** Write a summary of why and how the English language has changed through the centuries. Remember to include only the most important points in the text. Use the space provided on page 72 to write your response.

HINT Think about how you will organize your summary to explain the main ideas and details.

▶ **Read**

Hair Today, Gone Tomorrow
by Jan Russ

1   Just as clothing fashions change, so do hair fashions. People in the past sometimes used their hair to make unusual statements—much like today.

2   Before the invention of scissors, people just let their hair grow long and tied it back. But after a while, people began to style their hair. Some hairstyles were very complex.

3   The largest and most elaborate hairstyles appeared in the late 1700s. Women wore their hair piled high on top of their heads. As the style became even more extreme, they wove hair onto large wire frames. Some of these hairpieces towered three feet above a woman's head! The style also called for fancy ornaments. Tucked into the hairpieces were flowers, birds, and waterfalls—even complete battle scenes!

4   In the 1920s, women started a fashion of cutting hair short, called hair bobbing. Women "bobbed" their hair to show the newly independent spirit of the time. The fashion of short hair was then replaced by a return to long hair.

5   In the 1960s, many women wore their hair long and very straight. Because not everyone is born with straight hair, many teenagers would iron their hair to make it straight. They would lay their curly hair on an ironing board and press the curls straight. Soon, young men, like young women, also let their hair grow long, partly as a sign of rebellion. This rebellion was a statement against the social rules of the time—as many fashions are.

Close Reader Habits

What details are important enough to include in a summary? Reread the article. **Underline** sentences that tell more about the main idea.

Think Use what you learned from reading the history article to respond to the following questions.

1 Read the statements in the box.

> In the 1960s, young people rebelled by letting their hair grow long.
> In the 1700s, women wore large, elaborate hairstyles.
> Women in the 1920s cut their hair to show their independence.
> Teenagers of the 1960s pressed their curly hair to make it straight.
> Hair fashions change over time and are used to make unusual statements.

> As you reread, decide which details are important to include in a summary and which are not. Remember, key details directly support the main idea.

Identify the main idea and **three** key details that support it. Write them in the boxes below to complete the chart.

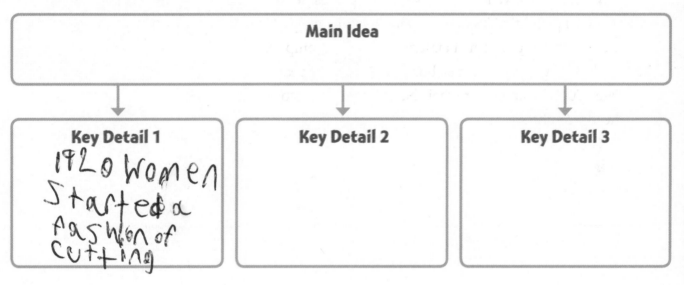

Main Idea

Key Detail 1

1920 women started a fashion of cutting

Key Detail 2

Key Detail 3

Talk

2 Take turns summarizing the text. Be sure to include the main idea of the text and at least **three** key details.

 Write

3 **Short Response** Write a summary of the article "Hair Today, Gone Tomorrow." Use information from the passage in your summary. Use the space provided on page 73 to write your answer.

> **HINT** Begin by planning the order in which you should present the key details.

Write Use the space below to write your answer to the question on page 69.

New Ways with Words

> **HINT** Think about how you will organize your summary to explain the main ideas and details.

3 **Short Response** Write a summary of why and how the English language has changed through the centuries. Remember to include only the most important points in the text.

_____

_____

_____

_____

_____

_____

_____

> Don't forget to check your writing.

Write Use the space below to write your answer to the question on page 71.

Hair Today, Gone Tomorrow

3 **Short Response** Write a summary of the article "Hair Today, Gone Tomorrow." Use information from the passage in your summary.

> **HINT** Begin by planning the order in which you should present the key details.

_____

_____

_____

_____

_____

_____

_____

_____

Check Your Writing

☐ Did you read the prompt carefully?

☐ Did you put the prompt in your own words?

☐ Did you use the best evidence from the text to support your ideas?

☐ Are your ideas clearly organized?

☐ Did you write in clear and complete sentences?

☐ Did you check your spelling and punctuation?

▶ **Read**

Genre: History Article

from It All Began with Spacewar!

by Peter Roop, *Cobblestone*

WORDS TO KNOW

As you read, look inside, around, and beyond these words to figure out what they mean.

- **established**
- **demonstrations**
- **introduced**

1   Two enemy spaceships slowly circled each other on a black and white screen. One spaceship accelerated as the other rotated to the right. The first spaceship fired a silent missile at its opponent. The missile missed its target. The second spaceship returned fire. Its missile hit the enemy and erased it from the screen.

2   This was the scene on the screen of *Spacewar!*, the world's first video game. This historic game ushered in the age of electronic games. . . .

3   The basic rules were quickly established: two enemy spaceships controlled by switches firing missiles at one another. The team then added stars to the background and introduced gravity and hyperspace to make *Spacewar!* more challenging and realistic.

4   *Spacewar!* was an immediate hit at computer conventions and demonstrations. It not only showed what a computer could do, but it was also fun to play.

Time Line

1950s
Researchers use computers to play checkers and other games.

1962
Spacewar! is invented.

1971
Ralph Baer begins work on a computer game to play on a home TV.

5   Games had been played on computers long before *Spacewar!* was created. Researchers in the 1950s had programmed their "giant electronic brains" to play checkers, tic-tac-toe, and chess. Computers were so new in 1960 that nobody was certain just how many tasks these machines could perform. Games were ideal for discovering the "intelligence" of computers. . . .

1975

A home version of
the game *Pong*
becomes available.

1977

A revolutionary home
video game system with
joysticks and game
cartridges is introduced.

1979

A variety of new
video games begin
to flood the market.

6   *Spacewar!* proved too bulky and complicated for the average person to play. For years, it remained a researchers' game. Then, in 1971, Ralph Baer, an electronics engineer, began working on hooking a computer to a home television.

7   Describing his work, Baer said, "The thought came to me that you should be able to do something else with television besides watch it. You ought to be able to play games." With this idea in mind, Baer invented *Odyssey*, a game with a bouncing ball and paddles that could be played on any television screen. *Odyssey* was the first video game consumers could buy and play at home.

8   About the same time, Nolan Bushnell and Ted Dabney, two electrical engineers, designed the game *Computer Space*. Bushnell described the game as "a cosmic dogfight between a spaceship and a flying saucer." *Computer Space*, however, did not catch on with game players. So Bushnell and Dabney invented an electronic table tennis game, which they called *Pong*. An expert on arcade games, Bushnell matched the excitement of table tennis with the fun of a pinball machine. *Pong* was so successful that Bushnell founded the Atari company to manufacture and sell the game. *Pong* is considered the first truly successful coin-operated video game.

9   The boom in video games was on! Dozens of companies entered the business of making video games for homes and arcades. *Space Invaders*, *Asteroids*, *Sea Wolf*, *Carnival*, and many other video games began thrilling players in every corner of America. . . . [But *Spacewar!* was] the game that helped introduce the wonders of the computer to the world.

Think Use what you learned from reading the history article to respond to the following questions.

1 Read the statements in the box below.

> Many companies began making computer video games.
> Stars and gravity were added to make the game more realistic.
> *Spacewar!* helped introduce computer games to the world.
> *Pong* was so successful, Bushnell started a company to make and sell it.
> *Spacewar!* showed what a computer could do and was fun to play.
> *Pong* was invented by electrical engineers.

Select the main idea and **three** key details that you would include in a summary about the passage. Write them to complete the chart below.

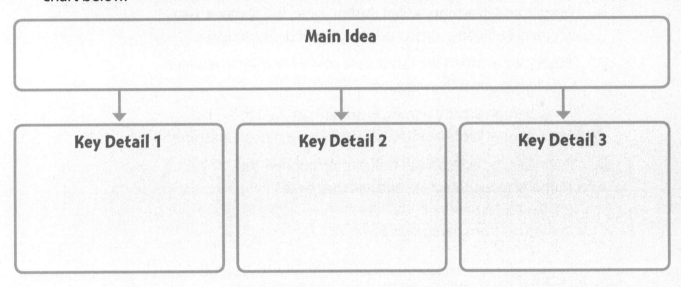

Main Idea

Key Detail 1

Key Detail 2

Key Detail 3

2 Which of these details is **not** important enough to include in a summary of the article?

A *Spacewar!*, the world's first video game, began the age of electronic games.

B Games were ideal for exploring what computers could do.

C *Space Invaders, Asteroids, Sea Wolf,* and *Carnival* were all arcade games.

D *Spacewar!* was too difficult for most people to play.

3 The following question has two parts. First, answer Part A. Then answer Part B.

Part A
Which sentence **best** summarizes key details in paragraph 8?

    A Nolan Bushnell and Ted Dabney designed *Computer Space.*

    B Dabney's and Bushnell's failure with *Computer Space* led them to create *Pong*, which was successful.

    C *Computer Space* was not a hit with game players.

    D Games created by the Atari company were ideal for discovering the intelligence of computers.

Part B
Which sentence from the passage **best** supports your answer in Part A?

    A "About the same time, Nolan Bushnell and Ted Dabney, two electrical engineers, designed the game *Computer Space.*"

    B "Bushnell described the game as 'a cosmic dogfight between a spaceship and a flying saucer.'"

    C "An expert on arcade games, Bushnell matched the excitement of table tennis with the fun of a pinball machine."

    D "*Pong* was so successful that Bushnell founded the Atari company to manufacture and sell the game."

4 Read the sentences from paragraph 6.

> *Spacewar!* proved too bulky and complicated for the <u>average</u> person to play. For years, it remained a researchers' game.

What does the word <u>average</u> mean as it is used in the sentence?

    A younger

    B ordinary

    C outstanding

    D important

Write

5 **Short Response** Write a summary of "It All Began with *Spacewar!*"
Use details from the text to support your response.

_____

_____

_____

_____

_____

_____

_____

_____

 Learning Target

**In this lesson, you learned how to use main ideas and key
details to develop a summary. Now, explain how you developed
a deeper understanding of ways to share information about
history texts.**

_____

_____

_____

_____

👥 **Introduction**

LAFS.4.RI.1.1 Refer to details and examples in a text when explaining what the text says explicitly and when drawing inferences from the text.

Lesson 6
Supporting Inferences
About Informational Texts

Learning Target

Making inferences based on key details and examples in an informational text will help you better understand the author's ideas about the topic.

▶ **Read** When you read informational texts, you can learn important information about a topic. Often, a text will state facts, **examples**, and other **details** directly. Other times, however, you must figure out an important idea on your own. To do this, use **text evidence** and what you already know from experience to make an **inference**, or a "sensible guess."

Study the cartoon below. Use what you see and what you know to make an inference about what is happening to the boy.

▶ **Think** Consider what you've learned so far about making inferences. What is happening to the boy? Complete the *Inference Chart* below to make an inference based on cartoon details and what you already know.

What the Cartoon Shows (Evidence)	What I Know (Experience)	My Inference

▶ **Talk** Share your inference and chart with a partner.

- Did you agree on what happened in the cartoon?
- Did you agree about the details added to your charts?
- Why did you agree or disagree?

◎ **Academic Talk**
Use these words and phrases to talk about the text.

- **examples**   • **details**   • **text evidence**
- **inference**

▶ **Read**   **Genre: History Article**

The Travels of the POTATO

by Marie Schaeffer

1   The potato plant is native to the Andes Mountain region of South America. This is where it first appeared and thrived. The ancient Incas were the first people known to eat the potato. It is an excellent food source, one that provides both energy and vitamins. During the 1500s, Spanish explorers to that region encountered the potato. They had never seen it before. By the 1600s, potatoes were grown in many places in Spain.

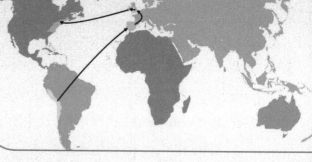

2   Early on, some Europeans shunned the potato. Scientists learned that it was closely related to some poisonous plants. But some European doctors accepted the potato as a medicine and used it to treat common illnesses. By the early 1700s, potatoes were being raised in England as a food crop. The plants grew well in the cool, moist climate. Soon, the potato became a major food staple, particularly in Ireland. Finally, in 1719, immigrants from England and Ireland introduced the potato to the New England area of North America.

Close Reader Habits

Think about key details in the passage that help you make inferences. Then **underline** key details that describe the events that brought the potato to Europe.

Explore   How do the details in the article help you make inferences about why the potato came to be used in Europe and elsewhere?

Look for details that help you make inferences about how the potato traveled.

Think

1 Complete the Inference Chart below to help you make inferences about the spread of the potato as a food crop.

What the Text Said (Evidence)	What I Know (Experience)	My Inference
• "The potato plant is native to the Andes Mountain region of South America." • "Spanish explorers. . . . had never seen it before." • "By the 1600s, potatoes were grown in many places in Spain."		
• "By the early 1700s, potatoes were being raised in England as a food crop." • "The plants grew well in the cool, moist climate."		

Talk

2 Explain what you can infer about how and why the use of the potato spread. Identify text details you used to support your inferences.

 ## Write

3 **Short Response** Explain how and why the use of the potato spread to other countries. Include at least three text details as support. Use the space on page 86 to write your response.

HINT To organize your writing, identify details about the climate where the potato thrives.

Fruit of the Bog

by Alden Sims

1   The first people known to eat cranberries were the Native Americans in northern regions of what is now the United States. Centuries before the Pilgrims arrived in 1620, Native Americans ate a bread made with cranberries mashed into cornmeal. They also munched on dried cranberries throughout the winter. But cranberries were useful for more than just food. Native Americans made dye from the berries to color blankets and rugs. And, they used the berries as a medicine for the treatment of wounds.

2   In 1810, Henry Hall from Cape Cod, Massachusetts, became the first person known to cultivate cranberries. (The word *cultivate* means "to grow as a farm crop.") Cranberries grow only in particular conditions. They grow best in bogs. They need an acid, peat soil, a steady water supply, and a covering of sand. The growing season must last from April to November, followed by a dormant period in the winter. The winter chill is needed for the fruit buds to mature.

3   Do you know how cranberry farmers know when the berries are ripe and ready to harvest? The small berries float to the surface of the bog and bob along there. The farmers are able to pull off this nifty harvest trick because inside each berry is a tiny pocket of air.

4   For years, the number-one cranberry-producing state in the United States was Massachusetts. However, since 1995, the state of Wisconsin has been the top cranberry producer. In 2010, Wisconsin harvested more than 4 million barrels of cranberries.

Close Reader Habits

What are growing conditions like in Massachusetts and Wisconsin? As you reread the article, **underline** details that tell about conditions all cranberries need to grow.

Think Use what you learned from reading the article to respond to the following questions.

1 This question has two parts. Answer Part A. Then answer Part B.

> Good inferences are those you can back up with words, phrases, or sentences from the text.

Part A
What inference can you make about Wisconsin based on details in the article?

- **A** It was first settled by Native Americans who ate berries and corn.
- **B** It was a major producer of blankets and rugs dyed red.
- **C** It provides the conditions needed for growing cranberries.
- **D** It has always been the number-one cranberry-producing state.

Part B
Choose one piece of evidence from the article that **best** supports the answer in Part A.

- **A** "The first people known to eat cranberries were the Native Americans in northern regions of what is now the United States."
- **B** "The growing season must last from April to November, followed by a dormant period in the winter."
- **C** "For years, the number-one cranberry-producing state in the United States was Massachusetts."
- **D** "However, since 1995, the state of Wisconsin has been the top cranberry producer."

Talk

2 Explain what you can infer about growing conditions in Massachusetts and Wisconsin based on the details in the article. Use the Inference Chart on page 87 to organize your thoughts. Make sure to include details that describe the growing conditions needed by cranberries.

 Write

3 **Short Response** Using information from your chart, explain your inferences about growing conditions in Massachusetts and Wisconsin. Use details from the passage to support your response. Use the space provided on page 87 to write your answer.

>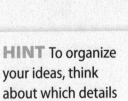
> **HINT** To organize your ideas, think about which details **best** explain your inference.

Write Use the space below to write your answer to the question on page 83.

The Travels of the POTATO

> **HINT** To organize your writing, identify details about the climate where the potato thrives.

3 **Short Response** Explain how and why the use of the potato spread to other countries. Include at least three text details as support.

_____

_____

_____

_____

_____

_____

_____

_____

_____

Check Your Writing

☐ Did you read the prompt carefully?

☐ Did you put the prompt in your own words?

☐ Did you use the best evidence from the text to support your ideas?

☐ Are your ideas clearly organized?

☐ Did you write in clear and complete sentences?

☐ Did you check your spelling and punctuation?

> Don't forget to check your writing.

Fruit of the Bog

2 **Use the Inference Chart below to organize your ideas.**

What the Text Said (Evidence)	What I Know (Experience)	My Inference

Write **Use the space below to write your answer to the question on page 85.**

3 **Short Response** Using information from your chart, explain your inferences about growing conditions in Massachusetts and Wisconsin. Use details from the passage to support your response.

> **HINT** To organize your ideas, think about which details best explain your inference.

_____

_____

_____

_____

_____

_____

_____

▶ **Read**

Why Salt?
Valuable ♪ Little Cubes

by Leigh Anderson and David Chandler, *Appleseeds*

WORDS TO KNOW
As you read, look inside, around, and beyond these words to figure out what they mean.

- **role**
- **regulated**
- **access**

The *Via Salarium*, shown in yellow, led from the sea coast to Rome, an important center of trade.

1   Today, salt is given out freely in shakers and packets at our favorite restaurants. We can buy it cheaply at any grocery store. But it hasn't always been so easy to get salt. This tiny crystal cube has played a much more important role in history than just flavoring our fries. Around the world, cities were founded, roads were built, wars were fought, and trade routes were established, all for one reason: humans can't live without salt. Literally. Because of this simple fact, salt became a valuable item a long time ago. People who controlled salt had power. Around 2,000 years ago, some of the people with salt—and power—were the Romans.

2   One way Rome controlled salt was by building villages along the Mediterranean coast. This gave them access to the sea where they could harvest salt. One of the first great roads built by Romans . . . is called *Via Salarium*, or "Salt Road." It is the oldest road in Italy today. As you might have guessed, it was built to transport salt.

3   As Rome grew, it became a great trading center, and salt was one of the main items traded there. Salt was so important in the daily lives of the Romans that soldiers were paid in blocks of salt. This pay was called *salarium argentums* or "salt money," giving us our word *salary*. In fact, the word *soldier* comes from the Latin *sol dare*, meaning "to give salt."

4   Throughout history and around the world, governments have regulated and taxed salt. . . . Salt played a role in the history of our country, too. In both the Revolutionary and Civil wars, keeping enough salt for the soldiers was important. In these and other wars, enemies have tried to keep salt away from each other. The history of the world is overflowing with stories of salt.

What's So Important About Salt?

5   Human beings can't live without salt. It is a basic ingredient in our bodies. Salt is in our tears, sweat, saliva, blood, and even in our urine. Without this mineral our cells, nerves, and muscles can't do their jobs properly. However, too much salt can cause kidneys to work overtime, blood vessels to swell, and blood pressure to go dangerously high.

Roman soldiers were paid in *salarium argentums* or "salt money."

6   Our health depends on having the right amount of salt in our bodies. Generally, the human body is very good at keeping our salt levels balanced. But sometimes that balance can be thrown off. Our diets, for example, might contain extremely low or extremely high amounts of salt. If this goes on for too long, there could be serious consequences—even death.

7   When early humans survived on the meat they hunted, their bodies got enough salt from the animals they ate. As people learned to grow their vegetables and grains and began to eat less meat, salt became more important. And it was often hard to find. The need for salt and the limited supply of it made salt very valuable!

When people began to grow crops, they ate less meat and needed to find new ways to get salt into their diets.

▶ **Think** Use what you learned from reading the history article to respond to the following questions.

1 This question has two parts. First, answer Part A. Then answer Part B.

Part A
What inference can you make based on the information in paragraph 3?

   A The soldiers used blocks of salt as payment so they could travel along the Salt Road.

   B Salt was so valued by Romans that it was used as a form of pay.

   C The soldiers did not have a healthy diet, so they were paid in blocks of salt.

   D The Roman government ran out of gold, so it paid soldiers in blocks of salt.

Part B
Which **two** sentences from the text provide the **best** support for your answer in Part A?

   A "This . . . was called *salarium argentums* or 'salt money.'"

   B "Throughout history and around the world, governments have regulated and taxed salt."

   C "This tiny crystal cube has played a much more important role in history than just flavoring our fries."

   D "The word <u>soldier</u> comes from the Latin *sol dare*, meaning 'to give salt.'"

   E "Human beings can't live without salt."

   F "The need for salt and the limited supply of it made salt very valuable!"

2 Underline **two** sentences in the paragraph below that **best** support the idea that our bodies need salt.

Our health depends on having the right amount of salt in our bodies. Generally, the human body is very good at keeping our salt levels balanced. But sometimes that balance can be thrown off. Our diets, for example, might contain extremely low or extremely high amounts of salt. If this goes on for too long, there could be serious consequences—even death.

3 Read the following inference.

The salt transported over the Salt Road helped Rome to become a great and important trading center.

Which **three** details from the text provide the **best** support for the inference?

A "People who controlled salt had power."

B "When early humans survived on the meat they hunted, their bodies got enough salt from the animals they ate."

C "Around 2,000 years ago, some of the people with salt—and power—were the Romans."

D "One way Rome controlled salt was by building villages along the Mediterranean coast."

E "Human beings can't live without salt."

F "As people learned to grow their vegetables and grains and began to eat less meat, salt became more important."

4 This question has two parts. First, answer Part A. Then answer Part B.

Part A

Read the sentence from paragraph 4 of the passage.

The history of the world is <u>overflowing</u> with stories of salt.

What does the word <u>overflowing</u> mean as it is used in this sentence?

A wide and vast

B overly full of

C covered completely

D in short supply

Part B

Underline **three** sentences in the paragraph below that provide the **best** support for your answer in Part A.

Throughout history and around the world, governments have regulated and taxed salt. . . . Salt played a role in the history of our country, too. In both the Revolutionary and Civil wars, keeping enough salt for the soldiers was important. In these and other wars, enemies have tried to keep salt away from each other. The history of the world is overflowing with stories of salt.

Write

5 **Short Response** How is the value of salt different today than it was in ancient Roman times? Include **three** details from the article to support your response.

_____

_____

_____

_____

_____

_____

_____

Learning Target

In this lesson, you learned to use text details and what you know to make inferences. Now explain how this can help you develop a deeper understanding of informational texts.

_____

_____

_____

▶ **Read**

Read the history article. Then answer the questions that follow.

from "And Away We Go: Rockets"

from *Kids Discover*

1   From blastoff to touchdown, a rocket is an awesome sight. The Saturn 5 rocket that sent astronauts to the moon stood 363 feet high, about the height of a 30-story building. It weighed more than six million pounds. With rocket engines, it sent a spacecraft weighing more than 100,000 pounds to a lunar landing.

2   In 1930, Robert Goddard was a Massachusetts-born scientist working almost totally alone. He was the first to set earthlings on a path out of this world and into space. Thirty-nine years after Goddard shot off his first rocket, United States astronaut Neil Armstrong took his first step on the moon. Since that time, rockets have lifted hundreds of spacecraft and satellites into orbit around Earth. They have carried space shuttles to and from the *International Space Station*. They have sent unmanned spacecraft to Mars and Jupiter. Satellites put in orbit by rockets beam back information about Earth's atmosphere and weather.

Each Saturn 5 rocket could be used only once.

3   Robert Goddard once called himself a "one-dream-man." His dream was to send a rocket into space. It began on October 19, 1899, when he was 17 years old. He climbed a ladder to trim branches from a cherry tree. As he looked up, he had a vision of traveling into space.

4   Throughout his career, Goddard worked mostly alone. He had little money or support. Rocket research was not considered a proper subject for a serious scientist. Goddard experimented with rockets in his free time. Most of his experiments took place on his aunt's Massachusetts farm.

Robert Goddard on March 16, 1926, holding the launch frame for a rocket of his own design.

Up, Up, and Away!

Launch a rocket in your backyard with these simple household materials.

Materials:
- empty quart or liter plastic bottle
- cork
- paper towels
- 3 or 4 streamers (made from paper towels or crepe paper)
- thumbtack
- 1/2 cup water
- 1/2 cup vinegar
- 1 teaspoon baking soda

Directions:

1. Make your rocket by attaching streamers to the top of the cork with the thumbtack. Make sure the cork will fit tightly into the bottle. If it is too tight, ask an adult to help you trim the cork with a knife. If it's too loose, wrap pieces of paper towel around it until it fits snugly in the bottle top.

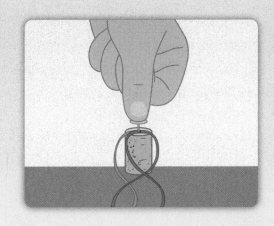

2. With the cork out of the bottle, put the water and the vinegar into the bottle.

3. Cut a 4-inch by 4-inch piece of paper towel. Wrap the baking soda in the paper towel, twisting the ends to keep the baking soda in.

4. Go outside where there is plenty of space. Drop the paper-towel-wrapped baking soda into the bottle. Fit the cork into the bottle top. Set the bottle upright away from any people.

5. WAIT. As the liquid soaks through the paper towel, the vinegar will react with the baking soda and produce carbon dioxide gas. As more and more gas forms, the pressure will build up inside the bottle. Eventually, the bottle will blow its cork. The streamers will help you trace its flight.

▶ **Think**

1 Which sentence **best** explains why the last step in making a rocket is to wait?

- **A** The cork has to fit tightly into the bottle top.
- **B** It takes time for gas to build up in the bottle.
- **C** It is safer to take the bottle outside to launch.
- **D** You must wrap the baking soda in a paper towel.

2 Read this sentence from paragraph 3.

Robert Goddard once called himself a "one-dream-man."

Which **two** sentences from the text explain why Goddard said this?

- **A** "Throughout his career, Goddard worked mostly alone."
- **B** "Most of his experiments took place on his aunt's Massachusetts farm."
- **C** "It began on October 19, 1899, when he was 17 years old."
- **D** "As he looked up, he had a vision of traveling into space."
- **E** "His dream was to send a rocket into space."
- **F** "Thirty-nine years after Goddard shot off his first rocket, United States astronaut Neil Armstrong took his first step on the moon."

3 This question has two parts. First, answer Part A. Then answer Part B.

Part A

Which sentence below **best** tells the main idea of the article?

    A   Robert Goddard helped build the rocket that took the astronaut Neil Armstrong to the moon.

    B   Robert Goddard was a scientist whose work led to the Saturn 5 rockets, which were 30 stories tall.

    C   Robert Goddard did most of his rocket research in his spare time on his aunt's farm in Massachusetts.

    D   Robert Goddard worked alone for many years to develop the rockets that led to space travel and exploration.

Part B

Which details in the chart below **best** support your answer to Part A? Draw an X next to two key details that support the main idea.

Detail from the Article	Supports the Main Idea
The Saturn 5 Rocket that sent astronauts to the moon stood 363 feet high, about the height of a 30-story building.	
Thirty-nine years after Goddard shot off his first rocket, United States astronaut Neil Armstrong took his first step on the moon.	
Satellites put in orbit by rockets beam back information about Earth's atmosphere and weather.	
Throughout his career, Goddard worked mostly alone.	

4 Answer Parts A and B below.

Part A
Which statement **best** explains why Robert Goddard worked "almost totally alone"?

    A Other scientists did not take rockets seriously.

    B Goddard did not like working with other scientists.

    C The farm was too far away from other people.

    D Goddard wanted to keep his research a secret.

Part B
Which sentence from the text **best** supports the answer to Part A?

    A "Throughout his career, Goddard worked mostly alone."

    B "Most of his experiments took place on his aunt's Massachusetts farm."

    C "Rocket research was not considered a proper subject for a serious scientist."

    D "Robert Goddard once called himself a 'one-dream-man.'"

5 Underline the sentence that **best** explains why the cork blows out of the bottle.

WAIT. As the liquid soaks through the paper towel, the vinegar will react with the baking soda and produce carbon dioxide gas. As more and more gas forms, the pressure will build up inside the bottle. Eventually, the bottle will blow its cork. The streamers will help you trace its flight.

6 Answer Parts A and B below.

Part A
The first instruction in "Up, Up, and Away!" is to attach streamers to the top of the cork. Why are the streamers important?

    A   They bring liquid into the bottle.

    B   They help people follow the flight of the cork.

    C   They make the cork fit tightly into the bottle top.

    D   They react with the baking soda and vinegar to make gas.

Part B
Which sentence from the text **best** supports the answer to Part A?

    A   "The streamers will help you trace its flight."

    B   "As the liquid soaks through the paper towel, the vinegar will react with the baking soda and produce carbon dioxide gas."

    C   "Make your rocket by attaching streamers to the top of the cork with the thumbtack."

    D   "Make sure the cork will fit tightly into the bottle."

7 In paragraph 2, what is the meaning of the word <u>earthlings</u>?

    A   animals

    B   people

    C   objects

    D   rockets

8 Which sentence **best** summarizes the first paragraph of the article?

    A Seeing a rocket is awesome because it is 363 feet tall and weighs more than six million pounds.

    B With rocket engines, the Saturn 5 rocket sent a 100,000-pound spacecraft to make a lunar landing.

    C The Saturn 5 rocket, which was tall and heavy, sent a spacecraft and astronauts to the moon.

    D Thanks to Robert Goddard, the Saturn 5 rocket was able to take human beings into space.

9 **Short Response** The sentence below is from Step 1 of "Up, Up, and Away!"

Make sure the cork will fit tightly into the bottle.

Why is it important for the cork to fit tightly? What would happen if it didn't fit tightly? Use details from the procedure to support your answer.

Write

10 **Extended Response** What is a rocket? What are some of the jobs that rockets have done throughout history? Use details from the article to support your answer.

In your answer, be sure to include
- a description of what a rocket is
- some of the jobs rockets have done in the past
- some of the jobs rockets do now
- details from the article to support your answer

Check your writing for correct spelling, grammar, capitalization, and punctuation.

_____

_____

_____

_____

_____

_____

_____

_____

_____

_____

_____

_____

_____

Key Ideas and Details in Literature

When you read stories, plays, and poems, what do you notice first? Most likely it's **details** about the characters, settings, and events. For example, imagine you tell a friend about the book *Tales of a Fourth-Grade Nothing*. First, you might talk about Peter and his little brother, Fudge. Then you might tell how Fudge does things that make Peter angry. Next, you might talk about an important event in the story, like when Fudge writes all over Peter's project poster. Finally, you might tell your friend that the book shows how Peter comes to like his little brother. Learning how to live with others—even people who annoy you—is a **key idea** of that book.

In this unit, you'll learn how and why readers pay attention to characters, settings, and events. You'll see that careful reading means paying close attention to what the characters think, say, and do. Finally, you'll practice summarizing the key ideas of a text and figuring out its theme.

✓ Self Check

Before starting this unit, check off the skills you know below. As you complete each lesson, see how many more skills you can check off!

I can:	Before this unit	After this unit
describe characters by referring to their thoughts, words, and actions.	☐	☐
use details from a story or play to describe a setting or an event.	☐	☐
figure out the theme of a story or poem.	☐	☐
explain how a theme is supported by details.	☐	☐
summarize a story, play, or poem.	☐	☐
refer to details and examples when explaining and inferring what a story, play, or poem is telling you.	☐	☐

104 Unit 2 Key Ideas and Details in Literature   ©Curriculum Associates, LLC   Copying is not permitted.

page 115

page 130

page 144

page 158

page 171

page 178

page 184

👥 **Introduction**

LAFS.4.RL.1.3 Describe in depth a character . . . in a . . . drama, drawing on specific details in the text (e.g., a character's thoughts, words, or actions).

Lesson 7
Describing Characters in Plays

 **Learning Target**

Describing details about the thoughts, feelings, and actions of characters in a drama will help you better understand what you read.

▶ **Read** When you read a **drama**, or play, you learn about the **characters** by what they say and do. A character is a person, animal, or made-up creature in the play.

Identifying details about a character's thoughts, feelings, words, and actions helps you figure out what each character is like. **Character traits** are special qualities of the characters, such as shyness or honesty. **Motivations** are the reasons why characters act, think, and feel as they do. Moreover, the traits and motivations of different characters affect how they behave as a result of earlier events in the story.

Study the cartoon below to identify details that tell you about Edmund.

▶ **Think**   What have you learned so far about identifying details that help you understand and describe characters? Think about the important information you identified as you looked at the cartoon. Complete the *Character Trait Chart* below to help you understand what Edmund is like.

Character: Edmund (alien)

Trait	Details from the Cartoon (Thoughts, Feelings, Words, Actions)

▶ **Talk**   Share your chart with a partner.

- Did you identify the same trait?
- Which thoughts, feelings, and actions did each of you include as clues that show Edmund's character trait?

◎ **Academic Talk**
Use these words and phrases to talk about the text.

- **drama**
- **character**
- **character traits**
- **motivations**

Read

The TREASURE

by Mabel Astor

1 [*Setting*: IRIS *and* GUS, *her younger brother, stand in a forest.* IRIS *holds a map.*]

2 IRIS [*studying the map*]: We're supposed to turn left up here by that big tree.

3 GUS [*nervous*]: But it's getting dark, and Mom told us to be back for dinner.

4 IRIS: [*annoyed*] Seriously, Gus? We're searching for buried treasure! The world won't end if we get home a little late.

5 GUS [*nodding his head*]: Yeah, I guess you're right. [*hesitantly*] But . . .

6 IRIS: That's more like it. Let's get going! We can't let Victor and Elsa beat us.

7 [*They start walking. A sudden breeze whips the map from* IRIS'S *hand.*]

8 IRIS: Oh no! The map! [*A huge wind gust whisks the map into a tree.*]

9 GUS: Now what are we going to do?

10 IRIS: I guess one of us is going to have to climb up there.

11 GUS: But I'm afraid of heights.

12 IRIS [*shivering*]: I am, too, but do you think I'm going to let that stop us? We're so close!! [*She takes a deep breath and starts climbing.*]

13 GUS: Look! It's, it's . . . [*points to a gold coin in the dirt under the tree*]

Close Reader Habits

Underline the details that tell what motivates Iris's behavior.

How would you describe Iris in the drama *The Treasure*?

Think

> Stage directions are clues that help you learn what each character is like.

1 Complete the Character Trait Chart below to help you describe Iris.

Character: Iris

Traits	Details from the Drama (Thoughts, Feelings, Words, Actions)
competitive	
	Iris shivers when she sees thinks about climbing the tree.
determined	
	"Oh no! The map!"

Talk

2 Describe Iris. Point out details in the drama that helped you understand her character traits. Use the chart above to help organize your thoughts.

Write

3 **Short Response** Write a short description of Iris's character traits. Include details from the drama that helped you identify what she is like. Use the space provided on page 112 to write your response.

> **HINT** Reread lines 8–12. What does her reaction to Gus tell you about Iris?

William Tell

adapted from a Swiss folktale

1 [*Setting: A busy marketplace in Altdorf, Switzerland*]

2 WILLIAM: Come, my son. I have sold the cowhides. Now we must buy the things your mother has asked us to get.

3 ALBERT: Yes, Father. And what about a toy for little Lewis?

4 WILLIAM: You are a good boy to remember your little brother.

5 OFFICER: Stop, man! Why do you not salute the cap of your king! [*The OFFICER points to a pole. On top is a cloth cap. It belongs to the Austrian king, who has conquered Switzerland.*]

6 WILLIAM: I love my country. But I refuse to honor the Austrian king, who forces suffering upon my people.

7 OFFICER: Then I'll arrest you as a traitor! What is your name?

8 WILLIAM [*standing tall*]: William Tell.

9 OFFICER: And this is your son? [*looks to a nearby* SOLDIER] Soldier! Tie the boy to that tree over there!

10 WILLIAM: Leave him be! He is only a child!

11 OFFICER: I hear you are a famous shot. Perhaps you can shoot an apple from the head of your son? If so, I will let you go free.

12 WILLIAM: Never, you villain! I would rather die than risk hurting him. Now let him go, and take me to jail!

13 OFFICER: You will both die unless you shoot the apple as I say.

14 WILLIAM [*thinking aloud*]: Oh, dear life, what am I to do?

15 ALBERT [*trembling*]: Father, I want to go home.

16 WILLIAM: Stand still, my brave boy. I promise I'll not hurt you. [*He shoots, and then he falls to his knees, sighing with relief.*]

17 SOLDIER: The apple is split! That was a fine shot!

18 OFFICER [*frowning*]: I did not believe anyone could make it. I suppose I must honor my word and set you free.

> **Close Reader Habits**
>
> What kind of people are the officer and William Tell? Reread the play. **Underline** details that show the traits and motivations of both characters.

▶ **Think** Use what you learned from reading the drama to respond to the following question.

Imagine what happens on a stage. Think about what the characters say and do.

1 This question has two parts. Answer Part A. Then answer Part B.

Part A
Which phrase **best** describes a character trait of the officer?

    A sly, but fair-minded

    B heartless and cruel

    C bossy, but friendly

    D respectful and polite

Part B
Identify **three** lines from what the officer says that **best** support your answer in Part A. Write your evidence in the box below.

▶ **Talk**

2 Discuss the character traits of William Tell. What details from the drama reveal more about his thoughts, feelings, and actions? Use the Character Trait Chart on page 113 to organize your ideas.

 ▶ **Write**

HINT Identify the details that explain why William Tell reacts to the officer's words as he does.

3 **Short Response** Describe the character of William Tell. Include details from the drama in your response to support your description. Use the space provided on page 113 to write your response.

Write **Use the space below to write your answer to the question on page 109.**

The
TREASURE

3 **Short Response** Write a short description of Iris's character traits. Include details from the drama that helped you identify what she is like.

> **HINT** Reread lines 8–12. What does her reaction to Gus tell you about Iris?

_____

_____

_____

_____

_____

_____

_____

Check Your Writing

Don't forget to check your writing.

- ☐ Did you read the prompt carefully?
- ☐ Did you put the prompt in your own words?
- ☐ Did you use the best evidence from the text to support your ideas?
- ☐ Are your ideas clearly organized?
- ☐ Did you write in clear and complete sentences?
- ☐ Did you check your spelling and punctuation?

William Tell

2 **Use the Character Trait Chart below to organize your ideas.**

Character: William Tell

Traits	Details from the Drama (Thoughts, Feelings, Words, Actions)

Write **Use the space below to write your answer to the question on page 111.**

3 **Short Response** Describe the character of William Tell. Include details from the drama in your response to support your description.

> **HINT** Identify the details that explain why William Tell reacts to the officer's words as he does.

_____

_____

_____

_____

_____

_____

_____

▶ **Read**

Robin Hood
and the
Mournful Knight

adapted from an English folktale

[*Scene 1:* A camp in Sherwood Forest, where ROBIN HOOD *and his* MEN *are crafting arrows*]

1 LITTLE JOHN [*a huge man*]: My poor empty stomach is growling for dinner! I'd not say no to roast venison with rosemary and spring onions in a delicate cream sauce. Would you, Master Robin?

2 ROBIN HOOD: Stop! You sound like a recipe! Now my stomach, too, rumbles and grumbles for a meal. But first we must find ourselves a wealthy traveler to pay the bill. Little John, please ride out and fetch us a Lord Moneybags.

3 LITTLE JOHN [*bowing*]: With pleasure, kind Master.

4 ROBIN HOOD: Remember, friend: take care not to bother any simple farmers or laborers you meet. Those who toil[1] for their few pennies deserve to live in peace. Fetch us some fat, selfish gentleman who treats the poor like dirt beneath his shoes.

[1] **toil:** work extremely hard

5 WILL SCARLET: Look! [*pointing*] I've never seen a knight in such rags! What ails him, I wonder?

6 [*Enter the* KNIGHT. *He looks weary and mournful. He wears fine clothes, but they are old, torn, and dirty.*]

7 ROBIN HOOD: Welcome, gentle knight. I am Robin Hood. Will you not dine with us? We were just discussing the menu. We have pheasant, partridge, venison—or all three.

8 KNIGHT: Thank heavens for generous fellows like you! I have not tasted a bite for days. If I ever return to Sherwood Forest, I shall certainly repay your kindness.

9 ROBIN HOOD: Pardon me, Sir Knight, but here in Sherwood, our rich guests customarily pay in advance.

10 KNIGHT: How I wish I could, but I no longer have a penny to my name.

11 WILL SCARLET: [*suspiciously*] He lies! All these gentlefolk lie through their teeth. Let me search his saddlebags, Master Robin.

12 ROBIN HOOD: Please do, Will. Pardon us, Sir Knight, but we do not offer charity to the rich.

13 WILL SCARLET [*searching, then sounding baffled*]: I can't believe it—he speaks the truth!

14 ROBIN HOOD: What has befallen you, sir? You are surely a landowner, yet you are poorer than a beggar. Pray, tell us your story.

15 KNIGHT [*sits wearily on a fallen tree*]: A year ago, I was a wealthy man. But then my only son became entangled with a gang of tricksters. To save the foolish lad, I pledged all my lands. Now, unless I pay four hundred pounds[2] to the Earl of York by next week, I shall lose everything.

16 ROBIN HOOD: Have you no friends?

17 KNIGHT: When I was rich, I had dozens of kind friends. Now that I am a pauper, they have forgotten me. When I need their help, they turn away.

[2] **pound:** a unit of English money, originally equal to a pound in weight of sterling silver

18 ROBIN HOOD: Fear not, gentle knight—today you have made a new set of friends. Say, Little John! Unlock the treasure chest and count out four hundred pounds.

19 WILL SCARLET [*whose suspicious attitude has completely changed; now he all but weeps with sympathy*]: Shall he not have cloth for a new coat, Robin? His clothes are badly torn.

20 ROBIN HOOD: Of course! Give our friend a length of fine fabric. Choose a shade of blue that will match his eyes.

21 LITTLE JOHN: Here is the money, good knight.

22 WILL SCARLET [*sniffling*]: Here is the cloth, poor Sir.

23 KNIGHT [*overwhelmed with gratitude*]: Indeed, I do not know how to thank you! Tell me, Robin Hood, when shall I come to repay the money you have so kindly lent?

24 ROBIN HOOD: Twelve months from now, let us meet beneath this tree. Until then, be merry!

25 KNIGHT: I shall not fail you. Thank you and farewell, my beloved new friends.

[*Scene 2: Same Sherwood Forest camp, one year later*. The KNIGHT and his wife, LADY LEA *approach* ROBIN and his MEN.]

26 LADY LEA [*with a deep curtsey*]: A thousand thanks for saving our family from ruin.

27 ROBIN HOOD: Madam, it was our pleasure. How is your son? [*in a joking tone*] I hope he isn't keeping company with swindlers these days.

28 KNIGHT: Thankfully he is not. But Sir, let us conclude our business. [*He hands* ROBIN *a heavy sack of gold.*]

29 ROBIN HOOD [*peering into the sack*]: Surely, Sir Knight, this is too much! We lent you only four hundred pounds!

30 KNIGHT [*shrugging*]: So I added a few extra coins. You may give them to the next few paupers you meet. . . . Ha! Do I smell venison roasting? May we invite ourselves to dinner?

Think Use what you learned from reading the drama to respond to the following questions.

1 The box below contains traits and details from *Robin Hood and the Mournful Knight*.

Traits	Details from the Drama
adventurous	"Surely, Sir Knight, this is too much!"
fair	"Unlock the treasure chest and count out four hundred pounds."
suspicious	"You may give them to the next few paupers you meet."
polite	"Welcome, gentle knight."
generous	"I hope he isn't keeping company with swindlers these days."

In the chart below, write character traits from the box that describe Robin Hood. Then add details from the box to support your answers. You will not use every detail or trait.

Traits	Details from the Drama

2 Read the sentence from the passage.

If I ever return to Sherwood Forest, I shall certainly <u>repay</u> your kindness.

What does the prefix *re-* mean in the word <u>repay</u>?

   A in

   B not

   C back

   D half

3 This question has two parts. First, answer Part A. Then answer Part B.

Part A
Which phrase **best** describes character traits of Will Scarlet?

    A distrustful, but rude

    B careful, but peculiar

    C easily fooled, but wise

    D suspicious, but kind

Part B
Choose **three** details from the text that **best** support your answer in Part A.

    A "You are surely a landowner."

    B "He lies! All these gentlefolk lie through their teeth."

    C "I've never seen a knight in such rags!"

    D "Choose a shade of blue that will match his eyes."

    E "Shall he not have cloth for a new coat, Robin?"

    F "Let me search his saddlebags, Master Robin."

 Write

Describe the character traits of the Knight in Scenes 1 and 2. How and why does he change?

4 **Plan Your Response** What are the details that tell you about the Knight in each scene? Use a chart to organize your thoughts about the Knight and how he changes.

5 **Write an Extended Response** Describe the character traits of the Knight in Scenes 1 and 2. Use your chart and details from the text to support your description of how he changes.

_____

_____

_____

_____

_____

_____

_____

_____

_____

_____

_____

_____

_____

_____

_____

_____

 Learning Target

In this lesson, you learned to describe details about the
thoughts, feelings, and actions of characters. Explain how
describing these details will help you better understand
characters in a drama.

_____

_____

_____

 **Introduction**

LAFS.4.RL.1.3 Describe in depth a . . . setting or event in a story or drama, drawing on specific details in the text . . .

Lesson 8
Describing Settings and Events in Stories

 **Learning Target**

Using details to describe the settings and events in a story helps you better understand the stories you read.

▶ **Read** When you read a literary text, you learn about important things that happen to the characters, the **problems** they face, and **solutions** they come to. These are the story **events**. You also find out about the **settings**, or where and when the events occur.

To get the most from a story, look for **details** about the story events, including the characters' actions and reactions, as well as their thoughts and feelings. Also look for details describing how a setting looks and when and where the story takes place. Paying attention to these details helps you make sense of what happens in the story.

Look at each photo below. What details tell you about the setting? What details tell you about each event ?

▶ **Think**   What have you learned so far about story settings and events? Think about the important details you saw in each photo. Which details tell when and where the event occurs? Which tell about what is happening? Complete the chart by adding details, settings, and events.

	Left Photo	Right Photo
Details		
Setting (Place and Time)		
Events (What is happening?)		

▶ **Talk**   Share your chart with a partner.

- Which details did each of you include?
- How did each of you describe the events and settings?
- How did the details in the photos affect your understanding of the time, place, and events being shown?

◎ **Academic Talk**
Use these words to talk about the text.

- **problems**   • **solutions**   • **events**
- **settings**   • **details**

Meeting Grandma

by Gillian Adams

1   Several years ago, when I was about seven, my grandma flew to St. Louis to visit us. That summer, it was so blazingly hot that we rarely bothered to go outside, so naturally we were thrilled to go with our parents to pick her up from the airport.

2   The airport was a new experience to my brother and me. We rushed excitedly from one shop to another, fascinated by all the things anyone with money could buy. Eventually, we turned our attention to the restaurants, pleading for a pretzel, ice cream, a cold drink— anything.

3   Our parents finally agreed to buy us each a fruit smoothie. We thought carefully about the flavors—blueberry, strawberry, banana—what to choose? After a while, we made up our minds and ordered. Then the server was o-so-slow in preparing the drinks, but finally, the delicious concoctions were ready. Gratefully, we sank into our seats and began slurping them down. They were really, really cold, so we took our "sweet" time.

4   And that is where Grandma found us twenty minutes later. We had completely lost track of the time! Grandma's plane had arrived, and worried that we were lost, she had come in search of us.

Close Reader Habits

Underline details that tell you about the story setting and events.

Explore **What is the setting, and how does it influence the story characters and events in "Meeting Grandma?"**

Think

> Think about how the setting—the time and place—influences what happens in the story.

1 Fill in the chart with details about the story setting and events.

	Setting	
Important Events	First	
	Next	
	Last	

2 How does the setting affect the family's actions, and how does that lead to the last important event in the story?

_____

_____

_____

Talk

3 Describe the story setting in "Meeting Grandma." How did it influence the characters and story events?

Write

4 **Short Response** Describe the way the story setting of "Meeting Grandma" affected the characters and events. Include details from the story to support your response. Use the space provided on page 126 to write your response.

> **HINT** Identify details that explain why the characters lost track of time.

▶ **Read**

Baseball Lessons

by Bianca Gomez

1   For weeks Elena's brothers had been promising to teach her how to play baseball. Today, though, when she pestered them to join a game, Jorge said no. "Go away, little one!" he exclaimed. "This game is for expert players." How dare he call her little one!

2   Elena slammed the door hard and stomped into the kitchen where her grandmother was busy making the evening meal. Elena threw down her backpack and slumped in a chair. "Jorge and Hector won't teach me how to play baseball, Abuela," she grumbled. "They won't let me play because I don't even know how to catch, throw, or hit the ball—but how will I ever learn unless someone teaches me?"

3   "Ah, Chica, this is your lucky day," smiled Abuela. "In my youth, I had quite the reputation for being a good pitcher. We'll have to start some practice sessions outside."

4   For the next three weeks, they practiced daily in Elena's backyard. Abuela taught Elena everything she knew about baseball, which happened to be quite a lot. Finally, she sent Elena off to find a game.

5   Elena soon located her brothers and their friends in a game at the park. When she asked to join in, Jorge tried to send her away, but then one of his friends threw Elena a long, high ball. Reaching up with her glove, she made the catch easily. "Wow!" said Jorge. "How did you learn to catch like that?"

6   "Abuela taught me. I can throw hard and smash the ball, too."

7   "Well, if Abuela taught you, you must be good because she taught Hector and me, too," he laughed and nudged her gently. "Welcome to the game."

Close Reader Habits

What is Jorge's attitude toward Elena at the beginning of the story? Why does it change? Reread the story. **Underline** details that show why Jorge's attitude toward Elena changes.

▶ **Think** Use what you learned from reading the story to respond to the following questions.

1 Reread paragraph 2. Which **two** events result from what Elena says about her brothers' unwillingness to teach her to play baseball?

    A Jorge calls Elena "little one" and tells her to go away.

    B Jorge and Hector find a friend who teaches Elena how to play.

    C Elena and Abuela practice baseball for three weeks.

    D Jorge tries to send Elena away when she asks to join a baseball game at the park.

    E Elena learns how to reach up and catch a long, high ball easily.

    F Abuela teaches Hector to play baseball.

> In some stories, a character's feelings and actions are what impact the story's outcome the most.

2 Which details **best** describe the settings in this story?

    A Elena's kitchen chair and the park

    B the park and Elena's backyard

    C Abuela's kitchen and the park

    D the park on two different days

▶ **Talk**

3 Which story events explain the change in Jorge's attitude toward Elena? What does Elena learn that makes him change his mind? List the events in the chart on page 127 to help organize your thoughts.

 ▶ **Write**

4 **Short Response** Describe the events that lead to a change in Jorge's attitude toward Elena. Include story details to support your response. Use the space provided on page 127 to write your response.

> **HINT** Identify the important events that take place in the story.

Write Use the space below to write your answer to the question on page 123.

Meeting Grandma

4 **Short Response** Describe the way the story setting of "Meeting Grandma" affected the characters and events. Include details from the story to support your response.

> **HINT** Identify details that explain why the characters lost track of time.

_____

_____

_____

_____

_____

_____

> Don't forget to check your writing.

Check Your Writing

- ☐ Did you read the prompt carefully?
- ☐ Did you put the prompt in your own words?
- ☐ Did you use the best evidence from the text to support your ideas?
- ☐ Are your ideas clearly organized?
- ☐ Did you write in clear and complete sentences?
- ☐ Did you check your spelling and punctuation?

Baseball Lessons

3 **Use the chart below to organize your ideas.**

Important Events		
First	
Next	
Last	

 Write **Use the space below to write your answer to the question on page 125.**

4 **Short Response** Describe the events that lead to a change in Jorge's attitude toward Elena. Include story details to support your response.

> **HINT** Identify the important events that take place in the story.

_____

_____

_____

_____

_____

_____

_____

▶ **Read**

Genre: Short Story

King Lear
by William Shakespeare

adapted from a retelling in *Beautiful Stories from Shakespeare*

WORDS TO KNOW
As you read, look inside, around, and beyond these words to figure out what they mean.

• **grudge**

• **proposed**

• **conduct**

1   King Lear was old and tired. He was aweary of the business of his kingdom. He wished only to end his days quietly near his three daughters. . . .

2   Lear called his three daughters together, and told them that he proposed to divide his kingdom between them. "But first," said he. "I should like to know how much you love me."

3   Goneril, who was really a very wicked woman, and did not love her father at all, said she loved him more than words could say. She loved him dearer than eyesight, space, or liberty, more than life, grace, health, beauty, and honor.

4   "I love you as much as my sister and more," professed Regan. "I care for nothing but my father's love."

5   Lear was very much pleased . . . and turned to his youngest daughter, Cordelia. "Now, our joy, though last not least," he said. "The best part of my kingdom have I kept for you. What can you say?"

6   "Nothing, my lord," said Cordelia.

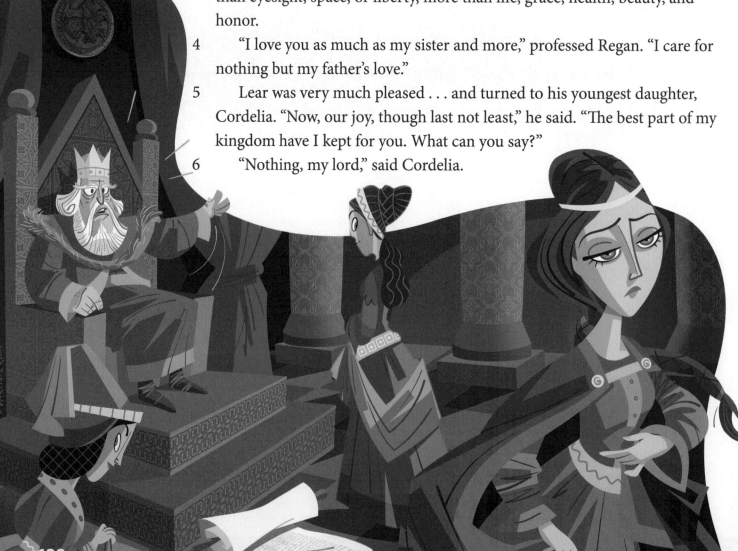

7   "Nothing can come of nothing. Speak again," said the King.

8   And Cordelia answered, "I love your Majesty according to my duty—no more, no less."

9   This she said, because she was disgusted with the way in which her sisters professed love, when really they had not even a sense of duty to their old father.

10   "I am your daughter," she went on. "You have brought me up and loved me. I return you those duties back as are right and fit, obey you, love you, and most honor you."

11   Lear, who loved Cordelia best, had wished her to make more extravagant professions of love than her sisters. "Go," he said. "Be forever a stranger to my heart and me." He divided the kingdom between Goneril and Regan, and told them that he should only keep a hundred knights at arms, and would live with his daughters by turns. . . .

12   The King now went to stay with this daughter Goneril, who had got everything from her father that he had to give. She now began to grudge even the hundred knights that he had reserved for himself. She was harsh and undutiful to him. Her servants either refused to obey his orders or pretended they did not hear them. . . .

13   "Goneril," said Lear, "I will not trouble you further—yet I have left another daughter."

14   So he set out with his followers for the castle of Regan. But she, who had formerly outdone her sister in professions of attachment to the King, now seemed to outdo her in undutiful conduct. She said that fifty knights were too many to wait on him, and Goneril . . . said five were too many, since her servants could wait on him.

15   Then when Lear saw that what they really wanted was to drive him away, he left them. It was a wild and stormy night, and he wandered about the heath half mad with misery. . . .

16   Here [Cordelia and her friends] found poor King Lear, wandering about the fields, wearing a crown of nettles and weeds. [She] brought him back and fed and clothed him. Then Cordelia came to him and kissed him.

17   "You must bear with me," said Lear. "Forget and forgive. I am old and foolish."

18   And now he knew at last which of his children it was that had loved him best, and who was worthy of his love. . . .

Think   Use what you learned from reading the story to respond to the following questions.

1   Reread paragraph 11. Which statement about story events **best** shows the relationship between King Lear and Cordelia at this point?

    A   King Lear began to believe that Cordelia had outdone her sisters in undutiful conduct.

    B   King Lear saw that each of his daughters really had wanted to drive him away all along.

    C   King Lear sent Cordelia away because she did not give him a strong enough expression of her love.

    D   King Lear knew at last that each of his daughters had never really loved him the way she had claimed.

2   Choose **two** statements that **best** describe the setting of the story.

    A   Lear's castle is too small for his daughters to live there.

    B   Regan's castle is surrounded by fields of nettles and weeds.

    C   The story takes place on a windy winter night.

    D   It is a time when kings rule and knights serve them.

    E   The castles are chilly places without much light.

    F   Lear's kingdom is large, wealthy, and beautiful.

    G   Goneril's castle is bigger and fancier than Regan's.

3   Read the sentence from paragraph 17 in the passage.

"You must <u>bear</u> with me," said Lear. "Forget and forgive. I am old and foolish."

Which dictionary definition **best** defines the word <u>bear</u> as it is used in the sentence?

    A   stand up to

    B   get over

    C   put up with

    D   provide for

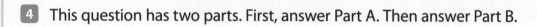

4 This question has two parts. First, answer Part A. Then answer Part B.

Part A
Which statement **best** describes why King Lear's feelings about Goneril started to change?

    A   She was a stranger to his heart.

    B   She began to be mean and disrespectful.

    C   She allowed fewer than fifty of her knights to serve him.

    D   She sent him outside to wander alone in the heath.

Part B
Underline **two** sentences in paragraph 12 that **best** support your answer in Part A.

> The King now went to stay with this daughter Goneril, who had got everything from her father that he had to give. She now began to grudge even the hundred knights that he had reserved for himself. She was harsh and undutiful to him. Her servants either refused to obey his orders or pretended they did not hear them. . . .

5 Which **two** sentences from paragraphs 15 and 16 **best** explain why King Lear's feelings toward his daughters changed at the end of the story? Write a sentence from each paragraph in the box below.

Write

6 **Short Response** What conclusions can be drawn about King Lear's experiences with his three daughters? What lesson did he learn? Use details about events from the story to support your response.

_____

_____

_____

_____

_____

_____

_____

 Learning Target

In this lesson, you learned to use details to describe the setting and events in a story. Now, explain how understanding the setting and events help you better understand a story.

_____

_____

_____

Lesson 9
Determining the
Theme of a Story

 **Learning Target**

Using details in the text to identify the theme of a story will help you understand the story's important message, or lesson.

▶ **Read** Most story authors want to share an important message or lesson about people or life called the **theme**. Normally, authors do not state the theme directly. Instead, they expect their readers to **infer** the theme from what happens in the story.

To figure out the theme of a story, look for details that show what the characters do, say, think, and feel. Think about how the characters solve their problems and what can be learned from their experiences.

Read the cartoon below. Find details that help you figure out the theme shown in the cartoon.

▶ **Think** What have you learned about how details help to develop the theme of a story? Think about the important details you identified in the cartoon. Complete the *Theme Chart* to identify the theme of the cartoon.

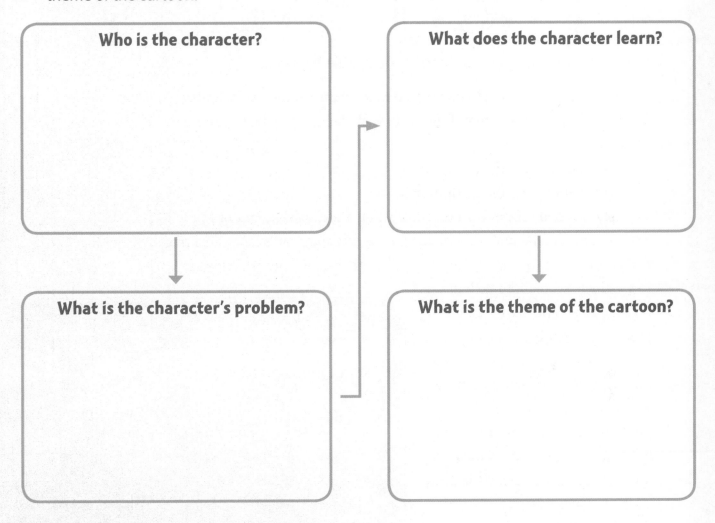

Who is the character?

What does the character learn?

What is the character's problem?

What is the theme of the cartoon?

▶ **Talk** Share your chart with a partner.

- Which details about the character did you include?
- How did each of you describe what the boy learned?
- Did you agree about the theme of the cartoon?

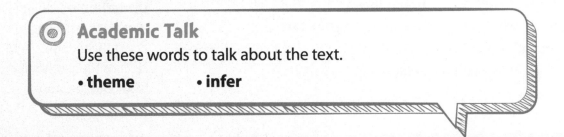

Academic Talk
Use these words to talk about the text.
- **theme**   - **infer**

> Read

The Two Travelers

adapted from a fable by Aesop

1   Two men planned a trip that would take them through wild, lonely country. They promised that if they met with danger they would stand by each other.

2   "To the end!" said the first man.

3   "To the end!" said the second man.

4   They traveled only a short distance when a bear rushed out of the woods at them. The first man, as soon as he saw the bear, rushed to a tree and climbed it as quickly as he could. The other man, who was slower to see the bear, realized he had no time to escape. He fell to the ground, pretending to be dead.

5   The bear came over to the man on the ground. The animal sniffed and smelled the traveler. The bear put his face right up to the man's ear. But the man held his breath and soon, losing interest, the bear walked away.

6   When the bear was safely out of sight, the first traveler slid down the tree and walked over to his companion, who was now sitting by the side of the road.

7   "Well, that was a close one, wasn't it?" the first man said. "What did that bear say when he had his mouth to your ear?"

8   "It's no secret," growled the second man. "He said I should never again believe anything said by a coward like you!"

Close Reader Habits

Underline words and phrases that tell you about the thoughts and feelings the second man has about the story events.

Explore **How do the details about the story characters and events help to develop the theme in "The Two Travelers"?**

> What happens in the story? How do characters act and feel? These questions will help you figure out the theme.

▶ Think

1 What do the characters promise each other as the story opens?

_____

_____

What happens that creates a problem for the characters?

_____

_____

2 How does each character attempt to solve the problem?

First Man: _____

Second Man: _____

3 At the end of the story, what has the second man learned about the first man's promises?

_____

_____

▶ Talk

4 Discuss story details that develop the theme of "The Two Travelers." How do the story events, especially the ending, help to reveal the author's lesson about life?

▶ Write

5 **Short Response** Describe a theme of "The Two Travelers." Include details about the story events and characters' actions that helped you infer the theme, or the author's life lesson. Use the space provided on page 140 to write your response.

> **HINT** Focus on what the characters do and what they say.

▶ **Read**

Claudine's Tack Attack

by Nadine Blanc

1   For three long years, the Nazis had occupied France. By now, everyone in my village was used to German trucks driving through, carrying ammunition and supplies to the front to supply Nazi soldiers in their battles against the American troops. From her window, my friend Claudine and I watched glumly as the trucks roared and rumbled by.

2   "Too bad we can't slow them down," I remarked one day.

3   Claudine's eyes became thoughtful. "Maybe we can!" She shared her idea, and we ran to her father's workshop.

4   "These might work," she announced, holding out a can of short, extremely sharp, steel tacks. "Papa uses them to shingle roofs."

5   Heading back to the road, I had second thoughts. How could two eleven-year-olds slow down a war machine with a bunch of tacks? Still, I followed Claudine up the hill to a spot above the road and crouched behind an old stone wall.

6   All too soon we heard the rumble of engines, so we raced to the road. "Like this," whispered Claudine. She began flinging handfuls of tacks onto the pavement, so I threw handfuls, too. Then, just in time, we ducked out of sight. Blam! The exploding tire sounded like a gunshot. Then another. Blam!

7   "Two blowouts!" Claudine whispered as we crept away. After dark, we crept back toward the road. The German soldiers were still struggling with the heavy rubber tires. Better yet, the road was so narrow that the other trucks could not pass. Claudine and I had delayed twelve trucks for half the day!

Close Reader Habits

How do the girls' actions relate to the theme? Reread the story. **Underline** details that explain what happens as a result of the girls' actions.

▶ **Think** Use what you learned from reading the story to respond to the following questions.

1 Which statement **best** explains why the girls wanted to slow down the German trucks?

> **A** The girls did not want the Nazi trucks to take French supplies back to Germany.
>
> **B** The girls wanted to make trouble for the German troops who were occupying France.
>
> **C** The girls wanted to help the Americans troops steal German supplies that were being carried on the trucks.
>
> **D** The girls wanted to slow down trucks delivering supplies to soldiers who were fighting American troops.

> Historical fiction is set in the past. Some parts are based on historical fact. Other parts have been made up by the author.

2 Which statement **best** describes how events in paragraphs 5, 6, and 7 are important to the theme of the story?

> **A** They show that the girls grew tired of looking out a window.
>
> **B** They show that the girls passed up a chance to be brave.
>
> **C** They show that the girls' dangerous risk paid off.
>
> **D** They show that the girls' clever plan was only temporary.

▶ **Talk**

3 Discuss the theme of the story. Identify important details about events and the girls' motivations and behavior that help reveal the theme. Organize the information in the Theme Chart provided on page 141.

 ▶ **Write**

4 **Short Response** Use the information in your chart to write about the theme, or lesson, that can be learned from the girls' experience. Support your response with details from the story. Use the space provided on page 141 to write your response.

> **HINT** Characters' thoughts, feelings, and actions can help reveal why they behaved as they did.

Write **Use the space below to write your answer to the question on page 137.**

The Two Travelers

5 **Short Response** Describe a theme of "The Two Travelers."
Include details about the story events and characters' actions
that helped you infer the theme, or the author's life lesson.

> **HINT** Focus on what the characters do and what they say.

_____

_____

_____

_____

_____

_____

_____

_____

_____

_____

Don't forget to check your writing.

Check Your Writing

☐ Did you read the prompt carefully?

☐ Did you put the prompt in your own words?

☐ Did you use the best evidence from the text to support your ideas?

☐ Are your ideas clearly organized?

☐ Did you write in clear and complete sentences?

☐ Did you check your spelling and punctuation?

Claudine's Tack Attack

3 **Use the Theme Chart below to organize your ideas.**

Who is the character?	What does the character learn?

What is the character's problem?	What is the theme of the story?

 Write **Use the space below to write your answer to the question on page 139.**

4 **Short Response** Use the information in your chart to write about the theme, or lesson, that can be learned from the girls' experience. Support your response with details from the story.

> **HINT** Characters' thoughts, feelings, and actions can help reveal why they behaved as they did.

_____

_____

_____

_____

_____

_____

_____

▶ **Read**

FROM
Sir Ivaine

by Maude L. Radford,
King Arthur and His Knights

WORDS TO KNOW
As you read, look inside, around, and beyond these words to figure out what they mean.

- **courtesy**
- **determined**
- **disobedient**

1   Among Arthur's Knights of the Round Table was one who was a mixture of good and bad, as indeed most people are. His name was Sir Ivaine; brave, kind-hearted, and merry; but at the same time fickle, sometimes forgetful of his promises, and inclined to make light of serious things.

2   One night, in the early spring, the knights and ladies of Arthur's Court were sitting in the dining-hall. . . .

3   Sir Ivaine was telling of his experience with the Black Knight.

4   "It was when I was very young," he said; "indeed, I had just been made a knight. Some one told me of the wicked Black Knight who lived, and still lives, in a wood a long way from here. Knowing that he did much evil, I determined to kill him. I rode to the wood where he lived, and in which I found a marble platform. In the middle of it was a sunken space holding a fountain. I walked to this, and following the directions of some writing which was on the stone, picked up a cup that lay at hand, and filling it with water, poured it into the fountain.

5   "Then a great storm of wind and rain arose, and when it was at its height the Black Knight rode up and began to attack me. We fought for a little while, but he easily overthrew me. Thinking me dead, he rode back, leaving me on the ground. But after a time I was able to mount my horse, and went back to my mother's castle."

6   At this moment the king and the queen entered, unperceived by any one except Sir Ivaine. The young man, who was always polite, sprang to his feet; then the other knights rose. Sir Kay, who was not always sweet-tempered, said to Sir Ivaine:

7   "We all know that you are very polite, but you have more courtesy than bravery."

8   At that Sir Ivaine said: "I was almost a boy when the Black Knight overthrew me, but I could conquer him now."

9   "It is very easy to say that after you have eaten," said Sir Kay. "Almost any knight feels brave and self-satisfied when he has had a good supper of venison."

10   The king asked what the conversation was about, and Sir Ivaine repeated the story of his adventure, adding: "And, Sir King, I crave your permission to set forth to-morrow to slay this Black Knight who is a pest in the land."

11   "I have heard of this man," said the king, "and have often thought of sending some one to punish him. But he lives far away, and it has been necessary heretofore to right first the wrongs nearest home. Yet now his evil deeds and persecutions must cease. Tomorrow a company of us will set forth and conquer him and all his people."

12   The king named some half-dozen of his knights, Sir Ivaine among them, who were to undertake this adventure.

13   Sir Ivaine was displeased; he thought that the adventure should be his alone. So he rose in the middle of the night and stole away unattended, determined to go in advance of the others and kill the Black Knight. It did not occur to him that in proving himself brave, he was also proving himself disobedient.

14   He rode forth in the darkness, humming merrily to himself. . . . After many days of travel, Sir Ivaine reached the forest in the midst of which was the castle of the Black Knight. He rode to the platform of stone, [and] the Black Knight appeared.

15   He recognized the armor of Sir Ivaine, and said: "Aha! I see I did not kill you before, but you shall not escape me this time."

16   "The best man shall win," said Sir Ivaine, cheerfully.

17   Then the two began a great combat. . . . [They] fought so eagerly that they were not even aware of the storm. It was not long before the Black Knight began to grow weak from the many powerful and death-dealing strokes from Sir Ivaine's sword. At last, seeing that he was mortally wounded, the Black Knight turned his horse. [He] galloped in the direction of his castle.

18   . . . Sir Ivaine followed. But he could not quite catch up with the Black Knight, although gaining on him inch by inch. By the time the castle moat was reached, Sir Ivaine was only five feet behind. The horses thundered one after the other over the bridge. The Black Knight rode under the portcullis, or sharp iron gate, which was raised. The instant he was inside, the portcullis fell, in order to shut out Sir Ivaine.

19   But Sir Ivaine had already passed beneath it. [He] sprang to his feet and drew his sword to renew his attack upon the Black Knight, but he was already dead . . . .

20   Then Sir Ivaine realized what his recklessness had cost him. There he was, alone in a strange castle, the lord of which he had killed. Soon the people of the castle would come and capture him, for he could not escape, since the portcullis was down. . . .

▶ **Think** Use what you learned from reading the legend to respond to the following questions.

1 This question has two parts. First, answer Part A. Then answer Part B.

Part A

In paragraph 7, Sir Kay says that Sir Ivaine is more polite than brave. Which statement below describes how Sir Ivaine tries to show that Sir Kay is wrong?

A Sir Ivaine wants to prove that he can be both kind-hearted and polite.

B Sir Ivaine wants to prove that he can defeat the Black Knight by himself.

C Sir Ivaine wants to prove that he can be brave after a good meal of venison.

D Sir Ivaine wants to prove that he can lead the company of knights.

Part B

Which statement below **best** supports the answer in Part A?

A "Among Arthur's Knights of the Round Table was one who was a mixture of good and bad, as indeed most people are."

B "'I have heard of this man,' said the king, 'and have often thought of sending someone to punish him.'"

C "'. . . . Sir King, I crave your permission to set forth to-morrow to slay this . . . pest in the land.'"

D "It did not occur to him that in proving himself brave, he was also proving himself disobedient."

2 Read the sentence from the passage.

> Sir Ivaine was <u>displeased</u>; he thought that the adventure should be his alone.

What does the prefix *dis-* mean in the word <u>displeased</u>?

    A   over

    B   not

    C   again

    D   under

3 Reread paragraph 13. How is Sir Ivaine's response to the king's plan important to the theme of the story?

    A   It shows he thought the knights named by the king were cowardly.

    B   It shows he thought the Black Knight could be defeated quickly and easily.

    C   It shows he did not think that evil deeds should go unpunished.

    D   It shows he did not think carefully about what he was about to do.

4 Read the sentence from paragraph 20.

> Then Sir Ivaine realized what his recklessness had cost him.

Which **three** statements **best** describe how the consequences of Sir Ivaine's actions support a story theme?

    A   Sir Ivaine had learned how to win a fight.

    B   Sir Ivaine needed to find a new company of knights.

    C   Sir Ivaine had shown the king he was disobedient.

    D   Sir Ivaine needed to prove himself again to the king.

    E   Sir Ivaine had put his life in great danger.

    F   Sir Ivaine would be embarrassed if he returned home.

    G   Sir Ivaine would have little hope of escape.

Write

5 **Short Response** What lesson does Sir Ivaine learn in this passage? How does his experience relate to the theme in the story? Use details from the passage to support your answer.

_____

_____

_____

_____

_____

_____

_____

 Learning Target

In this lesson, you learned to identify the theme of a story by using details in the text. How did learning to identify the theme help you better understand the story?

_____

_____

_____

👥 **Introduction**

LAFS.4.RL.1.2 Determine a theme of a . . . poem from details in the text . . .

Lesson 10
Determining the Theme of a Poem

Learning Target

Using details in a poem to determine its theme will help you develop a deeper understanding of the poet's ideas.

▶ **Read** On one level, a poem may share a poet's thoughts and feelings about a simple experience. On another level, the poet's words suggest a deeper meaning, or the **theme** of the poem. A poet usually won't state the theme. Instead, *you* must connect the poem's details to a message about life and how to live it.

To discover the theme of a poem, think of what it mostly tells about and the ideas shared by the poet. Then dig deeper. Ask yourself: How do details in the poem connect to a larger life lesson?

Read the poem carefully. Think about how choosing a road to take is similar to making choices in life.

A Fork in the Road

The road down which to go,

I simply do not know.

How do I make up my mind

When I know not what I'll find?

▶ **Think** Consider what you've learned so far about reading poetry. Then complete the chart to examine the levels of meaning in the **lyric poem** "A Fork in the Road."

Levels of Meaning

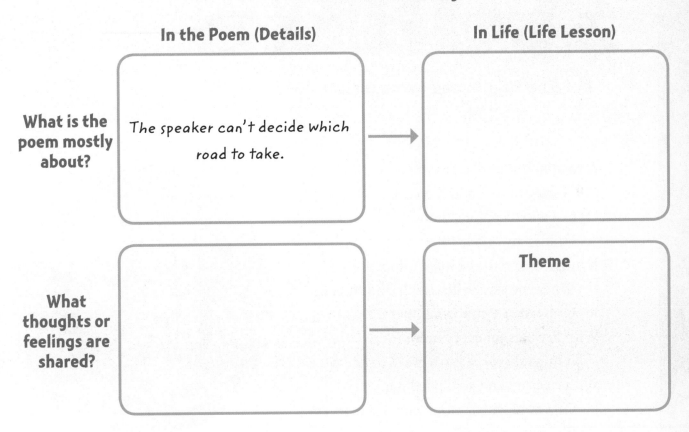

In the Poem (Details)

In Life (Life Lesson)

What is the poem mostly about?

The speaker can't decide which road to take.

What thoughts or feelings are shared?

Theme

▶ **Talk** Share your chart with a partner.

- How did each of you describe details in the poem and a lesson about life? Did you find similar connections?
- Did you agree on the thoughts and feelings the poet shared?
- What conclusions did you make about the theme?

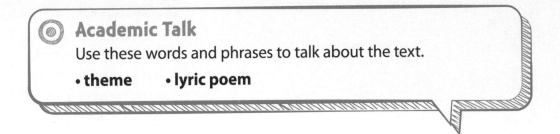

◉ **Academic Talk**
Use these words and phrases to talk about the text.
- **theme**   - **lyric poem**

Roads

by Rachel Field, *Favorite Poems, Old and New*

1 A road might lead to anywhere,—
    To harbor towns and quays,
 Or to a witch's pointed house
    Hidden by bristly trees.
5 It might lead past the tailor's door,
    Where he sews with needle and thread,
    Or by Miss Pim the milliner's,
 With her hats for every head.
    It might be a road to a great, dark cave
10 With treasure and gold piled high,
    Or a road with a mountain tied to its end,
    Blue-humped against the sky.
 Oh, a road might lead you anywhere—
    To Mexico or Maine.
15 But then, it might just fool you, and—
    Lead you back home again!

Close Reader Habits

As you reread, **circle** phrases that show where a road may lead. Then think about why a road leading back home might be a surprise.

Explore	**How do the details in the poem help you determine the theme, or life lesson, shared in "Roads"?**

> Look for details about where roads—and life—may lead. The details will lead you to the theme.

▶ Think

1 Complete the chart below by writing what the poem describes, what thoughts or feelings are shared, the life lesson, and the theme.

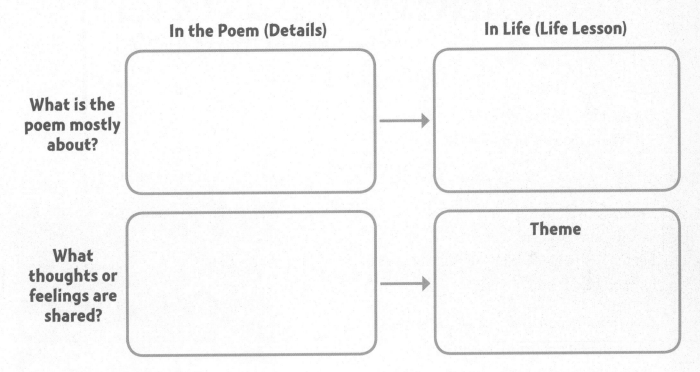

Levels of Meaning

In the Poem (Details) → **In Life (Life Lesson)**

What is the poem mostly about?

What thoughts or feelings are shared? → **Theme**

▶ Talk

2 Explain how the descriptions about where the different roads lead relate to a theme about life. Take notes about your discussion.

▶ Write

3 **Short Response** Explain why the descriptions of where roads may lead are important to the theme of "Roads." Consider how the poet's descriptions help you understand her message about life experiences. Use the space provided on page 154 to write your response.

> **HINT** Before you begin, review your chart to recall details about the poem and the theme.

The House by the Side of the Road

by Sam Walter Foss, *Dreams in Homespun*

1 Let me live in a house by the side of the road
       Where the race of men go by—
  The men who are good and the men who are bad,
       As good and as bad as I.
5 I would not sit in the scorner's seat[1]
       Nor hurl the cynic's ban[2]—
  Let me live in a house by the side of the road
       And be a friend to man.

  I see from my house by the side of the road,
10   By the side of the highway of life,
  The men who press with the ardor of hope
       The men who are faint with the strife,
  But I turn not away from their smiles nor their tears,
       Both parts of an infinite plan—
15 Let me live in a house by the side of the road
       And be a friend to man.

[1] **sit in the scorner's seat:** think bad things about other people
[2] **hurl the cynic's ban:** say mean things about other people

Close Reader Habits

What is the poem mostly about? Reread the poem. **Underline** key details that suggest something about the poem's theme, or message about life.

Think Use what you learned from reading the lyric poem to respond to the following questions.

Lyric poems express feelings and ideas. Read the poem once to get an idea of the topic. Then reread it to find the message.

1 This question has two parts. Answer Part A. Then answer Part B.

Part A

How is the theme of the poem shared through the speaker's words?

   A The speaker believes that hope gives all people a reason to live.

   B The speaker believes it's good to offer criticism to help people improve.

   C The speaker believes that he should only sit and observe what people do and say.

   D The speaker believes that people should be accepted as they are.

Part B

Choose **three** lines from the poem that **best** support your answer from Part A. Write them in the box below.

Talk

2 What is the theme of the poem? What thoughts does the speaker share? What do the poem's details tell you about the speaker's attitude about life? Use the chart on page 155 to gather your thoughts about the theme.

 Write

3 **Short Response** What is the theme of the poem? Use the information in your chart to explain how the details in the poem help to develop the theme. Include details from the poem in your response. Use the space provided on page 155 to write your response.

HINT Remember, the theme is a general statement that expresses the deeper meaning of the poem.

Write **Use the space below to write your answer to the question on page 151.**

Roads

3 **Short Response** Explain why the descriptions of where roads may lead are important to the theme of "Roads." Consider how the poet's descriptions help you understand her message about life experiences.

> **HINT** Before you begin, review your chart to recall details about the poem and the theme.

_____

_____

_____

_____

_____

_____

_____

_____

_____

Check Your Writing

☐ Did you read the prompt carefully?

☐ Did you put the prompt in your own words?

☐ Did you use the best evidence from the text to support your ideas?

☐ Are your ideas clearly organized?

☐ Did you write in clear and complete sentences?

☐ Did you check your spelling and punctuation?

Don't forget to check your writing.

The House by the Side of the Road

2 **Use the chart below to organize your ideas.**

Levels of Meaning

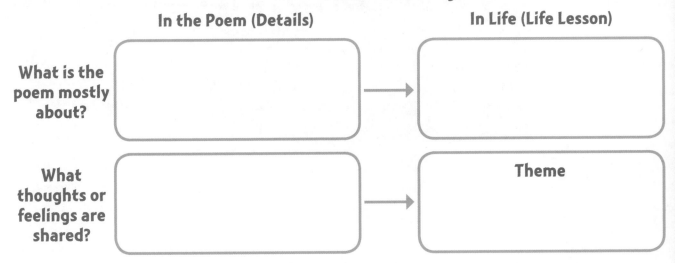

In the Poem (Details)		In Life (Life Lesson)
What is the poem mostly about?	→	
What thoughts or feelings are shared?	→	**Theme**

 Write **Use the space below to write your answer to the question on page 153.**

3 **Short Response** What is the theme of the poem? Use the information in your chart to explain how the details in the poem help to develop the theme. Include details from the poem in your response.

> **HINT** Remember, the theme is a general statement that expresses the deeper meaning of the poem.

_____

_____

_____

_____

_____

_____

_____

_____

▶ **Read**

WORDS TO KNOW
As you read, look inside, around, and beyond these words to figure out what they mean.

- **lure**
- **myriad**
- **treads**

The Path That Leads to Home

by Edgar Guest, from *A Heap O Livin'*

1 The little path that leads to home,
  That is the road for me,
  I know no finer path to roam,
  With finer sights to see.
5 With thoroughfares[1] the world is lined
  That lead to wonders new,
  But he who treads them leaves behind
  The tender things and true.

  Oh, north and south and east and west
10   The crowded roadways go,
  And sweating brow and weary breast
  Are all they seem to know.
  And mad for pleasure some are bent,
  And some are seeking fame,
15 And some are sick with discontent,
  And some are bruised and lame.

[1] **thoroughfares:** main roads; highways

Across the world the gleaming steel
        Holds out its lure for men,
But no one finds his comfort real
20   Till he comes home again.
And charted lanes now line the sea
        For weary hearts to roam,
But, Oh, the finest path to me
        Is that which leads to home.

25 'Tis there I come to laughing eyes
        And find a welcome true;
'Tis there all care behind me lies
        And joy is ever new.
And, Oh, when every day is done
30   Upon that little street,
A pair of rosy youngsters run
        To me with flying feet.

The world with myriad paths is lined
        But one alone for me,
35 One little road where I may find
        The charms I want to see.
Though thoroughfares majestic call
        The multitude to roam,
I would not leave, to know them all,
40   The path that leads to home.

▶ **Read**

Genre: Lyric Poem

Landscape

by Eve Merriam

1   What will you find at the edge of the world?
    A footprint,
    a feather,
    desert sand swirled?
5   A tree of ice,
    a rain of stars,
    or a junkyard of cars?

    What will there be at the rim of the earth?
    A mollusc,
10 a mammal,
    a new creature's birth?
    Eternal sunrise,
    immortal sleep,
    or cars piled up in a rusty heap?

▶ **Think** Use what you learned from reading the poems to respond to the following questions.

1 Read lines 13 and 14 from "The Path That Leads to Home."

> And mad for pleasure some are <u>bent,</u>
> And some are seeking fame,

Which word or phrase **best** states the meaning of <u>bent</u> as it is used here?

   A badly crooked or curved

   B strongly willing to try

   C dishonest

   D moved out of line

2 The table below contains themes and lines from "The Path That Leads to Home."

Themes	Lines
Traveling away from home is a waste of time.	I know no finer path to roam, With finer sights to see.
The world is full of exciting places to visit.	And sweating brow and weary breast Are all they seem to know.
Nothing is more pleasing than being home with family.	Across the world the gleaming steel Holds out its lure for men,
It is only by leaving home that we learn to love it.	But no one finds his comfort real Till he comes home again.

In the table below, write the theme that **best** describes the poem and the lines that **best** support the theme.

Themes	Lines

3 Which statement **best** describes the speaker's message about travel on the world's thoroughfares in "The Path That Leads to Home"?

   A   The world offers wonderful sights but not what is most important.

   B   Some travel only because they are searching for pleasure or for fame.

   C   Many must leave their homes because they are ill or injured.

   D   Weary people can find happiness by traveling across the sea.

4 Read the following line from "Landscape."

   What will you find at the edge of the world?

   Identify the statement that **best** describes other lines in the stanza.

   A   The world offers only piles of rusty junkyard cars.

   B   The world has contrasting climates, from cold to hot and dry.

   C   The world is full of natural beauty, but there is also ugliness.

   D   The world will be left with a footprint made by a single person.

5 Which statement **best** expresses the theme of the poem "Landscape?"

   A   The ends of the earth are worth visiting but might hold some unusual surprises.

   B   The natural wonders of the world might be spoiled by the choices people make.

   C   Going out into the world opens up new opportunities for people to better their lives.

   D   Traveling to far away places brings adventure and excitement.

Write

6 **Short Response** What is the theme shared in "The Path That Leads to Home?" (Think about what the speaker values in life.) Use details from the poem to support your answer.

_____

_____

_____

_____

_____

_____

_____

_____

 Learning Target

In this lesson, you used details to determine the theme of a poem. Now, describe how this skill helped you develop a deeper understanding of poems.

_____

_____

_____

Lesson 11
Summarizing Literary Texts

Learning Target

Identifying the most important events and details in a story or play helps you summarize and better understand what you read.

▶ **Read** When you **summarize** a literary text, you briefly retell story details and events in your own words.

A good summary includes only important story details. It tells about the main characters and setting. It also describes the **plot**, or story events, including the **problem** the characters face and its **solution**.

Read the story below. Think about which details to use to summarize it in two or three sentences.

A Jacket in the Boot

When we visited my parents' friends in England, their son James and I became fast friends. One afternoon, he and I decided to go to the park. It was cool outside, so James was looking for his jacket. Then he said, "Oh, I think I left it in the boot." I looked at him, puzzled. Why would he leave his jacket in a boot?

James started laughing. Then he told me that, in England, the trunk of a car is a *boot*. We had taken a drive in the countryside earlier. Because it had been warmer then, he had left his jacket in the trunk instead of wearing it.

▶ **Think** To summarize the story, think about the details that were important to understanding it. Complete the *Story Map* below to identify important story details. Then write the summary.

Characters	Setting
An American boy and James, an English boy	

Plot

Problem

Events

Solution

Summary: _____

_____

_____

_____

_____

▶ **Talk** Share your Story Map and summary with a partner. Did you agree about which details were important to include in your summaries?

⊚ **Academic Talk**
Use these words to talk about the text.
- **summarize**
- **problem**
- **plot**
- **solution**

▶ **Read**

The MIX-UP

by Frank Auster

1   Last month, Jenna announced to her mom that she planned on taking a long bike ride around the neighborhood.

2   "In that case," her mom responded, "would you please deliver these packages for me? This one is for Great Aunt Sally, and this one is for your cousin, Joey." Her mom explained that both relatives had birthdays coming up next week, and she wanted to surprise them.

3   "No problem," replied Jenna quickly. Since all of Jenna's relatives had settled in the same small town, no one lived too far away from the others. She tucked the packages in her backpack, hustled out to the garage, and grabbed her new bike.

4   When Jenna arrived at Great Aunt Sally's house, she suddenly realized that neither package had a name on it. But she was certain that Sally's was the one in the striped wrapping paper. Or was it? Wanting to be on her way, Jenna gave her great aunt the striped package and soon dropped off Joey's present, too.

5   The following week, Great Aunt Sally invited Jenna and her mom over for lunch. Sally answered the door wearing a bright, new baseball jersey. "How did you know this is my new favorite team?" she asked smiling at her guests.

6   "Oh, just a guess," said Jenna's mom sarcastically. She glared at Jenna, who quickly recognized her mistake.

Close Reader Habits

Underline the most important details that help you summarize the story.

Explore Which details should be included in a summary of "The Mix-Up"?

▶ **Think**

> In your Story Map, list only important parts of the story, not unimportant details.

1 Complete the Story Map below by adding important details.

Characters	Settings
	• Jenna's house and neighborhood

Plot	**Problem**
	Events
	Solution

▶ **Talk**

2 Compare the details from the story that you included in your Story Maps. How did you decide which details are the important ones?

 Write

3 **Short Response** Write a short summary of "The Mix-Up." In it, be sure to include important characters and events from the text. Use the space provided on page 168 to write your answer.

> **HINT** Remember to tell the story events in the order they occurred.

The Blind Men and the Elephant

based on an Indian folktale

1 [*Four blind men stand by a road. A man on an elephant rides by.*]

2 RIDER: Make way! Make way! I must take my elephant by.

3 FIRST MAN: I have never seen an elephant, sir.

4 OTHER MEN: Nor I!

5 RIDER: Never? Do you not know what he is like?

6 ALL FOUR MEN: No, sir.

7 RIDER: Come, then, stand by him, and touch him.

8 FIRST MAN [*placing his hand on the elephant's side*]: How interesting! Now I know all about him! He is exactly like a wall!

9 SECOND MAN [*feeling the tusk*]: Hah, not at all like a wall! He is round and smooth and sharp. He is like a spear.

10 THIRD MAN [*feeling the trunk*]: Oh, no! He is like a snake.

11 FOURTH MAN [*feeling a leg*]: Oh, how wrong you are! He is round and tall like a tree! [*All four men start arguing.*]

12 RIDER: Yet none of you can see! Ha, ha, ha! [*He rides on, laughing.*]

13 FIRST MAN: Ha, ha, ha! Hear how he laughs at you all!

14 SECOND MAN: He laughs at you and the others.

15 THIRD MAN: He laughs not at me!

16 FOURTH MAN: I say he laughs at all three of you!

17 [*The four men shake their fingers angrily and shout at each other.*]

Close Reader Habits

Why do the four blind men disagree about what an elephant looks like? Reread the drama. **Underline** details that explain why the men disagree.

▶ **Think** Use what you learned from reading the drama to respond to the following questions.

1 Choose the **three** most important events to use in a summary of the drama.

> A Story Map can help you organize details to use in a summary. Be sure to list story events in order.

   A An elephant rider allows four blind men to touch the elephant.

   B The blind men touch different parts of the elephant.

   C One man says the elephant must be like a snake.

   D One man declares the elephant is round and tall, like a tree.

   E Each man claims that only he knows what an elephant is like.

   F The blind men cannot agree about why the rider is laughing.

2 Which statement **best** summarizes why the elephant rider laughs?

   A Each man believes the rider is laughing at the other men.

   B Three of the men agree the rider is laughing at what the fourth man has said.

   C None of the men can see the elephant, but all four claim to be experts on its appearance.

   D The four men foolishly thank the rider for allowing them to get close to his pet elephant.

▶ **Talk**

3 Discuss the details in the drama that are important enough to include in a summary. Use the Story Map on page 169 to organize your ideas.

▶ **Write**

4 **Short Response** Use the information in your Story Map to summarize the drama. Include details from the text to support your summary. Use the space provided on page 169 to write your answer.

> **HINT** Retell the important events and ideas in the drama using your own words.

Write Use the space below to write your answer to the question on page 165.

The MIX-UP

HINT Remember to tell the story events in the order they occurred.

3 **Short Response** Write a short summary of "The Mix-Up." In it, be sure to include important characters and events from the text.

_____

_____

_____

_____

_____

_____

_____

Check Your Writing

☐ Did you read the prompt carefully?

☐ Did you put the prompt in your own words?

☐ Did you use the best evidence from the text to support your ideas?

☐ Are your ideas clearly organized?

☐ Did you write in clear and complete sentences?

☐ Did you check your spelling and punctuation?

Don't forget to check your writing.

The Blind Men and the Elephant

3 **Use the Story Map below to organize your ideas.**

Characters	Setting
Plot	**Problem**
	Events
	Solution

Write **Use the space below to write your answer to the question on page 167.**

4 **Short Response** Use the information in your story map to summarize the drama. Include details from the text to support your summary.

> **HINT** Retell the important events and ideas in the drama using your own words.

_____

_____

_____

_____

_____

_____

_____

Genre: Fable

WORDS TO KNOW

As you read, look inside, around, and beyond these words to figure out what they mean.

- **certainly**
- **conversation**
- **native**

The Two Frogs

a Japanese Fable

1   Once upon a time in the country of Japan, there lived two frogs. One made his home in a ditch near the town of Osaka, on the seacoast. The other dwelt in a clear little stream that ran through the city of Kyoto. At such a distance apart, they had never heard of each other. But funnily enough, the idea came into both their heads that they should like to see a little more of the world. After much thought, the frog who lived at Kyoto decided he wanted to see Osaka and the sea. At the same time, the frog who lived at Osaka decided he wanted to go to Kyoto . . . .

2   So one fine morning, they both set out along the road that led from Kyoto to Osaka. Half way between the two towns, there arose a mountain that had to be climbed. It took them a long time and a great many hops to reach the top, but they were there at last. Each was surprised to see another frog standing before him!

3   They looked at each other for a moment without speaking. Then they fell into conversation, explaining the cause of being so far from home. It was delightful to find that they both felt the same wish—to learn a little more of their native country. As there was no hurry, they stretched themselves out in a cool, damp place for a good rest before they parted.

4   "What a pity we are not bigger," said the Osaka frog. "We could see both towns from here and tell if it is worth our while going on."

5   "Oh, that is easy," returned the Kyoto frog. "We have only to stand up on our hind legs and hold on to each other. Then we can each look at the town we are traveling to."

6   This idea pleased the Osaka frog. He jumped up and put his front paws on the shoulders of his friend, who had risen also. There they both stood, stretching themselves as high as they could and holding each other so they might not fall down. The Kyoto frog turned his nose toward Osaka, and the Osaka frog turned his nose toward Kyoto. But the foolish things forgot that when they stood up, their great eyes lay in the backs of their heads. Though their noses might point to the places they wanted to go, their eyes beheld the places from which they had come.

7   "Dear me!" cried the Osaka frog. "Kyoto is exactly like Osaka. It is certainly not worth such a long journey. I shall go home!"

8   "If I had had any idea that Osaka was only a copy of Kyoto, I should never have traveled all this way," exclaimed the frog from Kyoto. As he spoke, he took his hands from his friend's shoulders, and they both fell down on the grass. They gave a polite farewell and set off for home again. And to the end of their lives, they believed that Osaka and Kyoto, which are as different as two towns can be, were as alike as two peas.

▶ **Think** Use what you learned from reading the fable to respond to the following questions.

1 Create a summary of important story events by choosing sentences from the box below. Write **three** sentences that describe the events in the box titled "Summary." Write the sentences in the order they happened.

The frogs rested in the cool, damp shade.

They decided not to continue their journeys.

It took time for the frogs to climb the mountain.

They tried to see the town they hoped to visit.

Two frogs were traveling to new towns.

They were surprised to see another frog.

Summary

2 Which statement **best** summarizes paragraphs 7 and 8 in the text?

A Both frogs show each other proof that their hometowns and the towns they are traveling to are copies of each other.

B Both frogs decide to stop traveling because they incorrectly believe the new towns are like their hometowns.

C Both frogs politely say goodbye and leave for their hometowns after falling on the grass.

D Both frogs say they wish they had never started on their journeys, and then they leave for home.

3 This question has two parts. First, answer Part A. Then answer Part B.

Part A

Which statement **best** describes why the frogs make the mistake they did?

    A   Kyoto looked exactly like Osaka, so the frogs did not think such a long journey was worth it.

    B   Each frog stood up on his hind legs and held on to the other frog to see the town he wanted to visit.

    C   The frogs' noses pointed in the right direction, but their eyes only saw what was behind them.

    D   The frogs got confused about the direction each of them had been traveling.

Part B

Underline **two** details in paragraph 6 that **best** support your answer in Part A.

    . . . . There they both stood, stretching themselves as high as they could and holding each other so they might not fall down. The Kyoto frog turned his nose toward Osaka, and the Osaka frog turned his nose toward Kyoto. But the foolish things forgot that when they stood up, their great eyes lay in the backs of their heads. Though their noses might point to the places they wanted to go, their eyes beheld the places from which they had come.

4 In paragraph 1, what is the meaning of the word <u>dwelt</u>?

    A   ate

    B   lived

    C   slept

    D   swam

Write

5 **Short Response** Summarize important story events that occur after paragraph 4 when the frogs decide to view the towns from the mountain. Use story details to support your summary.

_____

_____

_____

_____

_____

_____

_____

_____

_____

Learning Target

In this lesson, you learned to summarize the most important events and details in a literary text. Explain how learning to summarize will help you better understand a story or drama.

_____

_____

_____

_____

👥 **Introduction**

LAFS.4.RL.1.1 Refer to details and examples in a text when explaining what the text says explicitly and when drawing inferences from the text.

Lesson 12
Supporting Inferences About Literary Texts

Learning Target

Use story details and examples to explain what the story says and to support inferences you make.

▶ **Read** An **inference** is a reasonable guess you've figured out based on what you already know and the **details** of what you see or read. When you make an inference, be sure you can support it with **evidence**, or details and **examples** given in the text.

Readers make inferences to figure out what a story does not say directly. Evidence from a text can often help you understand something that an author hints at but does not state directly.

Look at the cartoon below. What inferences can you make about the girl? Which details help you figure out her feelings?

©Curriculum Associates, LLC   Copying is not permitted.

▶ **Think** What have you learned about using details to make inferences? Consider what happens in the cartoon. How does the girl eventually feel about the movie? Use what you figured out about the girl to complete the *Inference Chart* below. Make inferences based on the details in the cartoon and what you already know.

What the Cartoon Shows (Evidence)	What I Know (Experience)	My Inference
	People often look forward to seeing a new movie, especially if they've heard good things about it.	

▶ **Talk** Did you and your partner write the same things in the "What I Know" column? How did that information affect what you wrote in the "What the Cartoon Shows" column? How did the evidence help you make inferences?

Academic Talk
Use these words to talk about the text.
- **inference**
- **details**
- **evidence**
- **examples**

▶ **Read**

The Penny Thief

by Charlotte Fairchild

1   My family got a parakeet on the very day that we moved into our new apartment. On our first night in the new place, we tried to name our new pet. I wanted to call it Tweetie, but no one else liked that name. We couldn't find a name that everyone agreed on, so we agreed to think about it for a while.

2   My father always emptied his pocket change into a large glass bowl in the hallway. When we wanted money for this or that, he would count it out for us from the bowl. The very next night, as he tossed his change into the bowl, he mumbled, "Funny! I'm sure there were mostly pennies on top." None of us knew where the pennies had gone.

3   Every day that week, my father complained that someone was taking pennies from his bowl. We all pleaded ignorance. And every day that week, we discussed a new name for our pet.

4   At the end of the week, we took everything out of the birdcage to clean it. In every corner of the cage was a pile of pennies. That's when we learned that my mother had let the bird out to fly around every morning. "Penny thief!" my father cried. And our pet was named on the spot.

Close Reader Habits

As you read, **underline** the details the characters used as clues to figure out what happened to the pennies.

Explore   **What details in the mystery help you make inferences about story events in "The Penny Thief"?**

> Think about your inferences. Is each one based on text details? Does it make sense?

Think

1 Complete the Inference Chart below. It will help you understand the inferences the main character made.

What the Text Says (Evidence)	What I Know (Experience)	My Inference
		The family wants to find out what is happening.
	Some birds are attracted to shiny objects.	

Talk

2 As you read the story, what inferences did you make about the missing pennies? What text details supported your inferences?

 Write

3 **Short Response** Explain what inferences you made about the parakeet. Include at least **two** pieces of text evidence to support your answer. Use the space provided on page 182 to write your response.

> **HINT** To explain your inferences, give story clues that tell about what the parakeet does.

> **Read**

● ● ●

Thinking Out Loud

by Ben Karlsen

1   Slipping off the helmet of her space suit, Shaundra took a deep breath, then another. As she had hoped, fresh air filled her lungs. It was true: This planet, which she and her crew had spied from the mother ship, had an atmosphere like Earth's. And because it had air, perhaps the planet resembled Earth in other ways. Was it possible that she, Miek, and Goran had found what humans had long sought? Could there be intelligent life here?

2   For hours, the three astronauts wandered through forests and meadows filled with flowers of every color, shape, and aroma, but they were disappointed. The astronauts saw nothing that looked or acted like Earth animals—not even the tiniest insect. Certainly, they met no living creature with a human form.

3   Finally, they returned to their landing site. Before entering the mother ship, they had to collect samples of the plants. Shaundra grasped the stem of a particularly lovely flower and placed her knife against it. Suddenly, her eyes opened wide in surprise. "Did you hear that?" she asked the other two. "Well, I don't mean hear, exactly. It was as if this flower spoke to my mind. It seemed to be asking me not to harm it."

4   Miek was about to tease Shaundra when his jaw dropped. "I heard it—no, I felt it speak! It wants to know where we come from and why we're here. How should we answer it?"

5   "That's obvious," replied Shaundra. "We need only to think our answers, and this creature will understand. This planet is full of intelligent life—and it's beautiful life, too."

Close Reader Habits

What details help you understand the inferences that the astronauts made? Reread the story. To help you answer the questions that follow, **underline** the details that tell what the astronauts expected to find.

▶ **Think** Use what you learned from reading the science fiction story to respond to the following questions.

> A science fiction story tells about fictional settings, characters, and events but is based on scientific knowledge or theories.

1 This question has two parts. Answer Part A. Then answer Part B.

Part A
What kind of intelligent life did the astronauts expect to find?

- **A** The astronauts expected to find plants that could communicate.
- **B** The astronauts expected to find life forms they had never seen before.
- **C** The astronauts expected to find life similar to that on Earth.
- **D** The astronauts expected to find dangerous creatures.

Part B
Identify **two** sentences from paragraphs 1 and 2 that **best** support your answer to Part A. Write them in the box below.

```



```

▶ **Talk**

2 Based on the astronauts' words and actions, what inferences did the astronauts make when they started collecting flowers? Use the Inference Chart on page 183 to organize your thoughts.

> **HINT** Think about what the astronauts already knew that helped them make inferences about what they observed.

▶ **Write**

3 **Short Response** Use the information from your chart to describe how the characters used evidence to make their inferences. Include at least **two** details from the story to support your answer. Use the space provided on page 183 to write your response.

Write **Use the space below to write your answer to the question on page 179.**

The Penny Thief

3 **Short Response** Explain what inferences you made about the parakeet. Include at least two pieces of text evidence to support your answer.

> **HINT** To explain your inferences, give story clues that tell about what the parakeet does.

_____

_____

_____

_____

_____

_____

_____

_____

Check Your Writing

☐ Did you read the prompt carefully?

☐ Did you put the prompt in your own words?

☐ Did you use the best evidence from the text to support your ideas?

☐ Are your ideas clearly organized?

☐ Did you write in clear and complete sentences?

☐ Did you check your spelling and punctuation?

Don't forget to check your writing.

Thinking **Out Loud**

2 Use the Inference Chart below to organize your ideas.

What the Text Says (Evidence)	What I Know (Experience)	My Inference

Write Use the space below to write your answer to the question on page 181.

3 **Short Response** Use the information from your chart to describe how the characters used evidence to make their inferences. Include at least two details from the story to support your answer.

_____

_____

_____

_____

_____

_____

_____

▶ Read

Genre: Realistic Fiction

They Glow by Night

by Lorrie Doyle

WORDS TO KNOW
As you read, look inside, around, and beyond these words to figure out what they mean.

- **immediately**
- **restore**

1   My name is Aimee. My real name is Amy, but I prefer Aimee since it's more original and seems kind of French. Sometimes when I write Aimee I use a little heart to dot the *i*, but I think I might be growing out of that—I am, after all, almost ten.

2   You would think an almost-ten-year-old wouldn't need a baby-sitter, but then again, you're not my parents. They are convinced that I still need a sitter. "It's your money," I keep pointing out to them. "If you want to throw it away on a baby-sitter, that's up to you!"

3   Anyway, Emily's not so bad. Sometimes we actually have fun, since she always brings a supply of the newest shades of nail polish for me to try. But on this particular night, I was having a hard time concentrating on the "Glowing Green Goddess" Emily was applying to our fingers and toes. Outside, it poured rain. Lightning flashed across the sky, and thunder cracked so loudly it seemed to be exploding right in the living room. I could feel myself getting more and more nervous—not for myself, of course—I was worried about my parents being out in the storm, however.

4   Just as Emily was putting the finishing touches on my right pinky toe, there was a flash of lightning followed immediately by the loudest crack of thunder I'd ever heard. The television went blank and silent, and the hallway light went out, too. I noticed the familiar hum of the refrigerator was missing. The house was completely dark and silent. Emily stumbled to the window and peered outside.

5   "All the street lights are out. None of the other houses have lights either, so the power must be out in the whole neighborhood." She slowly bumped her way over to the phone and picked up the receiver. "No dial tone," she said glumly. "The telephone lines must be down too." She stopped and thought for a moment. "Your parents must have a flashlight around here somewhere. Do you know where they keep it?"

6   Before I could tell her I had no idea where the flashlight was, I started to cry. Yes, it's true. I cried, I wailed, I boo-hooed like a baby. I pressed my hands over my eyes to stop the flow, and still the tears kept coming. We were stuck here in the dark and quiet forever. And, to top off my fear and misery, what did I hear? Emily! Laughing! That was the last straw.

7   "Here we are," I sobbed, "stranded in the dark with my parents lost, no doubt, in the storm, and you're laughing!"

8   "Look Amy," she said. She reached out for my hand. And there, glowing in the dark, were my ten fingernails, and down at my feet were my ten glowing toenails. I looked over at Emily, whose toes and fingers were all aglow too! "Glowing Green Goddess" was fluorescent!

9   "See, we're not completely in the dark!" she said. "We can use our toes and our fingers to guide us. At least we won't bump into each other. Here, grab that bottle of nail polish. We'll search for the flashlight by the light of 'Glowing Green Goddess.'"

10   And we did. We found the flashlight, but we didn't even use it because we preferred getting around the house by "toe-light." My parents eventually got home, and the telephone and electrical service were restored. But ever since that night, I have kept an extra bottle of "Glowing Green Goddess" around because you never know when you might need some polish power!

▶ **Think**

Using what you learned from reading the story, respond to the following questions.

1 Which sentence **best** supports the inference that Amy isn't having fun with Emily that night?

A "They are convinced that I still need a sitter."

B "Sometimes we actually have fun, since she always brings a supply of the newest shades of nail polish for me to try."

C "But on this particular night, I was having a hard time concentrating on the 'Glowing Green Goddess' . . . . "

D "I noticed that the familiar hum of the refrigerator was missing."

2 The following question has two parts. First, answer Part A. Then answer Part B.

Part A
Which of these inferences about Emily is supported by paragraph 9?

A Emily is bossy and loud.

B Emily is clumsy and stubborn.

C Emily is clever and creative.

D Emily is kind and caring.

Part B
Underline **one** sentence in the paragraph that **best** supports your answer from Part A.

"See, we're not completely in the dark!" she said. "We can use our toes and our fingers to guide us. At least we won't bump into each other. Here, grab that bottle of nail polish. We'll search for the flashlight by the light of 'Glowing Green Goddess.'"

3 The following question has two parts. First, answer Part A. Then answer Part B.

Part A
What is the meaning of the word <u>aglow</u> as it is used in paragraph 8 of "They Glow by Night"?

    A very excited

    B shining with light

    C bright green

    D painted

Part B
Which detail from the story helps the reader understand the meaning of <u>aglow</u>?

    A The girls' nails helped them see in the dark.

    B The nail polish was a very flashy color.

    C The girls were painting their nails.

    D The girls were very excited to paint their nails.

4 From which sentence can you infer that Amy isn't as grown-up as she thinks she is?

    A "Sometimes when I write Aimee I use a little heart to dot the *i*, but I think I might be growing out of that. . . . "

    B "I could feel myself getting more and more nervous—not for myself, of course—I was worried about my parents being out in the storm, however."

    C "Before I could tell her I had no idea where the flashlight was, I started to cry."

    D "But ever since that night, I have kept an extra bottle of 'Glowing Green Goddess' around. . . ."

Write

5 **Short Response** Make an inference about how Amy feels about needing a baby-sitter **after** the events of this story. Explain your thinking. Include **two** details from the story to support your answer.

_____

_____

_____

_____

_____

_____

_____

 Learning Target

In the lesson, you learned how to use details and examples from a story to make inferences about what the story is telling you. Write about how making inferences helped you develop a better understanding of a story.

○ ○

_____

_____

_____

_____

▶ **Read**

Read the following story. Then answer the questions that follow.

from The Moffats

by Eleanor Estes

1   [Jane Moffat] watched Mr. Brooney, the grocery man, drive up with his horse and wagon. The Moffats called Mr. Brooney's horse the dancey horse, because of the graceful way he threw his legs about when he cantered up the street. Mr. Brooney stopped between Mrs. Squire's house and the yellow house. He threw down the heavy iron weight to keep his horse from dancing away and took several baskets of groceries from the wagon. He crossed the street and disappeared in Mrs. Frost's back yard. He was gone a long time. The horse stood there with the greatest patience. Occasionally he flicked his long tail to rid himself of a pesky fly. Or now and then he wriggled an ear when Sylvie, who was practicing her graduation music, hit a high note. And sometimes he raised one dainty foot or another and then planted it firmly on the ground. For the most part, however, he stood there dreamily, looking neither to left nor to right.

2   Jane watched him and watched him.

3   He had wings and could carry her away.

4   He was the wooden horse of Troy and many men could step out of him.

5   He was a bridge that she could walk under.

6   Sitting up there on the hitching post, watching the horse and watching the horse, Jane repeated to herself, "The horse is a bridge for me to walk under, and I'm goin' to walk under it."

7   So she jumped down and marched over to the horse. He stood there immobile. Except for his eyes, which followed her around like those of the velvet-clad lady in the picture in the sitting-room.

8   Jane walked under him and came out on the other side. This gave her an extraordinary feeling of satisfaction and elation.

9   At that moment when Jane was walking under the horse, Mama came to the window of the front parlor and shook her duster out vigorously. "Thank heavens!" she said to herself. "Thank heavens, it's spring again and that long hard winter is over." No more fussing with stoves and wondering where the next coal was coming from, she thought, slapping the duster against the green shutters. . . .

10   But goodness! Could Mama believe her eyes? What was Janey doing? Walking under that horse! Of all things! Mama was speechless with amazement and dropped the duster out of the window at the sight. Joe and Rufus saw her from the other side of the yard and became all tangled up in their stilts in consequence. Sylvie, who was practicing her singing way back in the kitchen, was the only one who did not see her.

11   "Jane! Whatever on earth!" Mama cried. "You mustn't do such things. You mustn't walk under horses. They might kick or start walking or something."

12   Jane stepped thoughtfully up the walk. "All right, Mama," she said.

13   She had no desire to keep on walking under horses. It was just something she felt she had to do at that moment, just that once. And she knew that horse. She'd been watching him and watching him. So she had walked under him and from the feeling inside of her she thought it had turned out to be an all right sort of thing to do—just that once.

▶ **Think**

1 This question has two parts. First, answer Part A. Then answer Part B.

Part A
Which phrase **best** describes Mr. Brooney's horse?

    A   small but dangerous

    B   useful but unpredictable

    C   elegant and calm

    D   heavy and slow

Part B
Identify three sentences from the text that **best** support your answer in Part A. Write your evidence in the box below.

2   Why does Mr. Brooney's horse wriggle his ears?

     A   He hears Sylvie sing a high note.

     B   He is bothered by a pesky fly.

     C   He is impatient waiting for Mr. Brooney.

     D   He is listening to Jane talking to him.

3   Read these sentences from the story. They tell Jane's thoughts about the horse.

     He had wings and could carry her away.

     He was the wooden horse of Troy and many men could step out of him.

     He was a bridge that she could walk under.

   What can readers infer about Jane based on her thoughts?

     A   She is fond of Mr. Brooney's horse.

     B   She wants to run away.

     C   She is very imaginative.

     D   She wishes she lived in another time.

4   This question has two parts. First, answer Part A. Then answer Part B.

Part A
Which phrase best describes the setting of the story?

     A   a neighborhood in the past

     B   a farm in the past

     C   a playground in the present

     D   a big city in the past

Part B
Underline **three** sentences from the text that best support your answer in Part A.

[Jane Moffat] watched Mr. Brooney, the grocery man, drive up with his horse and wagon. The Moffats called Mr. Brooney's horse the dancey horse, because of the graceful way he threw his legs about when he cantered up the street. Mr. Brooney stopped between Mrs. Squire's house and the yellow house. He threw down the heavy iron weight to keep his horse from dancing away and took several baskets of groceries from the wagon. He crossed the street and disappeared in Mrs. Frost's back yard. He was gone a long time. The horse stood there with the greatest patience. . . .

5 Read the following table based on the story.

Jane's Actions
• She watches and watches Mr. Brooney's horse.
• She sits on the hitching post.
• She jumps off the post and marches over to the horse.
• _____

Which of these key details belongs on the blank line?

    A   She watches her brothers play on stilts.

    B   She helps her mother dust the parlor.

    C   She walks underneath the horse.

    D   She rides the horse down the street.

6 This question has two parts. First, answer Part A. Then answer Part B.

Part A

Which sentence is the **best** description of Mama's response to Jane's actions?

    A   Mama is too busy dusting the front parlor to notice what Jane is doing.

    B   Mama does not see Jane because she is in the kitchen with Sylvie.

    C   Mama is proud of Jane for taking a risk and being so brave.

    D   Mama is shocked and upset with Jane for not being more careful.

Part B

Which sentence from the story **best** supports the correct answer to Part A?

    A   "At that moment when Jane was walking under the horse, Mama came to the window of the front parlor and shook her duster out vigorously."

    B   "Mama was speechless with amazement and dropped the duster out of the window at the sight."

    C   "Joe and Rufus saw her from the other side of the yard and became all tangled up in their stilts in consequence."

    D   "Sylvie, who was practicing her singing way back in the kitchen, was the only one who did not see her."

7 Select **four** details that should be included in a summary of the story.

    A Jane's mother is inside the house dusting the front parlor.

    B Jane and her brothers are outside playing.

    C While Mr. Brooney delivers groceries, Jane and her brothers feed the horse carrots.

    D Jane sits on the hitching post and watches Mr. Brooney's horse.

    E Jane is outside in order to avoid helping her mother with the spring cleaning.

    F The horse flicks his long tail and stomps his feet.

    G As Jane watches the horse, she imagines him as a bridge for her to walk under.

    H Jane stays outside to avoid hearing Sylvie practice her graduation music.

    I Jane jumps off the hitching post and walks under the horse.

    J Walking under the horse gives her a good feeling.

8 This question has two parts. First, answer Part A. Then answer Part B.

Part A
Which statement **best** describes a theme in the story?

    A Never walk under a horse.

    B Some risks are dangerous but worth taking.

    C Mr. Brooney's horse is a beautiful creature.

    D Sometimes Jane's mother worries too much.

Part B
Which **two** quotations from the story support your answer to Part A?

    A "Jane watched him and watched him."

    B "But goodness! Could Mama believe her eyes? What was Janey doing?"

    C "You mustn't walk under horses. They might start to kick or start walking or something."

    D "She had no desire to keep on walking under horses."

    E "So she had walked under him and from the feeling inside of her she thought it had turned out to be an all right sort of thing to do—just that once."

9 What gives Jane "an extraordinary feeling of satisfaction and elation" in the story? Why does Jane feel this way? Use details from the story to support your answer.

_____

_____

_____

_____

_____

_____

_____

_____

_____

10 This question has two parts. First, answer Part A. Then answer Part B.

Part A
What does <u>immobile</u> mean in paragraph 7?

    A unpleasant

    B graceful

    C helpless

    D motionless

Part B
Which detail from the story **best** helps the reader understand the meaning of <u>immobile</u>?

    A "The horse stood there with the greatest patience."

    B "The Moffats called Mr. Brooney's horse the dancey horse, . . ."

    C "So she jumped down . . ."

    D ". . . marched over to the horse."

11 The box below contains traits and details from *The Moffats* that describe Jane.

Traits	Details from the Play
imaginative	". . . Jane repeated to herself, 'The horse is a bridge for me to walk under, and I'm goin' to walk under it.'"
observant	"He was the wooden horse of Troy and many men could step out of him."
determined	"She'd been watching him and watching him."

In the chart below, write the character traits from the box. Then add details from the box that support each trait.

Traits	Details from the Play

Write

12 **Extended Response** What lesson does Jane learn at the end of the story? How does her experience with the horse teach her this lesson? Be sure to include key details from the story in your answer.

In your answer, be sure to
• explain what Jane learns
• tell how the horse helps teach this lesson
• use key details from the story in your answer

Check your writing for correct spelling, grammar, capitalization, and punctuation.

_____

_____

_____

_____

_____

_____

_____

_____

_____

_____

_____

_____

UNIT 3

Craft and Structure in Informational Text

How are buildings like informational texts? Buildings have frameworks to hold them up. Similarly, informational texts have frameworks called **text structures**. The type of framework a building has depends on the type of building it is. Skyscrapers have frameworks of steel and concrete. Houses have frameworks mostly of wood. And, like a building, the structure a text has depends on what that text needs to do. Writers **craft** their texts to accomplish particular goals. Does a writer want to compare video games? Then the writer puts that information into a compare–contrast structure. Does a writer want to explain how volcanic eruptions create diamonds? Then the writer uses a cause–effect structure. A text structure is more than just organization—it is always organization with a purpose.

In this unit, you'll practice identifying unknown words. You'll describe text structures. And, you'll learn the differences between first- and secondhand accounts of events. So, put on your hard hat—or rather, your thinking cap—as we read all sorts of informational texts.

✔ Self Check

Before starting this unit, check off the skills you know below. As you complete each lesson, see how many more skills you can check off!

I can:	Before this unit	After this unit
find the meaning of unfamiliar words and phrases in an informational text.	☐	☐
describe cause–effect and compare–contrast text structures.	☐	☐
describe chronological and problem–solution text structures.	☐	☐
compare and contrast the differences between firsthand and secondhand accounts of the same topic.	☐	☐

page 210

page 225

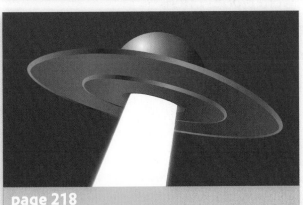

page 218

page 239

page 246

page 253

👥 **Introduction**

LAFS.4.RI.2.4 Determine the meaning of general academic and domain-specific words or phrases in a text relevant to a grade 4 topic or subject area.

Lesson 13
Unfamiliar Words

Learning Target

Using context clues to figure out the meaning of unfamiliar words and phrases will deepen your understanding of the texts you read.

▶ **Read** Informational texts often have words people don't use in everyday life.

- Some words usually appear only in texts in one **subject area**. For example, you'll see the word *fossil* in science texts and the word *geography* in social studies texts.

- Other words, called **academic words**, are useful in many subject areas. For example, the academic word *process* often appears in both science and social studies texts.

As you read, you can use **context clues** to figure out the meanings of unfamiliar words and phrases. Clues might be synonyms, antonyms, examples, or definitions.

Read the passage below. Circle the phrase <u>conceived of</u>, and underline context clues that help you learn its meaning.

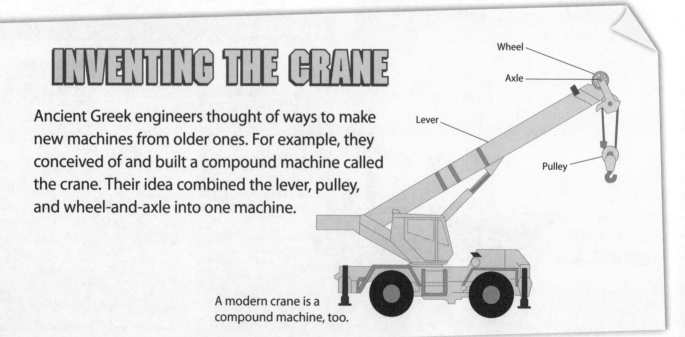

INVENTING THE CRANE

Ancient Greek engineers thought of ways to make new machines from older ones. For example, they conceived of and built a compound machine called the crane. Their idea combined the lever, pulley, and wheel-and-axle into one machine.

Wheel
Axle
Lever
Pulley

A modern crane is a compound machine, too.

▶ **Think** What have you learned about figuring out the meaning of unfamiliar words? Complete the chart below to figure out the meaning of the phrase <u>conceived of</u> as it is used in the passage. Then explain what the phrase most likely means.

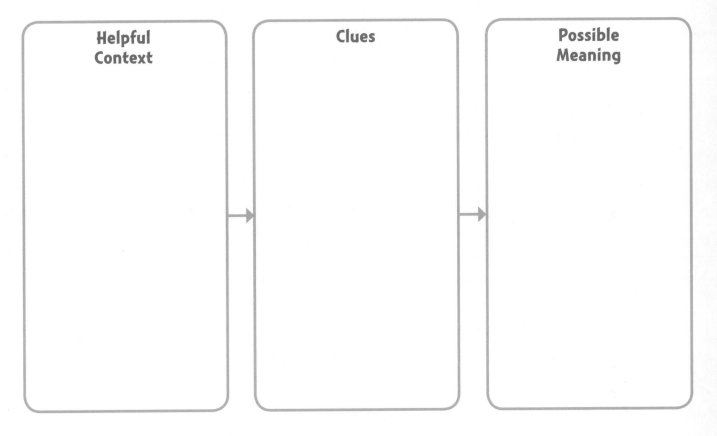

Helpful Context	Clues	Possible Meaning

The meaning of the phrase: _____

_____

▶ **Talk** Share your chart and meaning with a partner.

- Did you agree about the helpful context?
- Did you agree about the meaning of the phrase?

◎ **Academic Talk**
Use these phases to talk about the text.

- **subject area**   • **academic words**
- **context clues**

> **Read**

Fire and Air

by Johanna Joyner

1   Starting a fire is a bit like following a recipe. Getting anything to combust takes three ingredients: fuel, heat, and oxygen. All three are needed for burning to begin, but where do these ingredients come from? Fuel is anything that burns easily, including wood, paper, or grass. Heat can come from many places, but most people use matches. And oxygen, of course, is a gas in the air around us.

2   If a fire doesn't have enough of any one of the three ingredients, it will be weak. To strengthen the fire, just add one or more of the ingredients. It is simple to add more fuel or heat, but how do you add more oxygen? From a safe distance, blow on the fire. You will see it strengthen because blowing adds oxygen to the fire, making it burn vigorously. Your fire will grow bigger, brighter, and stronger.

3   To understand the role oxygen plays in keeping a fire burning, try this experiment:

An Experiment with Fire

4   **Materials You Will Need**

   • **MOST IMPORTANT:** A TEACHER HELPING YOU
   • three small candles (tealights)
   • three saucers
   • two glass jars, one larger than the other

5   **Procedure to Follow**

   Put each candle on a saucer, and have your teacher light each one. Place a jar over two of the candles. Pay attention to the candles to monitor what happens over time. You will observe that the candle with the least air available—the one covered by the smaller jar—is the first one extinguished. Keep watching to see which candle goes out next. Blow out the last candle.

> ### Close Reader Habits
>
> As you read, **circle** unfamiliar words or phrases. Then **underline** words or phrases that give you clues about their meanings.

Explore | How did context clues help you figure out the meaning of unfamiliar words in the science text?

Think

> A chart will help you identify the parts of the text that provide context clues.

1 Complete the chart below. Write the helpful context and clues you used to figure out the meaning of each unfamiliar word.

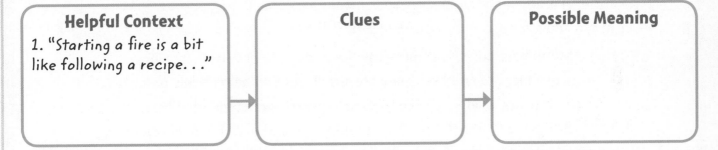

Combust means:

Helpful Context	Clues	Possible Meaning
1. "Starting a fire is a bit like following a recipe. . ."		

Monitor means:

Helpful Context	Clues	Possible Meaning
1. "Pay attention to the candles. . ." 2. ". . . happens over time."	1. attention	

Talk

2 Explain how figuring out the meaning of unfamiliar words helped you understand the text. Which context clues were the most helpful? Why?

Write

> **HINT** Replace an unfamiliar word with its possible meaning to see if it makes sense.

3 **Short Response** Briefly explain how you figured out the meaning of <u>combust</u> and <u>monitor</u>. Use text details to support your answer. Use the space on page 208 to write your answer.

Over Bridge, Under Tunnel

by Lloyd Frank

1   Mountains, lakes, and rivers can get in the way of people traveling from one place to another. There are structures that help people pass such obstacles. Bridges and tunnels help people overcome such barriers.

2   Bridges and tunnels are different in design and placement. A bridge is built over a body of water, a highway, or a railroad track. A tunnel, in contrast, is a passageway under the ground, under a body of water, or through a mountain. Bridges vary in shape and are often placed above ground or water. Some are even famous. The Golden Gate Bridge is one of the most renowned bridges in the world. This celebrated structure crosses over the entrance to San Francisco Bay and connects San Francisco to northern California. The Golden Gate is known for its length and height. But it is best known for its beauty. People come from all over the world not just to cross the Golden Gate but simply to look at it.

3   Of course, not even the world's most famous tunnel gets many visitors who just want to look. It's hard to get a good view of a subterranean passage. But since the Channel Tunnel opened in 1994, it has transported millions of people. The Channel Tunnel, or "Chunnel," runs beneath the English Channel and connects France and England. The Chunnel is a rail tunnel. The only automobiles that cross it are carried on special railway cars. The Chunnel is not the longest tunnel in the world, but it is one of the few tunnels that connects two countries.

Close Reader Habits

How can context clues help you? **Circle** words that are unfamiliar. Reread the article. **Underline** clues that help you figure out the meaning of the words.

Think Use what you learned from reading the science article to respond to the following questions.

1. What is the meaning of <u>obstacles</u> as it is used in paragraph 1 of the text?

    A   things made below or above ground

    B   things that slow or stop movement

    C   things that help people travel

    D   things built through mountains or over water

> Synonyms are context clues with meanings that are almost like the unfamiliar words. Antonyms are context clues with meanings that are opposite to the unfamiliar words.

2. Underline **four** context clues in paragraph 2 that **best** help you understand the meaning of the word <u>renowned</u>.

    A bridge is built over a body of water, a highway, or a railroad track. . . . Bridges vary in shape and are often placed above ground or water. Some are even famous. The Golden Gate Bridge is one of the most renowned bridges in the world. This celebrated structure crosses over the entrance to San Francisco Bay and connects San Francisco to northern California. The Golden Gate is known for its length and height. But it is best known for its beauty.

Talk

3. Discuss the meaning of the word <u>subterranean</u> as it is used in this sentence from paragraph 3:

    It is hard to get a good view of a <u>subterranean</u> passage.

> **HINT** Use a chart to organize your thoughts about context clues.

 Write

4. **Short Response** Write a definition of the word <u>subterranean</u>. Identify the context clues you found. Describe the strategy you used to figure out the meaning of the word. Use details from the text to support your response. Use the space provided on page 209 to write your answer.

Write Use the space below to write your answer to the question on page 205.

Fire and Air

3 **Short Response** Briefly explain how you figured out the meaning of <u>combust</u> and <u>monitor</u>. Use text details to support your answer.

> **HINT** Replace an unfamiliar word with its possible meaning to see if it makes sense.

_____

_____

_____

_____

_____

_____

_____

Check Your Writing

☐ Did you read the prompt carefully?

☐ Did you put the prompt in your own words?

☐ Did you use the best evidence from the text to support your ideas?

☐ Are your ideas clearly organized?

☐ Did you write in clear and complete sentences?

☐ Did you check your spelling and punctuation?

Don't forget to check your writing.

over Bridge, Under Tunnel

3 **Use the chart below to organize your ideas.**

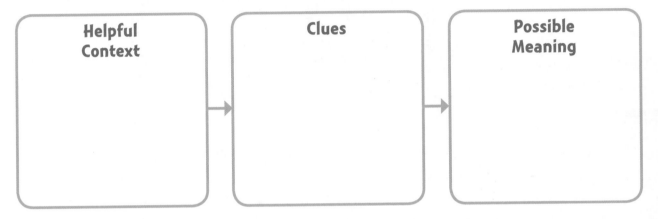

Helpful Context	Clues	Possible Meaning

Write **Use the space below to write your answer to the question on page 207.**

4 **Short Response** Write a definition of the word <u>subterranean</u>. Identify the context clues you found. Describe the strategy you used to figure out the meaning of the word. Use details from the text to support your response.

_____

_____

_____

_____

_____

_____

_____

_____

▶ **Read**

Seashells

by Bela Moté

WORDS TO KNOW
As you read, look inside, around, and beyond these words to figure out what they mean.

- **series**
- **hinged**
- **foreign**

1   If you walk along the seashore, you will probably see many kinds of shells. Seashells were once the homes of live animals. The animals that live inside shells have soft bodies, so they need their shells to protect them from harm. Their shells save them from storms or predators such as starfish, birds, and otters. Shells also give the animals a shape. In that way, shells are like skeletons on the outside of the body. When the animals die, the shells remain.

2   Creatures with shells belong to a group of animals called **mollusks**. Not all mollusks have shells. Of the mollusks that do have shells, there are two main groups.

worm shell

slipper shell

helmet shell

Univalves

3   More than three-quarters of all mollusks are **univalves**, a word that means "having a shell that is all one piece." The shell is coiled, and inside the coil is the soft body of the mollusk. Many univalves are named for their appearance. Look at the examples above. Does the helmet shell remind you of a helmet? How about the worm and slipper shells?

4   Some univalves have small holes in their shells. Abalone shells have a series of holes. Water and wastes are expelled, or pushed out, through the holes. The inside of an abalone shell gleams with different rainbow colors. This iridescent substance is called mother-of-pearl.

abalone shell

angel wing
shell

jackknife
shell

Bivalves

5 After univalves, **bivalves** are the next largest group of mollusks. When a bivalve is alive, the two parts of its shell are hinged. After the animal dies, you may find just one part of the shell lying on the beach.

6 Many bivalves have names that reflect their appearance. A jackknife is a knife that folds into its own case. The jackknife clam has an appropriate name because it has about the same shape as a closed jackknife. Are angel wing and kitten's paw fitting names for the shells shown here?

7 There are many different kinds of clams, from very small to very large. The giant clam is the largest bivalve. Some are four feet long and weigh 500 pounds. The giant clam even grows its own food. Tiny plants get caught in the clam. The plants get what they need from the clam, but eventually the clam eats the plants.

8 Another common bivalve is the oyster. All oysters can make pearls, but the pearl oyster makes the most beautiful ones. A pearl is an accident. A grain of sand or something else gets inside the oyster shell. An oyster is creating new shell material all the time. To protect itself from the foreign body, the oyster covers it with the same material that the oyster's shell is made of. The result is a pearl.

kitten's paw
shell

giant oyster shell

pearl oyster shell

▶ **Think** Use what you learned from reading the science text to respond to the following questions.

1 Read the sentence from paragraph 1 in the passage.

> Their shells save them from storms or <u>predators</u> such as starfish, birds, and otters.

What does the author suggest to the reader by using the word <u>predators</u>? Pick **two** choices.

    A Predators can harm some animals.

    B Predators need to find shelter from storms.

    C An animal's shell helps protect it.

    D All predators have skeletons.

    E When the animal dies, the shell remains.

2 This question has two parts. First, answer Part A. Then answer Part B.

Part A
What is the meaning of the word <u>iridescent</u> as it is used in paragraph 4?

    A not letting light through

    B easy to notice or understand

    C shining with many varying colors

    D a small amount of something

Part B
Which phrase from the passage helps the reader understand the meaning of <u>iridescent</u>?

    A "next largest group of mollusks"

    B "have small holes in their shells"

    C "the inside of an abalone shell"

    D "gleams with different rainbow colors"

3 This question has two parts. First, answer Part A. Then answer Part B.

Part A

What is the meaning of the word <u>bivalve</u> as it is used in paragraph 5?

    A   having a hard outer shell

    B   having a shell with two pieces

    C   having a soft outer shell

    D   having a shell that is all one piece

Part B

Underline the **two** phrases in paragraph 5 that **best** support your answer in Part A.

> After univalves, **bivalves** are the next largest group of mollusks. When a bivalve is alive, the two parts of its shell are hinged. After the animal dies, you may find just one part of the shell lying on the beach.

4 Read the sentence from the passage.

> The jackknife clam has an <u>appropriate</u> name because it has about the same shape as a closed jackknife.

What does the author tell the reader by using the word <u>appropriate</u>? Pick **two** choices.

    A   Bivalves are the largest group of mollusks.

    B   Jackknife describes the shape of the clam.

    C   An angel wing is a good name for the clam.

    D   Jackknife is a good name for the clam.

    E   The clam looks like an open jackknife.

    F   A jackknife folds into its own case.

Write

5 **Short Response** What does the author tell the reader by using the underlined word in the sentence below from paragraph 8? How do the details in the paragraph further develop this idea? Include **one** or more context clues from the text to support your response.

A pearl is an <u>accident</u>.

_____

_____

_____

_____

_____

_____

_____

 Learning Target

In this lesson, you learned to use context clues to figure out the meaning of unfamiliar words or phrases. Explain how using context clues deepened your understanding of the text.

LAFS.4.RI.2.5 Describe the overall structure (e.g., comparison, cause/effect . . .) of events, ideas, concepts, or information in a text or part of a text.

Lesson 14
Text Structures, Part 1: Cause–Effect and Compare–Contrast

Learning Target

Identifying the main way an author organizes events and ideas in an informational text will help you better understand the topic.

▶ **Read** Authors use different **text structures** to organize the ideas and details they want readers to understand about a topic.

- A **comparison** text structure describes how two or more things are similar and different. Words such as *like, both,* and *unlike* signal a comparison.

- A **cause–effect** structure connects events that happen (effects) with why they happen (causes). Words such as *because, as a result, therefore,* and *if . . . then* often signal this structure.

Read each passage below. Circle words that signal its text structure.

Passage 1
The earliest sound recordings were made on tin foil. Because the foil ripped easily and sounded bad, inventors looked for better materials. Later recordings were therefore put on harder metal or wax, which lasted longer and sounded better.

Passage 2
Thomas Edison invented the phonograph in 1877. It played sound when the listener spun a hand crank that turned a metal tube. In 1886, Alexander Bell invented the graphophone. Like the phonograph, the graphophone played sound and was powered by the listener. Unlike the phonograph, the graphophone was operated by means of a foot pedal that turned a wax-covered tube.

▶ **Think** Consider what you've learned about how authors use different text structures to organize their writing. Match each graphic organizer to the passage featuring that text structure. Then complete the graphic organizers using details from each passage.

Passage _____ : Comparison Text Structure

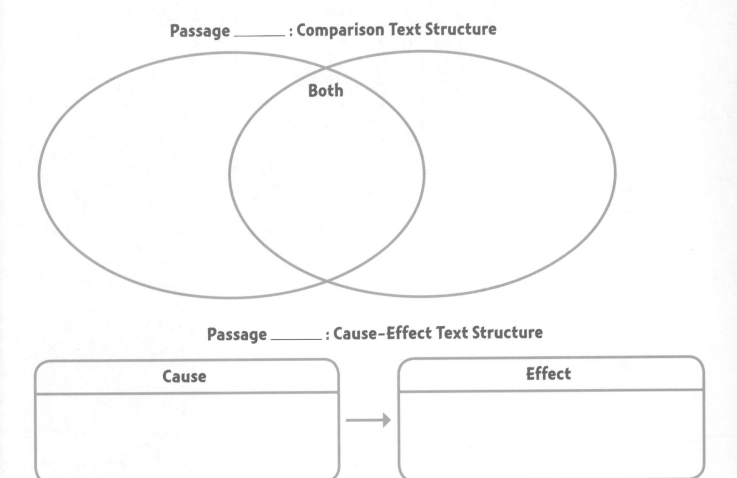

Both

Passage _____ : Cause–Effect Text Structure

Cause		Effect
	→	

▶ **Talk** Share your graphic organizers with a partner. Did you choose the same graphic organizers for the passages? What information did you list in the *Venn diagram*? What information did you list in the cause–effect chart? Which signal words in each passage helped you?

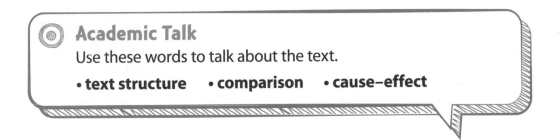

◎ **Academic Talk**
Use these words to talk about the text.
- **text structure**   - **comparison**   - **cause–effect**

Genre: **Magazine Article**

The Night the Martians Landed

by Scott Carey

1   October 30, 1938, was perhaps the most frightening night that thousands of Americans would ever experience. It was the night that the science fiction novel *The War of the Worlds* was presented in the form of a radio news broadcast.

2   Orson Welles, who would later become a famous movie actor and director, made the broadcast from a studio in New York City. The story was about Martians invading the Earth. Before the program began, Welles explained that the "news broadcast" was fiction. But many listeners tuned in late. Therefore, they missed Welles's explanation that this was a radio play. As a result, thousands of people thought that the Earth was really being invaded by Martians!

3   As people listened, some began to panic because the broadcast seemed real. Some people called their friends and relatives to warn them. Others alerted local police stations to the danger. Still others reportedly ran out into the streets, into parks, and into their cars, hoping to escape the "invasion." Newspapers reported huge traffic jams and overloaded telephone lines. It was a terrifying night for both citizens and police alike.

4   The next day, the newspapers told of the "fake" news broadcast. The headlines claimed that thousands of people had heard and believed it—but none of it was true.

Close Reader Habits

Circle signal words and phrases in paragraph 2 that show the text structure.

Explore How does the author use a cause-effect text structure to organize the ideas and details in "The Night the Martians Landed"?

Think

> Authors use different structures in different parts of a text to make their ideas clear.

1 Complete the chart below by adding text details that tell what happened and why. Remember that one event may result in others.

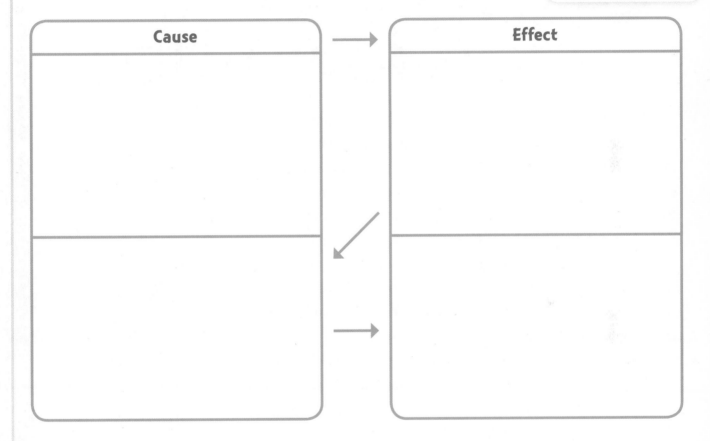

Cause	Effect

Talk

2 How has the author organized most of the ideas and details in the text? Which signal words helped you determine the structure? Why do you think the author chose this type of text structure?

 ## Write

3 **Short Response** Describe the overall text structure the author uses to organize ideas and details in the passage. Include text evidence in your response. Use the space on page 222 to write your response.

> **HINT** Make sure you explain where in the passage your evidence comes from.

> **Read** |

CARTOONS for Grown-Ups

by Jacob Miller

1   On September 29, 1959, the American Broadcasting System (ABC) aired the first cartoon on prime-time television.[1] *Rocky and His Friends* starred a playful flying squirrel named Rocky and his sidekick, Bullwinkle the Moose. These talking animals lived in the present-day (and imaginary) small town of Frostbite Falls, Minnesota. The pair faced tense situations caused by two mischievous Russian agents, Boris Badenov and Natasha Fatale. Their adventures created many amusing stories. This cartoon, later called *The Bullwinkle Show*, inspired a feature film, comic books, and generations of fans.

2   A year later, another prime-time cartoon premiered on ABC: *The Flintstones*. Unlike *The Bullwinkle Show*, *The Flintstones'* main stars were humans. Fred and Wilma Flintstone and their neighbors Barney and Betty Rubble lived in the town of Bedrock. Much of the humor stemmed from the characters' use of modern technology in a stone-age setting. Like *The Bullwinkle Show*, *The Flintstones* also inspired films, comics, and fans.

3   Despite their differences, *The Bullwinkle Show* and *The Flintstones* followed similar recipes for success. Both shows had clever dialogue and interesting characters. They were simple enough for young children but sophisticated enough for adults. Those reasons are why the cartoons succeeded in the 1960s. It's also why cartoons such as *The Simpsons* appeal to both adults and children today.

Close Reader Habits

How are the ideas organized in the passage overall? **Circle** words that signal the type of text structure used.

---

[1] **prime-time television:** shows aired in the evening to interest large audiences

Think Use what you learned from reading the article to respond to the following questions.

1. This question has two parts. Answer Part A. Then answer Part B.

> As you read, ask: How are the ideas organized? How does the structure help to make the writer's ideas clear?

Part A
How does the structure of the passage help readers understand more about *The Bullwinkle Show* and *The Flintstones?*

   A By presenting the effects of showing the cartoons at night, the passage explains why more viewers watched the cartoons.

   B By describing details about the cartoon shows, the passage shows how fans can use new ideas to create comic books and feature films.

   C By giving contrasting details about the two cartoon shows, the passage draws attention to the different types of people who liked each show.

   D By pointing out that the cartoons were alike and different, the passage makes it clear that both shows were popular for similar reasons.

Part B
Underline **two** details from paragraph 3 of the passage that **best** support the answer in Part A.

Talk

2. How is most of the passage organized? Use the Venn diagram on page 223 to compare and contrast details about the two shows.

 Write

3. **Short Response** Use the information in your Venn diagram to explain the overall text structure in the passage. Use at least **two** details from the passage to support your explanation. Use the space provided on page 223 to write your response.

> **HINT** Which details describe how the two television shows are similar and different?

Write Use the space below to write your answer to the question on page 219.

The Night the Martians Landed

3 **Short Response** Describe the overall text structure the author uses to organize ideas and details in the passage. Include text evidence in your response.

> **HINT** Make sure you explain where in the passage your evidence comes from.

_____

_____

_____

_____

_____

_____

_____

_____

Don't forget to check your writing.

Check Your Writing

☐ Did you read the prompt carefully?

☐ Did you put the prompt in your own words?

☐ Did you use the best evidence from the text to support your ideas?

☐ Are your ideas clearly organized?

☐ Did you write in clear and complete sentences?

☐ Did you check your spelling and punctuation?

CARTOONS for Grown-Ups

2 Use the Venn diagram below to organize your ideas.

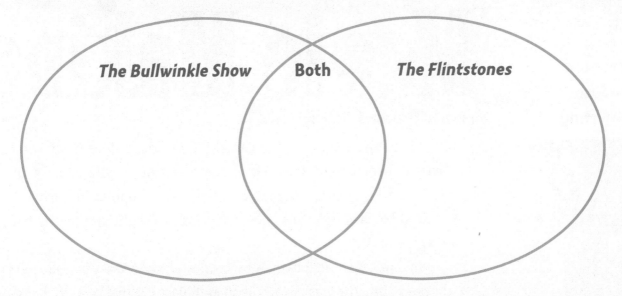

The Bullwinkle Show   Both   *The Flintstones*

Write Use the space below to write your answer to the question on page 221.

3 **Short Response** Use the information in your Venn diagram to explain the overall text structure in the passage. Use at least **two** details from the passage to support your explanation.

> **HINT** Which details describe how the two television shows are similar and different?

_____

_____

_____

_____

_____

_____

from

The History of Movie Making

by Gallimard Jeunesse

1   Lights! Action . . . but no camera. Centuries before Hollywood existed, people used light and screens to create moving images. In the 18th and 19th centuries, magic lanterns were popular in Europe. The earliest had a simple lens and used candles to light up pictures painted on glass slides.

2   In 1885, George Eastman of Rochester, New York, introduced paper-backed film. Thomas Alva Edison and his assistant, W. K. L. Dickson, used George Eastman's flexible film when they made a motion picture camera. Their Kinetograph, patented[1] in 1891, had a sprocket, or wheel with teeth. An electric motor turned the sprocket. The sprocket teeth hooked the perforations[2] and pulled the film through the camera.

[1] **patented:** protected by an official document granting the right of ownership
[2] **perforations:** a series of holes made in either side of the film

A Magic Lantern Projector

The First Picture Show

3   Paris, 1894: Louis Lumière peeps into an Edison Kinetoscope projecting machine. He's inspired! Paris 1895: Louis and his brother Auguste Lumière project the first publicly screened film, using their own invention, the *Cinématographe*. It combined the strong lamp and lens of a magic lantern with a shutter-and-film reel mechanism.[3] By 1898, the Lumières had collected almost 1,000 short films. Most of them were real-life footage or news events from around the world. But Georges Méliès, a Parisian theater magician, had some fantastic ideas that would take film beyond reality.

4   The Lumière brothers' hand-cranked invention (1895) was a combination of camera, projector, and printer. The camera could shoot film. The projector kept the film still, while a frame (image) was projected on screen; then the frame was quickly advanced. Some audiences were shocked by the realistic pictures. The train moved as if it would plunge right into the audience. Supposedly, some frightened viewers ran out of the theater!

[3] **mechanism:** a group of parts with which a machine operates

Poster of a Crowd Watching a Lumière Movie

Auguste Lumière poses with his invention, an early form of motion picture projector.

Méliès the Magician

5   The Lumières were the founders of realistic films. It took a magician to create a whole new type of film. Georges Méliès, a well-known Parisian magician and theater owner, tried to buy a *Cinématographe* from the Lumières in 1895. They would not sell it to him. So Méliès went to London and bought some Eastman film. He designed his own camera and built a studio, a 25 x 55-foot shed, in his garden. Then Méliès started making films. At first like the Lumières, he shot travel scenes or scenes from daily life. Then, quite by accident, Georges Méliès learned about special effects.

Hocus-Pocus

6   In 1896, Méliès' camera jammed while he was filming a Paris street. It took him a few seconds to fix it and continue shooting. Meanwhile, the street scene changed: A bus drove away and a hearse drove up. When Méliès projected his film, he was astonished to see the bus suddenly turn into a hearse! He began to experiment with this kind of stop-motion photography.

A Trip to the Moon

7   In 1902, Méliès produced the science-fiction classic *A Trip to the Moon*, which brought him worldwide fame. The approximately 11-minute silent film was based on the work of Jules Verne. It showed the adventures of six astronomers who pile into a rocket, get shot out of a cannon, and land smack in the eye of the man in the moon. Méliès' Star Film studio used extraordinary sets, props, and film effects to do things like make the moon's face move.

An image from the 1902 film *A Trip to the Moon*

▶ **Think** Use what you learned from reading the history text to respond to the following questions.

1 The sentences below are from paragraph 5 of the passage.

> At first like the Lumières, he shot travel scenes or scenes from daily life. Then, quite by accident, Georges Méliès learned about special effects.

Which of the following **best** describes the text structure of these sentences?

A Cause–effect: The sentences tell how the Lumières' films showed Méliès how to make special effects.

B Comparison: The sentences tell how Méliès' films were similar to and different from the Lumières' films.

C Cause–effect: The sentences tell how Méliès' films led the Lumières to film scenes of daily life.

D Comparison: The sentences tell how the Lumières' films and Méliès' films had nothing in common.

2 What effect does the text structure of the passage have on the reader's understanding of the history of movie making?

A By giving the causes and effects of early filmmaking techniques, the passage explains how readers can create their own stop-motion films using basic equipment.

B By describing the events in the order they happened, the passage makes it easy to understand every step in the history of making movies.

C By comparing early filmmakers and describing the causes and effects of their efforts, the passage gives a clearer picture of how movie making came about.

D By presenting all the problems and comparing and contrasting the filmmakers' solutions, the passage explains why the history of French movies is important.

3 Complete the chart below by identifying the type of text structure each detail supports. Write "cause–effect" or "comparison" beside each detail.

Detail	Text Structure
"[The *Cinématographe*] combined the strong lamp and lens of a magic lantern with a shutter-and-film reel mechanism." (paragraph 3)	
"The Lumière brothers' hand-cranked invention (1895) was a combination of camera, projector, and printer." (paragraph 4)	
"Georges Méliès . . . tried to buy a *Cinématographe* from the Lumières in 1895. They would not sell it to him. So Méliès . . . designed his own camera." (paragraph 5)	
"Meanwhile, the street scene changed: A bus drove away and a hearse drove up. When Méliès projected his film, he was astonished to see the bus suddenly turn into a hearse!" (paragraph 6)	
"In 1902, Méliès produced . . . *A Trip to the Moon*, which brought him worldwide fame." (paragraph 7)	

4 Read the sentence from the passage.

> In 1896, Méliès' camera <u>jammed</u> while he was filming . . . . It took him a few seconds to fix it and continue shooting.

Which phrase **best** describes the meaning of <u>jammed</u>?

   A squeezed tightly

   B stepped on the brakes

   C moved the gears

   D became stuck

Write

5 **Short Response** Describe the text structure in these sentences from paragraph 3 of the passage. Support your answer with at least **two** details from the sentences.

> By 1898, the Lumières had collected almost 1,000 short films. Most of them were real-life footage or news events from around the world. But Georges Méliès, a Parisian theater magician, had some fantastic ideas that would take film beyond reality.

_____

_____

_____

_____

_____

Learning Target

In this lesson, you identified comparison and cause–effect text structures. Now explain how identifying the text structure in a passage helps you better understand the ideas in a text.

👥 **Introduction**

LAFS.4.RI.2.5 Describe the overall structure (e.g., chronology, . . . problem/solution) of events, ideas, concepts, or information in a text or part of a text.

Lesson 15
Text Structures, Part 2: Chronology and Problem–Solution

Learning Target

Describing the way an author organizes events, ideas, or information will help you better understand the text.

▶ **Read** Writers use **text structures** to organize their ideas.

- **Chronology** is a text structure that describes events in the order they occur. Words such as *first, next, during,* and *finally* signal this text structure, as do dates that tell when the events happened.

- A **problem–solution** text structure describes a problem first and then its solution. Words such as *problem, solution, challenge, fixed, issue,* and *resolved* signal a problem–solution structure.

Read the passages below. Circle signal words that indicate the text structure of each passage.

I'll never forget the storm last October. Before the storm started, I found some blankets and flashlights. During the storm, I played games with my family. Finally, I turned on the radio and listened to the local weather report. Crack!

The ground shook as a tree in our front yard toppled over, falling across power lines and cutting off our electricity. We faced the challenge of getting through the night without lights or heat. We resolved that first issue with flashlights and candles. Dad fixed the second problem by making a fire in the fireplace.

▶ **Think** What have you learned about chronological and problem–solution text structures? Match each chart to the passage featuring that text structure. Then complete the charts using details from each passage.

Passage: _____

Problem–Solution Text Structure

Problem	Solution

Passage: _____

Chronological Text Structure

Order	Event
1	
2	
3	

▶ **Talk** Share your charts with a partner. Did you choose the same chart for the passages? Did you list the events in the same order in the *Chronology Chart*? Did you write a similar problem and solution in the *Problem–Solution Chart*? What signal words from each passage helped you?

◎ **Academic Talk**
Use these words to talk about the text.

- **text structures** - **chronology** - **problem–solution**

▶ **Read**

Treating the Red Fox

by Mark B. Champlin

1   I first spotted the red fox on a June morning. It was beside the tool shed, trembling. I approached the animal cautiously and saw its left hind leg was injured. I went inside my cabin and got my medical bag. Then, with caution, I returned to the fox. Next, I gently lifted its injured leg and decided to attach a splint. The fox settled back and let me proceed with my work. On my porch, I set up a wooden box padded with pillows so the fox could heal. Beside the box I placed bowls of food and water that I refilled daily.

2   One morning in July, I stepped out to the porch and saw that the red fox was gone. I checked the porch each day after, but the fox was nowhere to be found.

3   Late one August afternoon, I spied the red fox coming up the path to my cabin. A short distance behind, a silver fox was limping along. I watched as the animals approached the tool shed. The silver fox was fearful, but the red fox apparently resolved the issue by assuring it the area was safe. The silver fox settled down beside the tool shed. The red fox observed its friend for a few moments, and then returned to the dense woods. As I had done once before, I entered the cabin, located my medical bag, and returned outside to treat the silver fox.

Close Reader Habits

Circle signal words that the author uses to show the order of events in his memoir.

Explore Why did the author choose a particular text structure when he wrote "Treating the Red Fox"?

Think

> In a memoir, the writer shares specific events from his or her life.

1 Complete the chart below by listing the events from the memoir in the order in which they occur.

Order	Event
1	
2	
3	
4	
5	

Talk

2 How does the text structure chosen by the author help you understand events in the memoir? How do the signal words help?

Write

3 **Short Response** Explain how the author's choice of text structure is important to understanding "Treating the Red Fox." Include details from the text to support your response. Use the space provided on page 236 to write your response.

> **HINT** Number the events in the text to help you figure out when the events happened.

> **Read**

30 SECONDS OF FUEL

by Theresa Baker

1   In July 1969, three astronauts blasted off for the Moon. Their goal was not only to land on the Moon but also to walk on its surface. The journey from Earth to Moon was quiet, and the astronauts were patient and calm during the trip. The landing, however, would be quite exciting.

2   After getting near the Moon, the landing ship, named *Eagle*, separated from the command ship. The command ship then remained in orbit around the Moon. During the landing ship's descent to the Moon, the astronaut flying the ship made an announcement. Astronaut Neil Armstrong said, "The *Eagle* has wings." He meant that the landing ship was flying well and doing its job.

3   As the *Eagle* began its final approach, alarms sounded. By now, fuel was running low. Looking out the window, Armstrong realized the terrain was not good for landing. The problem was that it was rocky and dangerous. The landing site was supposed to be smooth.

4   There was less than a minute of fuel left for a landing. If they ran out, the *Eagle* would be forced to cancel its flight and go back to the command ship. Armstrong had to decide how to meet this challenge. Should he call off the landing? Or should he look for another landing spot? He quickly chose to fly the ship to another area. Just seconds later, the ship landed in an area of the Moon called the Sea of Tranquility. There were only about 30 seconds of fuel left. Armstrong announced, "The *Eagle* has landed."

Close Reader Habits

How does the structure of the last two paragraphs differ from the others? Reread the article. **Circle** the details that help you identify the structure of paragraphs 3 and 4.

▶ **Think** Use what you learned from reading the history article to respond to the following questions.

> Writers may use different text structures in different paragraphs to make their ideas clear.

1 The question has two parts. Answer Part A. Then answer Part B.

Part A
In paragraphs 1 and 2, the author describes events in time order. What structure does the author use to present information in paragraphs 3 and 4?

- **A** The author tells the order in which the events happened during the *Eagle's* attempt to land.
- **B** The author explains a challenge Armstrong faced and how he solved it.
- **C** The author tells what caused the *Eagle* to land and what happened as a result.
- **D** The author compares and contrasts the events that happened before and after the *Eagle* landed.

Part B
Which **two** sentences from the text **best** support the answer in Part A?

- **A** "As the *Eagle* began its final approach, alarms sounded."
- **B** "The problem was that it was rocky and dangerous."
- **C** "The landing site was supposed to be smooth."
- **D** "There was less than a minute of fuel left for a landing."
- **E** "He quickly chose to fly the ship to another area."
- **F** "Armstrong announced, 'The *Eagle* has landed.'"

▶ **Talk**

2 What did Armstrong do to land the *Eagle* on the Moon? Use the chart on page 237 to help organize your ideas about the text structure the author used to present this information.

▶ **Write**

3 **Short Response** Explain how the author presents the events that Neil Armstrong faced as he landed the *Eagle* on the Moon. Include at least **two** details from the text to support your response. Use the space provided on page 237 to write your response.

> **HINT** In your response, be sure to tell *where* in the passage you found your text evidence.

Write Use the space below to write your answer to the question on page 233.

Treating the Red Fox

> **HINT** Number the events in the text to help you figure out when the events happened.

3 **Short Response** Explain how the author's choice of text structure is important to understanding "Treating the Red Fox." Include details from the text to support your response.

_____

_____

_____

_____

_____

_____

_____

_____

Don't forget to check your writing.

Check Your Writing

☐ Did you read the prompt carefully?

☐ Did you put the prompt in your own words?

☐ Did you use the best evidence from the text to support your ideas?

☐ Are your ideas clearly organized?

☐ Did you write in clear and complete sentences?

☐ Did you check your spelling and punctuation?

30 SECONDS OF FUEL

2 **Use the chart below to organize your ideas.**

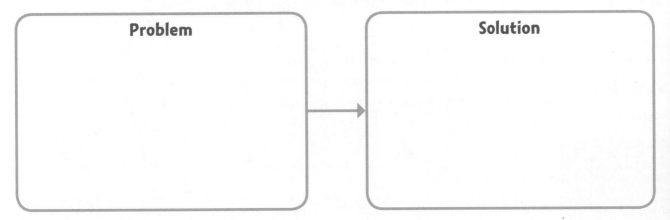

Problem	Solution

Write **Use the space below to write your answer to the question on page 235.**

3 **Short Response** Explain how the author presents the events that Neil Armstrong faced as he landed the *Eagle* on the Moon. Include at least **two** details from the text to support your response.

> **HINT** In your response, be sure to tell *where* in the passage you found your text evidence.

_____

_____

_____

_____

_____

_____

_____

_____

> **Read**

On May 29th, 1953, Tenzing Norgay, along with Sir Edmund Hillary, was one of the first two people to reach the summit of Mount Everest, the highest mountain on Earth. The following passage is taken from his autobiography.

from

TIGER of the SNOWS

The Autobiography of Tenzing of Everest

by Tenzing Norgay

WORDS TO KNOW

As you read, look inside, around, and beyond these words to figure out what they mean.

- **pinnacle**
- **summit**

1   On top of the rock cliff we rested again. Certainly, after the climb up the gap we were both a bit breathless, but after some slow pulls at the oxygen I am feeling fine. I look up; the top is very close now; and my heart thumps with excitement and joy. Then we are on our way again. Climbing again . . . .

Tenzing Norgay, the Famous Sherpa Mountaineer

2   Then the rocks, too, are beneath us. We are back among the snowy humps. They are curving off to the right, and each time we pass one I wonder, "Is the next the last one? Is the next the last?" Finally we reach a place where we can see past the humps, and beyond them is the great open sky and brown plains. We are looking down the far side of the mountain upon Tibet. Ahead of us now is only one more hump—the last hump. It is not a pinnacle. The way to it is an easy snow slope, wide enough for two men to go side by side. About thirty feet away we stop for a minute and look up. Then we go on . . . .

3   A little below the summit Hillary and I stopped. We looked up. Then we went on. The rope that joined us was thirty feet long, but I held most of it in loops in my hand, so that there was only about six feet between us . . . .

Tenzing Norgay and Edmund Hillary Pose After Their Climb

The pair climb beyond a deep fissure on Mount Everest.

4   We stepped up. We were there. The dream had come true . . . .

5   What we did first was what all climbers do when they reach the top of their mountain. We shook hands. But this was not enough for Everest. I waved my arms in the air and then threw them around Hillary, and we thumped each other on the back until, even with the oxygen, we were almost breathless. Then we looked around. It was eleven-thirty in the morning, the sun was shining, and the sky was the deepest blue I have ever seen. Only a gentle breeze was blowing, coming from the direction of Tibet, and the plume of snow that always blows from Everest's summit was very small . . . .

6   It was such a sight as I had never seen before and would never see again: wild, wonderful, and terrible. But terror was not what I felt. I loved the mountains too well for that. I loved Everest too well. At that great moment for which I had waited all my life my mountain did not seem to me a lifeless thing of rock and ice, but warm and friendly and living. She was a mother hen, and the other mountains were chicks under her wings. I too, I felt, had only to spread my own wings to cover and shelter the brood that I loved.

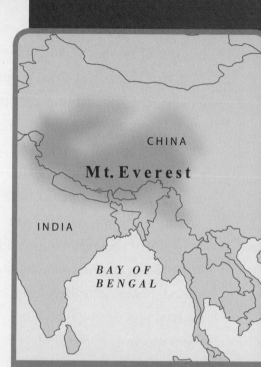

Mount Everest straddles the border between Nepal and China.

▶ **Think**   Use what you learned from reading the autobiography to respond to the following questions.

1   This question has two parts. First, answer Part A. Then answer Part B.

Part A
How is the first paragraph different from the ones that come after it?

A   It describes events that led Norgay and Hillary to climb Mount Everest. The other paragraphs tell about problems they overcame on their climb.

B   It shows what a mountain climber has to do to stay alive on a dangerous climb. Later paragraphs tell what happened as they reached the top and why it happened.

C   It helps readers understand a problem the climbers faced and how they solved it. Later paragraphs tell the order of the events as the men climbed to the top of the mountain.

D   It compares what Tenzing Norgay felt as he reached the top of the mountain to what Hillary felt. Other paragraphs help readers understand why they made the climb.

Part B
Underline a detail in paragraph 1 that **best** supports the answer to Part A.

On top of the rock cliff we rested again. Certainly, after the climb up the gap we were both a bit breathless, but after some slow pulls at the oxygen I am feeling fine. I look up; the top is very close now; and my heart thumps with excitement and joy. Then we are on our way again. Climbing again . . . .

2   What does the word <u>plains</u> mean as it is used in paragraph 2?

A   grassy fields

B   aircraft

C   bodies of water

D   Tenzing's homeland

3 This question has two parts. First, answer Part A. Then answer Part B.

Part A
How does the author **mainly** organize the details in *Tiger of the Snows*?

    A by stating the problems he faced and how he solved them

    B by stating his point of view and comparing it to Hillary's

    C by explaining the events in the order they occurred

    D by explaining what happened and why it happened

Part B
Which **two** details from the text **best** support the answer to Part A?

    A "I look up; the top is very close now; and my heart thumps with excitement and joy." (paragraph 1)

    B "Finally we reach a place where we can see past the humps, and beyond them is the great open sky. . . ." (paragraph 2)

    C "The way to it is an easy snow slope, wide enough for two men to go side by side." (paragraph 2)

    D "We looked up. Then we went on." (paragraph 3)

    E "The dream had come true . . . " (paragraph 4)

    F "But this was not enough for Everest." (paragraph 5)

4 Put events from the autobiography in the order they happen by writing the numbers 1 to 4 on the lines before each sentence.

_____ Tenzing and Hillary shake hands at the top of the mountain.

_____ As Tenzing and Hillary climb above the rocks, Tenzing wonders if the next snowy hump will be the last one.

_____ Tenzing compares the mountain to a mother hen with chicks under her wings.

_____ After climbing up a gap, Tenzing and Hillary rest on a rock cliff and breathe in extra oxygen.

Write

5 **Short Response** Why do you think the author used a chronological text structure in this autobiography?

_____

_____

_____

_____

_____

_____

_____

_____

_____

Learning Target

In this lesson, you learned how authors use chronological and problem–solution text structures to organize information and ideas. Explain how this helped you better understand the texts.

_____

_____

_____

_____

LAFS.4.RI.2.6 Compare and contrast a firsthand and secondhand account of the same event or topic; describe the differences in focus and the information provided.

Lesson 16
Comparing Accounts of the Same Topic

Learning Target

Comparing and contrasting firsthand and secondhand accounts of the same event or topic will help you develop a deeper understanding of what happened.

▶ **Read** When you **compare** accounts of the same topic, you are studying the writer's viewpoint. A **firsthand account** is written by someone who witnessed or took part in an event as it happened. Someone who heard or read about an event writes a **secondhand account**. You can compare the **information** or facts each writer chooses to emphasize.

I am going to write down everything I have seen so that I can remember it.

In 1900, a powerful hurricane wrecked the city of Galveston, Texas. It destroyed many homes. This boy watched the hurricane as it was happening. His description of the event would be a firsthand account that includes his thoughts and feelings. He wants to retell what he experienced.

I learned about the Galveston hurricane by reading a new book about it.

The girl was not in Galveston in 1900. She knows about the hurricane from reading a book written about it many years later. The book would be a secondhand account with a broader **focus**. It would include background information and other details from research.

▶ **Think** Consider everything you've learned so far about firsthand and secondhand accounts. How are they the same? How is the focus of each account different? Use the *Venn diagram* below to compare and **contrast** each type of account and organize your thinking.

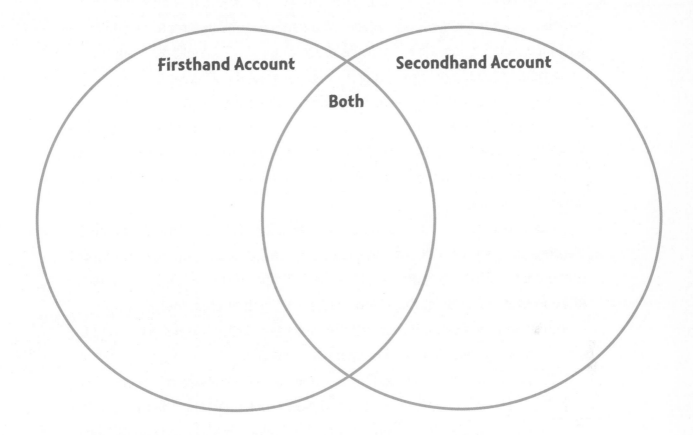

Firsthand Account   **Secondhand Account**

Both

▶ **Talk** Imagine that the boy and the girl write down their thoughts about the Galveston Hurricane of 1900. Based on the details in the cartoons, how would the two accounts be the same, and how would they be different?

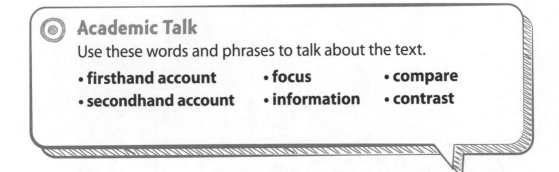

◉ **Academic Talk**
Use these words and phrases to talk about the text.

- **firsthand account**   • **focus**   • **compare**
- **secondhand account**   • **information**   • **contrast**

▶ **Read**

The Unsinkable *Titanic* by Julian Green

1   For more than a hundred years, the story of the *Titanic* has fascinated people. It was the largest passenger steamship ever built, already world-famous when it was launched. One magazine proudly called it "unsinkable." But that pride would crumble on *Titanic*'s first voyage across the Atlantic Ocean.

2   There were 2,240 passengers and crew on that voyage. The ship left Southampton, England, on April 10, 1912. It was scheduled to reach New York City ten days later. But at 11:30 on the night of April 14, the *Titanic* hit an iceberg that tore open the ship's massive hull. As the vessel took on water, it began to sink.

3   The ship's captain told his radio operator to call for help. Then he ordered the crew to lower the lifeboats. In the panic, fleeing passengers launched most of the boats with several empty seats. By 2:20 the next morning, three hours after striking the iceberg, the *Titanic* had sunk. Another ship, the *Carpathia*, was 58 miles away when it received the distress call. The *Carpathia* rushed to rescue the survivors. Only 705 people were saved.

4   Newspaper headlines around the world announced the loss of the unsinkable ship. It quickly became the subject of countless books and films. In fact, the first *Titanic* movie appeared just a month later, starring one of the survivors. British and American officials tried to discover the causes of the disaster. They looked at everything, from the way the ship was built to the actions of the crew. In the end, the main lesson of the *Titanic* was that no ship is truly unsinkable.

> **Close Reader Habits**
>
> As you read, **underline** clues that tell you whether this is a firsthand or secondhand account.

Explore How would a firsthand account and a secondhand account of the sinking of the *Titanic* differ?

▶ **Think**

> In a firsthand account, a writer describes the experience. In a secondhand account, the writer focuses on reporting many different details about the event.

1 Who would write a firsthand account about the sinking of the *Titanic*?

_____

_____

Who would write a secondhand account? _____

_____

_____

2 Reread the magazine article. Do you think this is a firsthand or secondhand account? Find evidence in the selection to support what you think.

_____

_____

_____

_____

_____

_____

▶ **Talk**

3 Imagine that a passenger on the *Titanic* writes about that experience. What kind of account would that be? Discuss how that person's account would be similar to and different from the article you just read.

 ▶ **Write**

4 **Short Response** How would the facts in paragraphs 2 and 3 of the passage differ if a passenger on the *Titanic* described the disaster? Use the space provided on page 250 to write your answer.

> **HINT** What would stand out in a passenger's mind about that night?

The Sinking of the Titanic

by James McGough, in
Sinking of the Titanic
and Great Sea Disasters

1   As the life-boats pulled away the officers ordered the bands to play, and their music did much to quell panic. It was a heart-breaking sight . . . to see the great ship go down. First she listed to the starboard, on which side the collision had occurred, then she settled slowly but steadily, without hope of remaining afloat.

2   The *Titanic* was all aglow with lights as if for a function. First we saw the lights of the lower deck snuffed out. A while later and the second deck illumination was extinguished in a similar manner. Then the third and upper decks were darkened, and without plunging or rocking the great ship disappeared slowly from the surface of the sea. . . .

3   The sea was calm—calm as the water in a tumbler. But it was freezing cold. None had dressed heavily, and all, therefore, suffered intensely. The women did not shriek or grow hysterical while we waited through the awful night for help. We men stood at the oars, stood because there was no room for us to sit, and kept the boat headed into the swell to prevent her capsizing. Another boat was at our side, but all the others were scattered around the water.

4   Finally, shortly before 6 o'clock, we saw the lights of the *Carpathia* approaching. Gradually she picked up the survivors in the other boats and then approached us.

Close Reader Habits

How are the two accounts of the sinking different? Reread the article and the memoir. **Underline** details in the memoir that give facts not told in the article.

Think

Use what you learned from reading the memoir and the article to answer the following questions.

> A memoir is usually a firsthand account of what the writer saw, felt, thought, and did. It often uses a personal tone.

1 The facts in the magazine article on page 246 came from earlier news reports and articles about the event. In the memoir on page 248, where did James McGough get his facts?

    A He read about the events in the magazine article.

    B He heard about the events from friends on the ship.

    C He imagined the events and wrote a story about them.

    D He experienced the events as they happened.

2 Which information did McGough give that was not in the article?

    A The *Carpathia* traveled to the *Titanic's* location.

    B Passengers were put into lifeboats.

    C The lights on the *Titanic* went out deck by deck.

    D The *Titanic* sank into the ocean.

3 Which words and phrases are clues to McGough's feelings on the night that the *Titanic* sank? Write **two** clues in the box below.

Talk

4 How are the two accounts of the *Titanic* the same? How are they different? Use the Venn diagram on page 251 to organize your thoughts.

Write

5 **Short Response** Use the information in your Venn diagram to describe how the firsthand and secondhand accounts of the disaster are the same and different. Use the space provided on page 251 to write your answer.

> **HINT** Choose a writing structure that shows similarities and differences.

Write **Use the space below to write your answer to the question on page 247.**

The
Unsinkable *Titanic*

4 **Short Response** How would the facts in paragraphs 2 and 3 of the passage differ if a passenger on the *Titanic* described the disaster?

> **HINT** What would stand out in a passenger's mind about that night?

_____

_____

_____

_____

_____

_____

_____

_____

_____

Check Your Writing

> Don't forget to check your writing.

☐ Did you read the prompt carefully?

☐ Did you put the prompt in your own words?

☐ Did you use the best evidence from the text to support your ideas?

☐ Are your ideas clearly organized?

☐ Did you write in clear and complete sentences?

☐ Did you check your spelling and punctuation?

The Sinking of the Titanic

4 Use the Venn diagram below to organize your ideas.

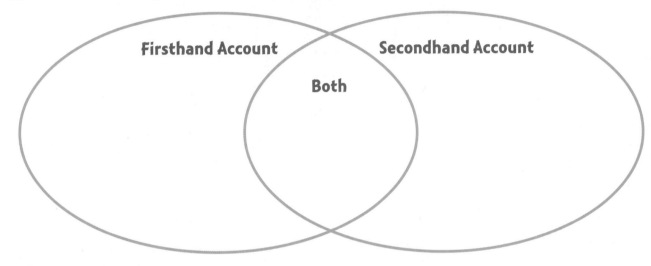

Firsthand Account   **Secondhand Account**

Both

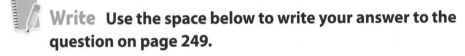

Write **Use the space below to write your answer to the question on page 249.**

5 **Short Response** Use the information in your Venn diagram to describe how the firsthand and secondhand accounts of the disaster are the same and different.

> **HINT** Choose a writing structure that shows similarities and differences.

_____

_____

_____

_____

_____

_____

_____

▶ **Read**

WORDS TO KNOW

As you read, look inside, around, and beyond these words to figure out what they mean.

- **launch**
- **brilliant**
- **atmosphere**

To Space and Back

by Sally Ride

1   Launch minus 10 seconds . . . 9 . . . 8 . . . 7 . . . The three launch engines light. The shuttle shakes and strains at the bolts holding it to the launch pad. The computers check the engines. It isn't up to us anymore—the computers will decide whether we launch.

2   3 . . . 2 . . . 1 . . . The rockets light! The shuttle leaps off the launch pad in a cloud of steam and a trail of fire. Inside, the ride is rough and loud. Our heads are rattling around inside our helmets. We can barely hear the voices from Mission Control in our headsets above the thunder of the rockets and engines. For an instant I wonder if everything is working right. But there's no time to wonder, and no time to be scared.

3   In only a few seconds we zoom past the clouds. Two minutes later the rockets burn out, and with a brilliant whitish-orange flash, they fall away from the shuttle as it streaks on toward space. Suddenly the ride becomes very, very smooth and quiet. The shuttle is still attached to the big tank, and the launch engines are pushing us out of Earth's atmosphere. The sky is black. All we can see of the trail of fire behind us is a faint, pulsating glow through the top window.

4   Launch plus six minutes. The force pushing us against the backs of our seats steadily increases. We can barely move because we're being held in place by a force of 3 g's—three times the force of gravity we feel on Earth. At first we don't mind it—we've all felt much more than that when we've done acrobatics in our jet training airplanes. But that lasted only a few seconds, and this seems to go on forever. After a couple of minutes of 3 g's, we're uncomfortable, straining to hold our books on our laps and craning our necks against the force to read the instruments. I find myself wishing we'd hurry up and get into orbit.

5   Launch plus eight and one-half minutes. The launch engines cut off. Suddenly, the force is gone, and we lurch forward in our seats. During the next few minutes the empty fuel tank drops away and falls to Earth, and we are very busy getting the shuttle ready to enter orbit. But we're not too busy to notice that our books and pencils are floating in midair. We're in space!

Sally Ride, the first American woman to go into space, shared her thoughts, feelings, and experiences in her memoir, *To Space and Back.*

THIS DAY IN HISTORY

| June 18,1983 | Memorable Milestones: Space Shuttle Missions |

1   A crowd of about 250,000 gathered early that bright June morning at Cape Canaveral, Florida, many wearing "Ride, Sally Ride" T-shirts. Across the nation, many others also watched and waited. Suddenly, the engines ignited, and smoke and steam billowed across the site. Then booster rockets lifted the huge space shuttle slowly into the air. Gathering speed, the *Challenger* blasted off into orbit for its second mission.

2   At the same moment, one crew member, mission specialist Sally K. Ride, was rocketing into history. Ride was America's first woman to travel into space. Sally Ride had earned the right to be aboard the space shuttle. A physicist, she had been in astronaut training for six years. She had also worked at Mission Control, relaying messages to shuttle crews during earlier shuttle flights. Ride had even helped develop a robotic arm to use in space. This knowledge and experience had led Captain Bob Crippen to choose her as a crew member. And Ride was ready for the challenge.

3   In just over eight minutes, launch engines were lifting *Challenger* to its 184-mile high orbit. During the ascent, Ride acted as flight engineer, calling out checklists to the pilots. She also joked with Mission Control about the exciting ride.

4   Once in orbit, the five astronauts wasted little time. In the busy days ahead, the crew completed a number of experiments. This included using radar and a high-resolution camera to study the earth's atmosphere. Ride helped launch two communications satellites. She also became the first woman to operate the shuttle's robotic arm by releasing a satellite into orbit.

▶ **Think**

Use what you learned from reading the memoir and the magazine article to respond to the following questions.

1 This question has two parts. First, answer Part A. Then answer Part B.

Part A
Which statement **best** describes the differences between the two accounts from *To Space and Back* and "Memorable Milestones: Space Shuttle Missions"?

    A   One is a news article. The other is from an eyewitness who watched the launch.

    B   Both are written by people who were at Cape Canaveral on June 18, 1983.

    C   One was written at the time of the launch. The other was written several years later.

    D   One is based only on facts. The other is based on facts and personal experience.

Part B
Write a sentence from each passage that supports your answer to Part A.

To Space and Back _____

_____

"Memorable Milestones" _____

_____

2 Which phrase from "Memorable Milestones: Space Shuttle Missions" helps the reader understand the meaning of the word <u>ascent</u> in paragraph 3?

    A   "ready for the challenge"

    B   "lifting *Challenger*"

    C   "acted as flight engineer"

    D   "Once in orbit"

3. Complete the chart to compare the different accounts of the same event. Write an X in the box next to a detail that describes *To Space and Back* or "Memorable Milestones: Space Shuttle Missions." Some details may describe both accounts.

Statement	*To Space and Back*	"Memorable Milestones"
Describes the launch of a space shuttle		
Explains how the launch affects the author's body		
Tells why the mission was unlike other missions		
Presents all events as taking place in the past		
Presents events as if they are taking place now		

 Write

Describe the difference in focus between Sally Ride's memoir and the account of the launch in "Mission Milestones." Reread the two texts. Underline details that show the difference in the focus of each account.

4. **Plan Your Response** How is the focus of Sally Ride's memoir different from the focus of the magazine article? Use a Venn diagram to organize your thoughts before you write.

5. **Write an Extended Response** Using evidence from the texts and information from your Venn diagram, describe how the focus of the firsthand and secondhand account is different.

_____

_____

_____

_____

_____

_____

_____

_____

_____

_____

_____

_____

_____

_____

_____

_____

_____

Learning Target

Now that you've compared and contrasted different accounts about the same events, write about how you developed a deeper understanding of what happened.

_____

_____

_____

_____

▶ **Read**

Read the history article. Then answer the questions that follow.

from "Ferris's Grand Idea"

by Marcia Amidon Lusted, *Cobblestone*

1   Daniel Burnham was stumped. He wanted the World's Columbian Exposition to have a centerpiece to rival the Eiffel Tower from the Paris exposition of 1889. The graceful iron-and-steel structure had become a landmark recognized around the world. France's engineering talent now looked superior to America's. "Some distinctive feature is needed," Burnham said to a group of engineers at a weekly dinner in 1891. "Something novel, original, daring, and unique must be designed and built if American engineers are to retain their prestige and standing."

2   Burnham wanted something that would "out-Eiffel Eiffel" . . . to draw people to Chicago.

3   George Washington Gale Ferris, a young engineer from Pittsburgh, Pennsylvania, was present at the banquet that night. Hearing Burnham's words, Ferris recalled an idea he had been working on. He quickly scribbled the design on his dinner napkin. It was something that had never been done before: a revolving . . . wheel, 250 feet in diameter. It would hold more than 2,000 people in 36 cars attached to the wheel's rim. Each car would be as large as a bus and hold 40 (seated) to 60 (standing) people at a time . . . .

4   The wheel was not finished in time for the fair's opening day, May 1, 1893, but by June the engineers were testing it. On the first day of testing with passengers aboard, crowds of spectators ignored the engineers' requests to stand back. Instead, they rushed the wheel and climbed into the cars for the 20-minute ride. Ten minutes were spent getting passengers off and on. This was followed by a 10-minute nonstop single revolution. Ferris's grand idea was a huge success and wildly popular. It quickly became the highlight of the fair.

5   It cost 50 cents to ride the wheel, the same as the price of admission to the fair itself. The huge wheel cost $400,000 to build and maintain during the exposition. That was an enormous expense in those days. But its total earnings were more than $700,000, making a tidy profit for the fair organizers, Ferris, and the investors who had helped him pay for the project.

6   After the fair closed in October, the wheel was dismantled. It was used several more times, including at the St. Louis World's Fair in 1904, but two years later it was sold for scrap metal. It took 200 pounds of dynamite to finally knock the huge wheel off its towers.

7   Ferris's wheel is gone, but its legacy lives on in almost every amusement park and carnival . . . . Next time you're awed by the views from the top, think of George Ferris and the vision he had to put you there.

▶ **Think**

1 What is the meaning of the word <u>recalled</u> as it is used in paragraph 3 of "Ferris's Grand Idea"?

    A called again

    B remembered

    C came up with

    D invented

2 This question has two parts. First, answer Part A. Then answer Part B.

Part A
What is the meaning of the word <u>revolving</u> as it is used in paragraph 3 of "Ferris's Grand Idea"?

    A large

    B new

    C turning

    D wonderful

Part B
Which word is a context clue for <u>revolving</u>?

    A "wheel"

    B "rim"

    C "diameter"

    D "attached"

3 This question has two parts. First, answer Part A. Then answer Part B.

Part A

What is the meaning of the word <u>dismantled</u> as it is used in paragraph 6
of "Ferris's Grand Idea"?

   A   moved off a stage

   B   emptied of people

   C   taken apart

   D   traveled around

Part B

Which of the phrases from the passage **best** helps the reader understand
the meaning of <u>dismantled</u>?

   A   "sold for scrap metal"

   B   "knock the huge wheel off"

   C   "used several more times"

   D   "closed in October"

4 **Short Response** The author of "Ferris's Grand Idea" organizes paragraphs 1
through 3 by identifying a problem and telling how the problem was solved. State
the problem and solution, supporting your response with details from the text.

_____

_____

_____

_____

_____

_____

_____

_____

_____

▶ **Read**

Read the history article. Then answer the questions that follow.

from "THE FERRIS WHEEL"

by Denton J. Snider, *World's Fair Studies* (1893)

1   While the Ferris Wheel was in process of construction many people said they would not trust it. A very old man, leaning on his staff one day and looking up at it, declared: "Life is too precious to be risked in that way." But the Wheel started and nearly everybody is taking a ride; men, women and children are seen going up and returning in safety to their friends. Yet some grow pale and get sick at the stomach during the trip; women cry and become hysterical, and sometimes they faint. For most people it is probably a little trial at the start; but there is a feeling that courage needs a taste of discipline when it fears to go where there is no danger. One can often see a workman carried around on the inside of the rim; when the Wheel starts he walks; when it stops for a moment, he inspects a bolt, or taps the megatherion[1] with his hammer, just to hear the ring of the monster's voice.

[1] **Megatherion:** An ancient Greek word that means "mighty beast."

▶ **Think**

5 Read these sentences from "The Ferris Wheel."

> While the Ferris Wheel was in process of construction many people said they would not trust it . . . . But the Wheel started and nearly everybody is taking a ride; men, women and children are seen going up and returning in safety to their friends.

How did the author organize the events described in these sentences?

A by cause and effect

B by compare and contrast

C by problem and solution

D by order of events

6 Read the following sentence from "The Ferris Wheel."

> One can often see a workman carried around on the inside of the rim; when the Wheel starts he walks; when it stops for a moment, he <u>inspects</u> a bolt . . . .

What does <u>inspects</u> mean in the context of this sentence?

A removes

B tightens

C looks over

D ignores

7 This question has two parts. First, answer Part A. Then answer Part B.

Part A
Which sentence **best** describes a difference in the way information is provided in the two texts?

A   Only "The Ferris Wheel" explains the reasons the Ferris Wheel was built.

B   Only "Ferris's Grand Idea" includes details based on facts and historical research.

C   Only "Ferris's Grand Idea" describes what people experienced while riding on the Ferris Wheel.

D   Only "The Ferris Wheel" tells how popular the first Ferris Wheel was with people who attended that World's Fair.

Part B
Select **two** sentences from the texts that support the answer to Part A.

A   "A very old man, leaning on his staff one day and looking up at it, declared: 'Life is too precious to be risked in that way.'"

B   "The wheel was not finished in time for the fair's opening day, May 1, 1893, but by June the engineers were testing it."

C   "For most people it is probably a little trial at the start; but there is a feeling that courage needs a taste of discipline when it fears to go where there is no danger."

D   "But its total earnings were more than $700,000, making a tidy profit for the fair organizers, Ferris, and the investors who had helped him pay for the project."

E   "But the Wheel started and nearly everybody is taking a ride; men, women and children are seen going up and returning in safety to their friends."

8 **Short Response** Identify the overall structure in "The Ferris Wheel," and explain how the first sentence of the text contributes to that structure. Use at least **two** details from the text in your response.

_____

_____

_____

_____

_____

_____

_____

9 Compare how the two passages tell about the same event.

Complete the chart by drawing Xs in the boxes next to the statements that describe "Ferris's Grand Idea" and "The Ferris Wheel." Statements may be used for both texts.

Statement	"Ferris's Grand Idea"	"The Ferris Wheel"
Presents events as a firsthand account		
Presents events as a secondhand account		
Tells why the Ferris Wheel was invented		
Tells about the Ferris Wheel that was built for the 1893 World's Fair		
Tells what happened to the Ferris Wheel after the fair ended		

Write

10 **Extended Response** Think about the articles "Ferris's Grand Idea" and "The Ferris Wheel."

How are the topics of the articles alike? How are the topics different? How are their points of view different? What are some ways in which those points of view differ? Use details from both articles to support your answer.

In your answer, be sure to
- tell how the topics of the articles are alike
- tell how the topics of the articles are different
- tell how their points of view are different
- explain the differences in their points of view
- use details from **both** passages to support your answer

Check your writing for correct spelling, grammar, capitalization, and punctuation.

_____

_____

_____

_____

_____

_____

_____

_____

_____

_____

_____

UNIT 4

Craft and Structure in Literature

How are builders and authors alike? For one thing, they both use tools to make a **structure**. Builders use tools such as hammers, nails, and drills. Authors carefully choose words to write literary texts. Builders and authors also use different materials to **craft** (make) their structures. A bridge builder might use steel, an apartment builder might use concrete, and a cabin builder might use wood. The materials from which authors make literary texts are called elements. A poet uses the elements of verses, stanzas, rhyme, and meter to craft a poem. A play writer uses the cast of characters, dialogue, and a setting description to craft a play. Writers of stories and books use paragraphs, dialogue, and chapters.

In this unit, you'll practice figuring out the meanings of unknown words. You'll review the elements used to craft literary texts. Finally, you'll compare how poems, plays, and prose present characters, settings, and events to readers.

✓ Self Check

Before starting this unit, check off the skills you know below. As you complete each lesson, see how many more skills you can check off!

I can:	Before this unit	After this unit
find the meaning of unfamiliar words and phrases in poems, plays, and prose.	☐	☐
compare and contrast first-person and third-person points of view in literary texts.	☐	☐
refer to the elements of poetry when writing or speaking about poems.	☐	☐
refer to the elements of plays when writing or speaking about plays.	☐	☐
explain major differences between poems, plays, and prose.	☐	☐

page 279

page 286

page 288

page 300

page 308

page 321

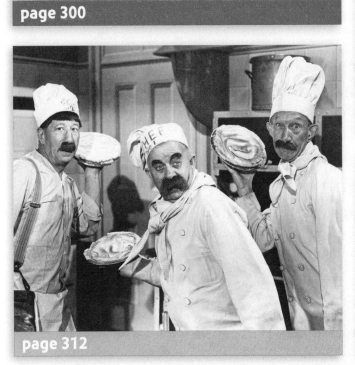
page 312

page 336

 **Introduction**

LAFS.4.RL.2.4 Determine the meaning of words and phrases as they are used in a text, including those that allude to significant characters found in mythology (e.g., Herculean).

Lesson 17
Understanding Vocabulary in Literary Texts

Figuring out the meanings of unfamiliar words and phrases in a literary text, including words about other traditional stories, helps you understand the text.

▶ **Read** A story, poem, or play may include a word or phrase you don't know. Try using **context clues** to help you figure out its meaning. Synonyms, antonyms, and other sentences surrounding it often suggest the meaning of an unknown word or phrase.

At times, an unknown word may **allude to**, or mention, a well-known person or place from **mythology**. These ancient stories describe human behavior or beliefs, and authors refer to them to make a special point. To understand an author's meaning, you must learn about those **significant**, or important, characters.

Read the story below. What are the meanings of *odyssey* and *locate*?

The Search

As I strolled home after a day of fun, I realized I'd lost my best baseball cap. So I went searching everywhere for it. My odyssey took me far and wide and finally back home. Despite my long journey, I'd failed to locate it, that is, until I sat down. It had been in my back pocket all along!

▶ **Think** How can context clues help you learn the meanings of unknown words and phrases? Complete the chart below to show what you have figured out about the meanings of <u>odyssey</u> and <u>locate</u>.

Unknown Word	Context	Possible Meaning	Clues
odyssey	"My odyssey took me far and wide . . ."		
locate			

▶ **Talk** Share your chart with a partner.

- Did your possible meanings agree?
- Which context clues did you use?
- Reread the "The Search." How does knowing the meanings of these two words help you better understand the passage?

◎ **Academic Talk**
Use these words and phrases to talk about the text.

- **context clues**
- **allude to**
- **mythology**
- **significant**

Read

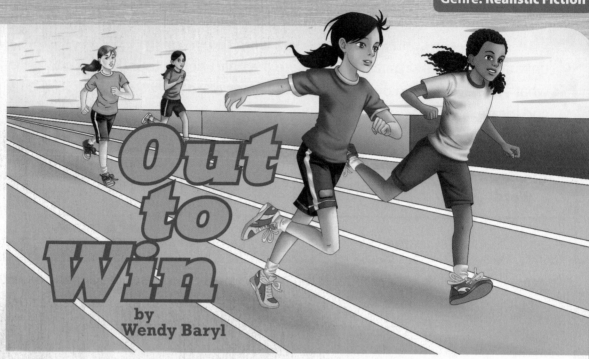

Out to Win

by
Wendy Baryl

1   As the annual school track meet approached, all I could think about was defeating Anna Banks. For the past three years, she'd beaten me in the 400-meter run, and always by just a step. No longer would I be satisfied with second place, however. Dissatisfied, I planned to win this year, and I couldn't think about anything else. I became obsessed with beating Anna. My thoughts focused on one goal all the time—winning. Naturally, I did more than just think. I practiced my starts daily, and I ran and ran and ran.

2   On the day of the race, I was eager to compete, and by the time we gathered at the starting line, I was really pumped. BAM—the starting gun fired and we were off! Anna and I quickly sprinted ahead of the other racers. When we shot across the finish line, I wasn't even certain who'd won at first. Then I heard the announcer—it was me!

3   Still breathing hard, Anna rushed over, smiling, and shook my hand. "You were great!" she declared. "Good race!" Right then, I realized that I'd been looking at the situation all wrong. Before, I'd been thinking of Anna as if she were some powerful enemy out to destroy me. But Anna wasn't my nemesis[1] at all; she had no urge to crush me. In fact, she had given me an opportunity to become a better sprinter than I ever would have been without her.

Close Reader Habits

Circle unfamiliar words and phrases. **Underline** phrases that give you clues to the word meanings.

[1]**nemesis:** a powerful rival; from the Greek goddess who punished overconfidence

Explore How do context clues help you figure out the meaning of unfamiliar words in "Out to Win"?

> Context clues can appear before or after the sentence having an unfamiliar word.

Think

1 Complete the chart below to show what you have figured out about the meanings of the words.

Unknown Word	Context	Possible Meaning	Clues
dissatisfied			
obsessed			
nemesis			

Talk

2 Explain the meaning of the word <u>opportunity</u> (paragraph 3). What context clues help you understand what the word means?

> **HINT** Reread paragraph 3 to find all the clues to the meaning of <u>opportunity</u>.

Write

3 **Short Response** Explain the meaning of <u>opportunity</u> (paragraph 3). Also include the context clues that helped you figure out the meaning of the word. Use the space provided on page 276 to write your response.

Read

The Catfish

by Oliver Herford, *The Book of Humorous Verse*

1 The saddest fish that swims the briny ocean,
      The Catfish I bewail.
   I cannot even think without emotion
      Of his distressful tail.
5 When with my pencil once I tried to draw one,
      (I dare not show it here)
   Mayhap it is because I never saw one,
      The picture looked so queer.
   I vision him half feline[1] and half fishy,
10   A paradox in twins,
   Unmixable as vitriol and vichy[2]—
      A thing of fur and fins.
   A feline Tantalus, forever chasing
      His fishy self to rend;
15 His finny self forever self-effacing
      In circles without end.
   This tale may have a Moral running through it
      As Aesop had in his;
   If so, dear reader, you are welcome to it,
20   If you know what it is!

Close Reader Habits

How does the poet describe the catfish? Reread the poem. **Underline** words and phrases that explain how he imagines a catfish to look.

[1]**feline:** catlike
[2]**vitriol and vichy:** an acid and an old word for mineral water; they are dangerous to mix

Think Use what you learned from reading the lyric poem to respond to the following questions.

1 In the poem, one word has this definition: "to cry out in sadness or pain." Underline the word that **best** fits the definition in the following lines from "The Catfish."

> The saddest fish that swims the briny ocean,
> The Catfish I bewail,
> I cannot even think without emotion
> Of his distressful tail.

> If a phrase mentions a character from mythology, you may need to look beyond the text to find information about it.

2 Read these lines from the poem.

> I vision him half feline and half fishy,
> A paradox in twins,
> Unmixable as vitriol and vichy—

What is the meaning of <u>paradox</u> as it is used in the poem?

A a creature with parts that don't seem to go together

B a furry fish with a brother that looks just like him

C a scaly cat that is confused and spins around

D a make-believe animal that has two different heads

Talk

3 Reread lines 13–14. Tantalus is a criminal in a Greek myth. He is punished by keeping delicious food and drink forever just out of his reach. Why does the poet describe the catfish as a "feline Tantalus"? Use the chart on page 277 to organize your ideas about the poem.

 Write

4 **Short Response** Use details from the poem and your discussion to explain why the poet calls the catfish a "feline Tantalus." Use the space provided on page 277 to write your response.

> **HINT** Think of what you know about a cat's usual reaction to a fish.

Write **Use the space below to write your answer to the question on page 273.**

Out to Win

3 **Short Response** Explain the meaning of <u>opportunity</u> (paragraph 3). Also include the context clues that helped you figure out the meaning of the word.

> **HINT** Reread paragraph 3 to find all the clues to the meaning of <u>opportunity</u>.

Check Your Writing

Don't forget to check your writing.

☐ Did you read the prompt carefully?

☐ Did you put the prompt in your own words?

☐ Did you use the best evidence from the text to support your ideas?

☐ Are your ideas clearly organized?

☐ Did you write in clear and complete sentences?

☐ Did you check your spelling and punctuation?

The Catfish

3 **Use the chart below to organize your ideas.**

Unknown Word	Context in Poem	Possible Meaning	Clues

Write Use the space below to write your answer to the question on page 275.

4 **Short Response** Use details from the poem and your discussion to explain why the poet calls the catfish a "feline Tantalus."

> **HINT** Think of what you know about a cat's usual reaction to a fish.

_____

_____

_____

_____

_____

_____

_____

▶ **Read**

A Golden Vase
and Two Bright Monkeys
adapted from a Tibetan folktale

WORDS TO KNOW
As you read, look inside, around, and beyond these words to figure out what they mean.

- **genuine**
- **recent**
- **pardon**

1   Long ago in Tibet, two friends named Dorje and Sonam hiked through the mountains looking to find a rare plant root used in medicines. They searched and dug for most of the day, with no results. Suddenly a clang rang out! Dorje's spade had hit something hard! Eagerly digging, the men unearthed a large vase.

2   "Surely this is pure gold!" Sonam exclaimed, as he brushed off the dirt. He held up the rare treasure, which shimmered in the bright sunlight. "We must have the touch of Midas," Sonam joked.

3   "Not so fast," Dorje said thoughtfully. Then a sly look crept across his face. "Before we start living like kings, we should test the vase," he added. "Remember, all that glitters is not gold. As it happens, I know a man who makes gold jewelry. If he tells me the vase is genuine, I will sell it, and then you and I will share the money."

4   Trusting his friend, Sonam gave Dorje the vase. The two friends parted, agreeing to meet in two days to divide any profits from the sale of the vase.

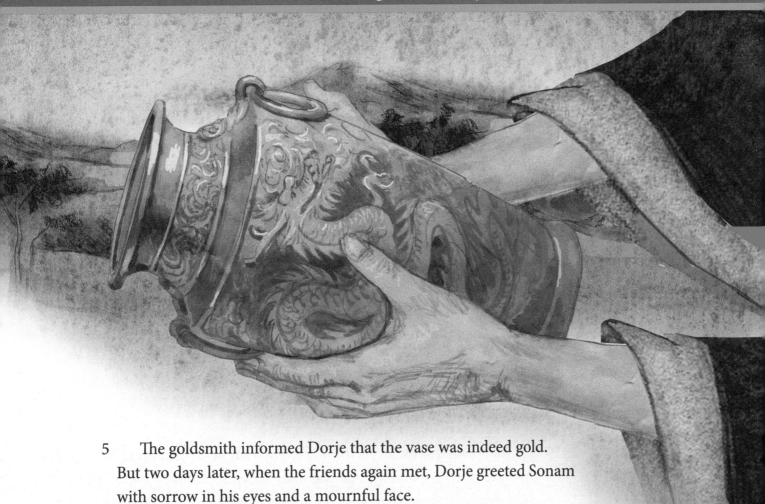

5   The goldsmith informed Dorje that the vase was indeed gold. But two days later, when the friends again met, Dorje greeted Sonam with sorrow in his eyes and a mournful face.

6   "What is wrong, Dorje?" asked Sonam.

7   "Alas!" sighed Dorje dramatically. "Our hopes have been bitterly crushed. By accident I set the vase too close to the fire, and it melted into a worthless lump of pewter. It was only cheap metal after all."

8   Sonam was not taken in by Dorje's tale, but he hid his suspicions. He just sighed and then softly replied, "Never mind. Since the vase was worth nothing, nothing has been lost."

9   Relieved that Sonam had taken the bad news so well, Dorje invited him to stay overnight with his family.

10   The next morning Sonam said, "Friend Dorje, I want to thank you for your efforts with the vase and repay you as you deserve. May I invite your two dear children to visit my home in the country? They can play with my pet rabbits, swim in my lake, and breathe fresh air. Let them come home with me for a nice vacation!"

11   As soon as the children heard of the plan, they pestered and pestered until their parents agreed.

12   Soon Sonam set off for home with the children for company. Eventually they came to a place called Monkey Hill, the home of many wild monkeys. Sonam captured two young creatures and put them in a small cage. "We will take these little fellows home as pets. You can play with them if you treat them kindly," he explained. "I will name a monkey after each of you, we'll teach them tricks, and they will be your twins!"

13   Quick learners, the young monkeys soon imitated the way the children tilted their heads or moved in a certain way. Sonam and the children spent many hours together, laughing at the way the monkeys mimicked whatever the children did.

14   Then came the last day of vacation. Sonam gave each child a basket and shooed them outside. "Walk up the mountain to gather berries and fruits," he said. "We will surprise your father with a tasty treat before you return home."

15   Then Sonam waited. Hearing Dorje approach, he sat down with the monkeys. Holding each one gently, he put on a tragic face.

16   "What is wrong, my friend?" asked Dorje.

17   "Alas!" sighed Sonam. "These are now your lovely children. You see, I took them to Monkey Hill. But I accidentally allowed them too near the beasts. Your children were transformed into these monkeys, right before my eyes!"

18   Sonam called the monkeys by name, and they began their tricks. They imitated the way Dorje's children jumped, walked, and even smiled, just as they had been taught. At first, Dorje was speechless. "H-h-how can this be?" he sputtered. "Is such a thing even possible?"

19   "It was a freak accident," Sonam replied. "After all, strange things do happen from time to time. Why, I know of a recent case in which a gold vase was turned into cheap metal." Then a twinkle crept into his eyes.

20   "Oh!" was all Dorje could say at first. Then a look of shame and relief spread over his face. "Now I understand, my friend," he said. "Keeping the money for the vase was dishonest. I will gladly hand over what I owe you, if you will pardon my foolish greed."

21   Just then, Dorje's children ran in and hugged their father. All was gradually forgiven, and Sonam and Dorje remained friends for life.

22   Dorje would often retell the tale of the bright monkeys. And he would always end by saying, "I learned a valuable lesson that day. As you know, a true friend is a treasure greater than gold."

▶ **Think** Use what you learned from reading the folktale to respond to the following questions.

1 In Greek mythology, King Midas was granted the power to turn any object into gold simply by touching it. Why did the author use the phrase "the touch of Midas" in paragraph 2?

    A to show that Dorje and Sonam have Midas-like powers because they turned the vase they found into gold

    B to compare Dorje and Sonam's good fortune in finding the vase to Midas's ability to make gold

    C to show that Sonam is well educated, while Dorje is unfamiliar with the story of King Midas

    D to compare Dorje and Sonam's rare golden treasure to similar treasures owned by rich kings like Midas

2 This question has two parts. First, answer Part A. Then answer Part B.

Part A
What is the **best** meaning of the word <u>pewter</u> in paragraph 7?

    A a metal that shines like gold

    B a metal that is soft and melts easily

    C a metal that is not costly

    D a metal that is not useful

Part B
Underline **two** story details that support the answer to Part A.

"Alas!" sighed Dorje dramatically. "Our hopes have been bitterly crushed. By accident I set the vase too close to the fire, and it melted into a worthless lump of pewter. It was only cheap metal after all."

3 This question has two parts. First, answer Part A. Then answer Part B.

Part A

What is the meaning of the word <u>mimicked</u> as it is used in paragraph 13 of "A Golden Vase and Two Bright Monkeys"?

  A tried

  B watched

  C found

  D copied

Part B

Circle **one** word in the paragraph below that helps the reader understand the meaning of <u>mimicked</u>.

>   Quick learners, the young monkeys soon imitated the way the children tilted their heads or moved in a certain way. Sonam and the children spent many hours together, laughing . . . .

4 In the paragraphs 17 and 18 shown below from the story, one word has the following definition: "to change completely in appearance or structure." Underline the word that **best** fits the definition.

>   "Alas!" sighed Sonam. "These are now your lovely children. You see, I took them to Monkey Hill. But I accidentally allowed them too near the beasts. Your children were transformed into these monkeys, right before my eyes!"
>   Sonam called the monkeys by name, and they began their tricks. They imitated the way Dorje's children jumped, walked, and even smiled, just as they had been taught.

Write

5 **Short Response** Paragraph 19 of the passage uses the phrase "freak accident." Explain what the phrase means as it is used in the passage. Support your possible meaning with context clues and details from the text.

_____

_____

_____

_____

_____

_____

_____

 Learning Target

In this lesson, you learned how to use context clues to figure out the meanings of unknown words and phrases. Explain how this will help you better understand a story or poem.

_____

_____

_____

Lesson 18
Comparing Points of View

Learning Target

Comparing narrators and their thoughts and feelings about what happens will help you develop a deeper understanding of story characters and events.

▶ **Read** In stories, the **narrator** is the person who tells the story. The narrator always has a **point of view**, or how he or she thinks or feels about story events. Some narrators are characters in the story. They experience what happens and are called **first-person** narrators. Other narrators are not characters in the story. They look in from outside the story. They are called **third-person** narrators.

When you read, pay attention not just to what narrators say but also how they say it. Their points of view will affect the way you interpret what happens and why.

Study the cartoons below. For each one, decide who the narrator is.

As I walked down the hall, my friends stared at me, but I wasn't at all surprised. I wanted everybody's attention!

As Martha walked down the hall, her friends stared at her. She wasn't at all surprised. After all, she wanted their attention!

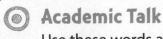 **Think**   What have you learned about first- and third-person narrators? Use the *Venn diagram* below to **compare** and **contrast** the narrators' points of view. Use information from the cartoons to help you.

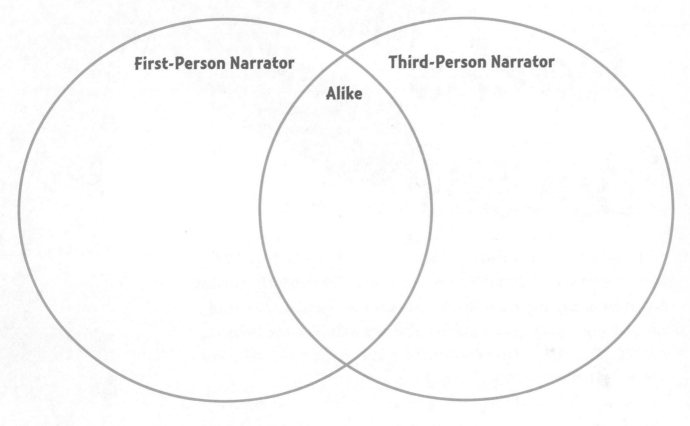

First-Person Narrator   Third-Person Narrator

Alike

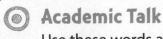 **Talk**   Share your Venn diagram with a partner.

• Did you and your partner identify the same similarities and differences?

• What details from the cartoons did you use to help you compare and contrast?

⊚ **Academic Talk**
Use these words and phrases to talk about the text.

• **narrator**   • **point of view**   • **compare**
• **first-person**   • **third-person**   • **contrast**

▶ **Read**

Just a Bunch of Rocks and Bones?

by Watley Hamish

1   I was looking forward to my first field trip at my new school. We were scheduled to visit the Museum of Natural History, which sounded extremely interesting to me, that is, until my new friend Barry started complaining about it. As our bus traveled along the highway, Barry insisted, "I'm telling you, LeBron, we went last year, and it's mostly just a bunch of boring rocks and bones. What a snoozer!"

2   *Oh, no,* I thought. *There's nothing worse than being bored, especially when I was really looking forward to something.* Suddenly, the trip seemed ruined. Moments later, our bus pulled into the museum's parking lot; we dragged ourselves outside and trudged up the museum steps.

3   Sweating under the hot sun, I glumly looked around. Then I noticed a statue of a small, perky dinosaur poking its head out of some bushes. *Hey,* I thought. *This might not be so bad.*

4   A tour guide met us and shepherded our class around the museum. Barry was right in one way. There were a lot of rocks and bones, but what rocks! We viewed cool fossils of creatures that had lived a million years ago. We also saw sparkling gemstones and meteors that had fallen from space. And the bones were even better! One gallery featured skeletons of mastodons and a saber-toothed cat. Another displayed dinosaurs, including part of a *T. rex.* Already I was hoping we'd come back to see more next year—but I don't think I'm ready to tell Barry that.

Close Reader Habits

Different words signal different types of narration. **Underline** the words that signal who is telling the story.

Explore How would an account of the museum trip told by a first-person narrator differ from an account told by a third-person narrator?

> The things a narrator and other characters do, say, think, and feel often reveal their points of view.

Think

1 Who is the narrator? _____

2 Does the story use a first-person or a third-person narrator? Explain your thinking, and include story evidence that supports it.

_____

_____

_____

3 How does LeBron's point of view about the museum change from the beginning of the story to the end? Why?

_____

_____

_____

_____

Talk

4 How would the story be different if it were told by a narrator with a different point of view? Why would it be different? List some story details that might change.

 ## Write

5 **Short Response** Describe how the story would have been different if it had been told by a narrator with a different point of view. Include text evidence in your response. Use the space provided on page 290 to write your response.

> **HINT** What could a narrator with a different point of view tell about Barry's thoughts and feelings?

If Only This Were Real

by Jing Wu

1　Hoshi stared at the clock over a panel in the spaceship. The school day was almost over, and she couldn't wait to meet with her friend, Jeri. Their newly created visual game awaited them on Deck C. Incredibly exciting, the game made space-time seem to pass much faster.

2　At least the new teacher, Vox-23, was more interesting than the last class-A instructional robot. Soon it completed the lesson. Then it announced what it always said: "Enjoy the rest of your afternoon, and have another lovely day!"

3　Hoshi glanced out the window into the blackness of space. Every hour of every day the view looked the same. Having spent half her life traveling to a lush planet in another galaxy, Hoshi recalled little else. She would be 15 by the time they arrived at their new home.

4　After class, Hoshi and Jeri raced straight to Deck C and entered one of the 3-D rooms, rooms that could create any scene a person imagined. Jeri excitedly pressed some buttons and called out, "Computer: run the program 'Old Earth School on a Big Hill.' Make it look real!" The bare room instantly changed into an old-fashioned classroom with a dusty blackboard mounted behind an old wooden desk. Sunlight from large windows filled the dusty air. As Hoshi and Jeri looked outside, they could see white clouds, blue sky, flowering trees, green grass, and a playground. They politely asked their human teacher, Mrs. Ryant, "May we go outside for recess?"

5　"If only this were real, Jeri!" Hoshi said wistfully. "Maybe sometime in the future, things truly will be this good."

Close Reader Habits

What is the narrator's point of view? Reread the story. **Underline** words that show how the narrator thinks or feels about characters and events.

Think Use what you've learned from reading the science fiction story to respond to the following questions.

1. This passage is told by a third-person narrator. Select **three** sentences that indicate the narrator is a third-person narrator.

    A "Hoshi stared at the clock over a panel in the spaceship."

    B "Incredibly exciting, the game made space-time seem to pass much faster."

    C "At least the new teacher, Vox-23, was more interesting than the last class-A instructional robot."

    D "Hoshi glanced out the window into the blackness of space."

    E "She would be 15 by the time they arrived at their new home."

    F "The bare room instantly changed into an old-fashioned classroom with a dusty blackboard mounted behind an old wooden desk."

> The narrator's choice of words reveals who is telling the story. Ask yourself: Is the narrator speaking from *outside* the story, or is the narrator a character *in* the story?

2. Reread paragraph 3. If the story were told in the first-person, which of the following would **most likely** be part of the story?

    A Hoshi's thoughts and feelings about traveling through space

    B details about Hoshi's and Jeri's actions, but not their point of view about the trip

    C different ways multiple characters viewed the trip

    D more information about the 3-D rooms on Deck C

▶ **Talk**

3. Compare the points of view of the narrators in "If Only This Were Real" and "Just a Bunch of Rocks and Bones?" Use the Venn diagram on page 291 to organize your thoughts. Explain how the points of view in the two stories compare.

▶ **Write**

4. **Short Response** Use the information from your discussion and diagram to compare the points of view of the narrators in "If Only This Were Real" and "Just a Bunch of Rocks and Bones?" Use at least **one** detail from each text to support your response. Use the space provided on page 291 to write your reponse.

> **HINT** Compare how you learn about the thoughts and feelings of the narrator in each story.

Write Use the space below to write your answer to the question on page 287.

Just a Bunch of
Rocks and Bones?

> **HINT** What could a narrator with a different point of view tell about Barry's thoughts and feelings?

5 **Short Response** Describe how the story would have been different if it had been told by a narrator with a different point of view. Include text evidence in your response.

_____

_____

_____

_____

_____

_____

_____

> Don't forget to check your writing.

Check Your Writing

☐ Did you read the prompt carefully?

☐ Did you put the prompt in your own words?

☐ Did you use the best evidence from the text to support your ideas?

☐ Are your ideas clearly organized?

☐ Did you write in clear and complete sentences?

☐ Did you check your spelling and punctuation?

If Only This Were Real

3 **Use the Venn diagram below to organize your ideas.**

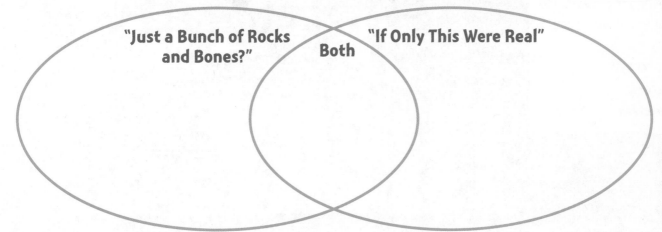

"Just a Bunch of Rocks and Bones?"   Both   "If Only This Were Real"

Write **Use the space below to write your answer to the question on page 289.**

4 **Short Response** Use the information from your discussion and diagram to compare the points of view of the narrators in "If Only This Were Real" and "Just a Bunch of Rocks and Bones?" Use at least **one** detail from each text to support your response.

> **HINT** Compare how you learn about the thoughts and feelings of the narrator in each story.

_____

_____

_____

_____

_____

_____

_____

▶ **Read**

TRICK or TREAT

by Bessie Chevalier

WORDS TO KNOW

As you read, look inside, around, and beyond these words to figure out what they mean.

- **current**
- **stern**
- **victim**

1   Terry hid his face behind his science book so no one would see him laugh. Everybody knew that if Terry chuckled when nobody else was laughing, somebody was about to get pranked. His current target was Mr. Mason, his teacher. Terry had put a rubber spider on Mr. Mason's chair and couldn't wait to see what happened when his teacher sat down.

2   "Good morning, class," said Mr. Mason as he breezed into the room. "Let's get started, shall we?" he added, grabbing his science book. He pulled his chair out and got ready to sit. Unable to help himself, Terry let out a squeaky snicker.

3   Mr. Mason froze. "Terry? Is there something you need to tell me?" he asked.

4   "No, Mr. Mason," Terry answered, but the huge smile on his face told the truth.

5   Mr. Mason leaned over and looked at the seat of his chair. There, right in the middle, was a big, black spider. Mr. Mason snatched up the rubber spider and walked over to Terry's desk.

6   "Terry, your pranks are getting tiresome," Mr. Mason said sternly. The other students nodded in agreement. At first, Terry's pranks had been funny. But nobody could remember a day when he hadn't played a trick on someone in the class. "I need you to go sit in the hall for ten minutes and think how your victims feel about your pranks."

7   Terry left the class and sat against the wall in the hallway. His smile was gone, but he didn't actually feel sorry. Mostly, he was disappointed that Mr. Mason had figured out his prank before he sat down. Terry had really wanted to see Mr. Mason's reaction.

8   A few minutes later, the classroom door opened. "You can come back in now, Terry," said Mr. Mason. Terry hopped up and walked back to his desk. "All right, let's get back to business," Mr. Mason continued. "Did all of you remember to bring your permission slips for the field trip to the ice cream factory tomorrow?"

9   Terry's eyes widened. Field trip? Ice cream factory? He didn't remember ever hearing about this. But all around him, his classmates were reaching into their desks and pulling out permission slips.

10   "Mr. Mason! I don't have a permission slip!" Terry wailed. He couldn't believe he was going to miss such a great trip.

11   "How does it feel to be pranked, Terry?" teased Mr. Mason, grinning.

12   Terry realized there was no field trip. He heaved a sigh of relief. "It felt awful, Mr. Mason," he answered. Suddenly, Terry realized that he was getting tired of his pranks, too.

Permission Slip

I _____ give permission

for my child _____ to go to

the _____ on _____

_____   _____
Parent Signature   Date

Genre: Realistic Fiction

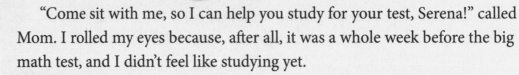

Putting It OFF

by Alan McMullen

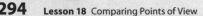

1   "Come sit with me, so I can help you study for your test, Serena!" called Mom. I rolled my eyes because, after all, it was a whole week before the big math test, and I didn't feel like studying yet.

2   "Mom!" I wailed. "Can't I finish watching this show on the science channel first? It's educational and *absolutely* fascinating! Plus, if I study now, I'll just forget everything before next week's test."

3   Mom sighed, "Go ahead and finish your program, I guess . . . but I won't be able to help you study after dinner."

4   "That's okay, Mom. I'll just study alone later before bedtime." She gave me a look that showed she suspected I didn't intend to study today. I wish she understood that I do my best work at the last minute.

5   Once again I relaxed into the couch. Truthfully, only half my attention was focused on the science channel program. Peeling stickers from a sheet and positioning them artfully on the cover of my math notebook seemed far more interesting, and it was a lot more entertaining than studying, for sure.

6   Once I'd arranged the cover stickers just the way I wanted, I put my notebook and stickers away and went to the kitchen to have dinner— macaroni and cheese, my favorite! Shortly after that, it was time for bed, but, naturally, I hadn't studied. Why would I, if the test was an entire week away?

7   The next morning, I sauntered into math class, well-rested and refreshed, but everyone else looked sleepy and tense. "What's going on?" I asked my friend Megan. "Why's everybody looking so tired?"

8   "I stayed up until almost 10 studying for the test," said Megan. "Didn't you?"

9   "Uh, no—it's next week, right?" I started to feel a little nervous.

10   "Serena, don't you remember? Mr. Gordon changed the day of the test from next Friday to this Friday! You didn't study at all?" Megan looked at me wide-eyed as I sank into my assigned seat.

11   If only I'd let Mom help me study last night, I might have a chance at passing this test. Never, never again will you catch me procrastinating before a big test! The next time, I promise I won't wait until the last minute.

▶ **Think** Use what you learned from reading the stories to respond to the following questions.

1 Which statement **best** describes the differences between the narrators' points of view in the two stories?

    A One story is told by a girl who is making observations from outside the story and describes how one person feels. The other story is told by a boy who is a character living through the events and describes how many people feel.

    B One story is told by a character who lives through the events and describes how many characters feel. The other story is told by a character who is an outsider observing the events and describes how one person feels.

    C One story is told by a character who lives through the events and describes how one person feels. The other story is told by a character who is an outsider observing the events and tells about how many people feel.

    D One story is told by a narrator who is actually the main character living through the events. The other story is told by a narrator who gives an account of the events from his imagination.

2 Underline the clues that helped you determine the narrator's point of view.

from "Trick or Treat"	from "Putting It Off"
Terry left the class and sat against the wall in the hallway. His smile was gone, but he didn't actually feel sorry. Mostly, he was disappointed that Mr. Mason had figured out his prank before he sat down.	"Come sit with me, so I can help you study for your test, Serena!" called Mom. I rolled my eyes because, after all, it was a whole week before the big math test, and I didn't feel like studying yet.

3 This question has two parts. First, answer Part A. Then answer Part B.

Part A

Read the sentence from paragraph 11 from "Putting It Off."

Never, never again will you catch me <u>procrastinating</u> before a big test!

What does the word <u>procrastinating</u> mean as it is used in the sentence?

    A   altering, revising, or editing something

    B   being slow or late about doing something

    C   taking control of something

    D   getting information about something

Part B

Underline the detail in the paragraph below that provides the **best** clue to the meaning of the word <u>procrastinating</u>.

If only I'd let Mom help me study last night, I might have a chance at passing this test. Never, never again will you catch me procrastinating before a big test! The next time, I promise I won't wait until the last minute!

4 Compare how the passages are similar and how they are different. Complete the chart by drawing Xs in the boxes next to statements that describe "Trick or Treat" and "Putting It Off." A statement may be used for both "Trick or Treat" and "Putting It Off."

Statement	"Trick or Treat"	"Putting It Off"
Includes a narrator who observes an event but does not experience the story		
Includes dialogue		
Includes the thoughts of the main character		
Includes a narrator who tells about the events as he or she experiences them		

Write

5 **Short Response** Compare and contrast the types of narration in "Trick or Treat" and "Putting It Off." Explain what each type reveals about the narrator's point of view. Use at least **one** detail from each story to support your answer.

_____

_____

_____

_____

_____

_____

_____

 Learning Target

In this lesson, you learned how first- and third-person narration differs. Now, describe how recognizing a narrator's point of view will help you develop a deeper understanding of story characters and events.

_____

_____

_____

_____

Lesson 19
Elements of Poetry

 **Learning Target**

Understanding about verse, rhythm, meter, and other features used in poems will help you write and talk about them.

▶ **Read** A poem has features you can both see and hear.

Each line in a poem is called a **verse**. Several verses grouped together form **stanzas**. These are **structural elements** you see.

Other elements in a poem are ones you hear. **Meter** sets up a pattern of strong and weak syllables in each verse. **Rhythm** is the regular pattern of sounds in the whole poem, like the beats in music. **Rhyme** repeats the same ending sounds in different words. Poets use these elements to express their ideas in new and surprising ways.

Read the poem below. Look and listen for structural elements.

Bigfoot's Complaint
by John Hansen

Why do they have to call me that?
I'm more than just a pair of feet.
If humans took a closer look,
They'd see my eyes are rather sweet.

But I walk these woods and hide my face
My footprints left in mud and snow.
The rest of me they'll never see
So I am called by what they know.

▶ **Think**   Use what you've learned about structural elements to complete the chart.

Element	Description	Example
verse		
stanza		
rhyme		

▶ **Talk**   Share your chart with a partner.

- Did you list the same elements, descriptions, and examples?
- Which parts of the poem do you see?
- Which parts do you hear?

◎ **Academic Talk**
Use these words to talk about the text.

- **structural element**   • **verse**   • **stanza**
- **meter**   • **rhythm**   • **rhyme**

> **Read**

Walking BIG WILLIE

by Clarisse Bartonelli

While I am working hard at school,
To master math and this and that,
At home Big Willie sleeps a lot
And dreams of chasing neighbors' cats.

5   Big Willie shakes himself awake
When through the door I come at three.
A furry bullet knocks me down.
A leash is dropped upon my knee.

We're on the street. No time to waste.
10   A million squirrels must be treed.
Some cats must be tormented next.
Will does this all at double speed.

Around the block and up the street,
He travels at the speed of sound,
15   And I, attached to him by leash,
Am led around and 'round and 'round.

I must confess I like the speed.
It's fun to travel zip–zam–zoom.
But sometimes when I'm out with Will,
20   I wonder, who is walking whom?

Close Reader Habits

As you read, **listen** for a pattern of rhyming words. Then **circle** any word at the end of a verse that rhymes with a word at the end of a different verse. Next, **draw lines** to connect the pairs of rhyming words.

Explore How do the elements in "Walking Big Willie" contribute to the poem's structure and meaning?

Think

> Poem verses often repeat the same meter. Together, the verses create a rhythm, or clear pattern of beats.

1 The pattern of strong (stressed) and weak syllables in a verse is its **meter**. Each verse in this poem has eight syllables, and every other syllable is **STRONG**. Study the meter of verse 1. Then underline the strong syllables in verse 2.

> Verse 1 While **I** am **WORK**ing **HARD** at **SCHOOL,**
> Verse 2 To master math and this and that,

2 Complete the chart below by adding information about the elements.

Element	Description	Effect
pattern of rhymes		Repeats sounds that help shape the poem stanzas
		Creates a pattern of strong and weak beats in a verse
		Creates a sense of sadness, excitement, or other feelings beyond the poet's words

Talk

3 Describe the structural elements used in "Walking Big Willie." How do they work together to create a feeling of exciting, speedy walks?

> **HINT** Reread the poem to figure out what elements of poetry the poet chose to use.

Write

4 **Short Response** Describe how the structural elements in "Walking Big Willie," including meter, create certain effects, or feelings. Use the space on page 304 to write your answer.

A TRAGIC STORY

by W.M. Thackeray,
The Book of Humorous Verse

There lived a sage[1] in days of yore,
And he a handsome pigtail wore;
But wondered much and sorrowed more,
Because it hung behind him.

5 He mused upon this curious case,
And swore he'd change the pigtail's place,
And have it hanging at his face,
Not dangling there behind him.

Says he, "The mystery I've found,—
10 I'll turn me round,"—he turned him round;
But still it hung behind him.

Then round and round, and out and in,
All day the puzzled sage did spin;
In vain—it mattered not a pin,
15 The pigtail hung behind him.

And right and left, and round about,
And up and down, and in and out,
He turned; but still the pigtail stout
Hung steadily behind him.

20 And though his efforts never slack,
And though he twist and twirl and tack,
Alas! still faithful to his back,
The pigtail hangs behind him.

[1] **sage:** a wise person

Close Reader Habits

How does the poet use rhythm in this poem for effect? As you reread the poem, **underline** the verse in each stanza that has a different beat than the others.

Think Use what you learned from reading the poem to respond to the following questions.

> Poets often group verses together to form stanzas. Each stanza usually presents a full thought or event.

1 Which statement **best** describes the last verse of each stanza?

  A It uses a different meter and does not rhyme with the last words of the other verses.

  B It uses the same meter and rhymes with words in the first verse of every stanza.

  C It uses the same meter, but only the last two verses in the stanza rhyme.

  D It uses a different meter, but the last verse rhymes with the other verses in the stanza.

2 What effect does the rhythm of each stanza have on a reader's understanding of how the sage feels?

  A The change in the last line creates a feeling of excitement.

  B The change in the last line creates a feeling of disappointment.

  C The change in the last line creates a feeling of boredom and restlessness.

  D The change in the last line creates a feeling of nervousness and concern.

Talk

3 Explain how the poet's use of structural elements adds to the meaning of the narrative poem. How do they combine to provide a clearer picture of the sage's problem in "A Tragic Story"? Make a list of your ideas.

> **HINT** Think of how the stanzas help to tell the story.

 Write

4 **Short Response** Describe how the poet's use of structural elements adds to the meaning of "A Tragic Story." Use at least **two** details from the passage to support your response. Use the space provided on page 305 to write your response.

Modeled and Guided Instruction

 Write Use the space below to write your answer to the question on page 301.

Walking BIG WILLIE

4 Short Response Describe how the structural elements in "Walking Big Willie," including meter, create certain effects, or feelings.

_____

_____

_____

_____

_____

_____

_____

_____

Don't forget to check your writing.

Write **Use the space below to write your answer to the question on page 303.**

A TRAGIC STORY

4 **Short Response** Describe how the poet's use of structural elements adds to the meaning of "A Tragic Story." Use at least two details from the passage to support your response.

_____

_____

_____

_____

_____

_____

_____

_____

_____

_____

Check Your Writing

☐ Did you read the prompt carefully?

☐ Did you put the prompt in your own words?

☐ Did you use the best evidence from the text to support your ideas?

☐ Are your ideas clearly organized?

☐ Did you write in clear and complete sentences?

☐ Did you check your spelling and punctuation?

▶ **Read**

REVENGE

by Felicia Witt

WORDS TO KNOW
As you read, look inside, around, and beyond these words to figure out what they mean.

- **constant**
- **innocent**

1   "A very fine Friday," Fiona did say,
    And set out to write up a plan for her day.
    "The first thing I'll do," said Fiona with flair
    "Is find out who planted this gum in my hair."

5   For Fiona, just moments ago, had tried prying
    Her head from her pillow, which made her start crying.
    For stuck 'twixt her head and the pillow so dewy
    Was a wad of gum—sticky, icky, and chewy.

    "Who did this thing?" asked Fiona, whose eyes
10 Narrowed to slits of the tiniest size.
    "Maybe a kid on whom I've played a prank—
    But that's nearly everyone!" Fiona's heart sank.

    Yes, it's true, our Fiona was known as a trickster
    Neither parents nor doctors nor teachers could fix her.
15 Every soul in her school had at some point been bitten
    By her tricks, though she seemed like an innocent kitten.

So it made all the sense in the world, she admitted,
That the gum in her hair was a message to quit it.
"I've played some great tricks on that crybaby, Jack.
20   Bet he put this old gum in my hair to get back."

She would have to get back at that back-getter, Jack,
And she thoughtfully planned out the perfect attack.
Jack's habits were something that Fiona knew
So she set out to replace his shampoo with glue.

25   But Fiona, in haste to avenge her gummed head,
Had missed all the gum wrappers under her bed.
She'd forgotten her own constant habit of chewing
And that the past night, that's what she'd been doing.

Genre: Poem

The Crocodile

by Lewis Carroll

from *The Hunting of the Snark and Other Poems and Verses*

How doth the little crocodile
Improve his shining tail,
And pour the waters of the Nile
On every golden scale!

5   How cheerfully he seems to grin!
How neatly spread his claws,
And welcomes little fishes in
With gently smiling jaws!

▶ **Think** Use what you learned from reading the poems to respond to the following questions.

1 Complete the chart below by using options from the box. Some options may not be used at all.

glue	scale	"And pour the waters of the Nile"
tail	flew	"Was a wad of gum— sticky, icky, and chewy."
sorrow	frail	playfulness
knew	anger	cleverness
grin	weak	

Element	"Revenge"	"The Crocodile"
What is an example of a verse in the poem?		
What are two words that rhyme in the poem?		
What is one effect the poet created by using meter and rhythm?		

2 In "Revenge," what is the feeling the poet **most likely** wanted readers to experience by using long verses and a fast rhythm?

    A how upset Fiona is about finding the gum in her hair

    B how tired Fiona is after waking up in the morning

    C how happy Fiona is about all the pranks she has played

    D how determined Fiona is to play even more pranks

3 What is the **main** purpose of the last stanza in "The Crocodile"?

    A   to show the crocodile is crafty

    B   to show the crocodile eats fish

    C   to show the crocodile is hungry

    D   to show the crocodile is a cheater

4 This question has two parts. First, answer Part A. Then answer Part B.

Part A
Read line 25 from the poem "Revenge."

    But Fiona, in haste to <u>avenge</u> her gummed head,

What does the word <u>avenge</u> mean as it is used in this line?

    A   to stick something together quickly

    B   to show who is now in control

    C   to teach an important lesson

    D   to punish for an earlier action

Part B
Which line from the poem "Revenge" provides the **best** clue for the meaning of <u>avenge</u>?

    A   "Neither parents nor doctors nor teachers could fix her."

    B   "That the gum in her hair was a message to quit it."

    C   "She would have to get back at that back-getter, Jack."

    D   "Had missed all the gum wrappers under her bed."

 **Write**

5 **Short Response** What structural elements do the poets of "Revenge" and "The Crocodile" use to create certain patterns and feelings? Include details from each poem to support your response.

_____

_____

_____

_____

_____

_____

_____

 Learning Target

In this lesson, you learned about the structural elements in poems. Describe how understanding about a poem's structure helps you write and speak about the poem.

 **Introduction**

LAFS.4.RL.2.5 . . . refer to the structural elements of . . . drama (e.g., casts of characters, settings, descriptions, dialogue, stage directions) . . . when writing or speaking about a text.

Lesson 20
Elements of Plays

 **Learning Target**

Understanding the purpose of different parts of a play will help you develop ways to talk and write about it.

▶ **Read** A drama, or play, is meant to be performed on a stage for an audience. Actors learn their parts by reading from a **script**, or written text. Special text features called **structural elements** tell the actors exactly what to say and do.

When you read a script, pay attention to all the structural elements, not just the **dialogue**, or words the characters speak. The **cast of characters** tells you who appears in the play, and the **setting** tells where and when it takes place. The **stage directions** tell the actors how to act and speak or what should happen on stage. Descriptions give details about how the characters or setting look. These structural elements work together to help you understand what an audience will experience.

Now read the script below. Look for the structural elements that differ from the way they'd be shown in a story.

The Surly Chefs

Setting: 1932, *a hotel kitchen*

Cast of Characters: HEAD CHEF, CHEF 2, CHEF 3, HOTEL GUEST

HEAD CHEF: [*staring angrily* at the HOTEL GUEST] So, you don't like our pies, do you? Maybe you'd like another taste, eh?

CHEF 2, CHEF 3: [*looking angry and upset*] Ready, Set, —

[*The three throw their pies at the* HOTEL GUEST.]

▶ **Think** Complete the chart below, which lists different structural elements in a play script. Add the purpose of each structural element and an example from *The Surly Chefs*. Remember to imagine the drama as the audience will see it.

Structural Element	Purpose	Example
Cast of characters		
Setting		
Dialogue		
Stage directions		
Descriptions		

▶ **Talk** Share your examples with a partner.

- How are your examples similar and different?
- How is the script of the play different from text in a story?

Academic Talk
Use these words and phrases to talk about the text.

- **structural elements**
- **dialogue**
- **cast of characters**
- **stage directions**
- **setting**
- **script**

> **Read**

Where's My Mummy?

by Silas Johnson

1 *Cast of Characters*: WILBUR, ROY, GLEN, *a* MUMMY
2 *Setting: The inside of a pyramid in Egypt*

3 [*Two workers,* WILBUR *and* ROY, *shovel dirt into a wheelbarrow. Oil lamps light the dark chamber, which includes a* MUMMY'S *tomb made of stone.*]

4 WILBUR [*shivering*]: Oooooh, Roy. This place gives me the creeps!

5 ROY: What's to be afraid of, Wilbur? Just get to work so we can get out of here.

6 [*The cover of the tomb creaks open. A wrapped hand reaches from inside.*]

7 WILBUR: Did you hear that? I heard something. [*He sees the* MUMMY'S *hand and starts shaking.*] And now I see something that I really don't want to be seeing!

8 [*The* MUMMY *climbs out of the tomb, moans, and walks toward them.* WILBUR *and* ROY *scream. Then the* MUMMY *starts laughing.*]

9 ROY: Hey, I'd know that laugh anywhere. Is that you, Glen?

10 GLEN [*unwrapping his head*]: Pretty good costume, don't you think?

11 ROY: Not bad. But what did you do with the real mummy?

12 GLEN: What mummy? There was nobody in there.

13 [*Just then a* MUMMY *walks slowly toward them from the shadows.* WILBUR, ROY, *and* GLEN *scream, turn, and run.*]

Close Reader Habits

As you read, **underline** the stage directions for Wilbur. Think about how the stage directions help you understand what Wilbur does and how he feels.

Explore How does your knowledge of structural elements in dramas help you understand what happens in *Where's My Mummy?*

Stage directions tell what the writer wants the audience to see and hear.

Think

1 Use the chart below to answer these questions. How should Wilbur perform his part? Which structural elements help you understand this?

Lines	Detail from the Text	What Wilbur Should Do	Structural Element
Line 4	[shivering]	Wilbur should act scared.	Stage directions
Line 7	Did you hear that? I heard something.		Dialogue
Line 7			
Line 8			

Talk

2 Discuss the way the play ends and how the stage directions help you understand what happens. List your ideas from the discussion.

Write

3 **Short Response** Describe how the structural elements of a play help you understand what is happening in *Where's My Mummy?* Use at least **two** details from the script in your response. Use the space provided on page 318 to write your response.

HINT Describe how the structural elements that guide a character's actions also help you.

Read

Genre: **Drama**

The Lightning Tantrum

by Hillary Sturm

1 *Cast of Characters*: YOUNG LIGHT, MOTHER LIGHT, FATHER LIGHT

2 *Setting: A colorful, cloud-filled sky at late evening. The light dims on three figures dressed in bright white gowns.*

3 YOUNG LIGHT: I'm tired of behaving! It's boring, and I don't want to be quiet! And I really don't want to go to bed yet!

4 MOTHER LIGHT: Young Light, I know you don't want to go to bed yet, but that's the way it has to be.

5 FATHER LIGHT: During the day you can play as much as you like. But when night comes, you've got to go to bed.

6 YOUNG LIGHT: But why? Why can't I play at night?

7 MOTHER LIGHT: Because there can't be light in the sky at night. That's when people on Earth are sleeping.

8 YOUNG LIGHT: It's not fair! [YOUNG LIGHT *stamps her foot. Then she begins pounding her fists against the sky.*]

9 FATHER LIGHT: Stop that! You'll wake up the whole sky!

10 YOUNG LIGHT: So? I want to wake up the sky! Hey, Clouds! Wake up! [*There's a low rumbling sound that gradually grows very loud. A flash of light is followed by a loud BOOM!*]

11 YOUNG LIGHT: Ha ha! I woke up the Clouds! RUMBLE!

12 MOTHER LIGHT [*shaking her head*]: Oh, dear. I guess the people on Earth will have a big thunder and lightning storm tonight.

Close Reader Habits

Which structural elements help you understand what is happening? Reread the script. **Underline** elements that help you understand events in the play.

Think Use what you learned from reading the drama to respond to the following questions.

1 Which statement **best** explains why the description in Line 2 is important to understanding the drama?

Imagine how the setting and action look onstage to the audience.

    A It tells how the actors will move on the stage.

    B It describes the setting and how the actors will look.

    C It describes the tone of voice actors will use when they speak.

    D It names the characters who will appear in the play.

2 Complete the chart by adding dialogue and stage directions to tell how Young Light should perform her part in lines 8–11.

Stage Directions	Dialogue	How Young Light Should Act

Talk

3 If you were putting on this play, what sounds, actions, and setting you would use? Why would each element be important?

 Write

4 **Short Response** Describe the sounds, actions, and setting you would use if you were putting on this play. Use script details as support. Use the space provided on page 319 to write your response.

HINT Create a word picture of what the audience will hear or see for each structural element.

Write Use the space below to write your answer to the question on page 315.

3 **Short Response** Describe how the structural elements of a play help you understand what is happening in *Where's My Mummy?* Use at least **two** details from the script in your response.

> **HINT** Describe how the structural elements that guide a character's actions also help you.

> Don't forget to check your writing.

Write Use the space below to write your answer to the question on page 317.

The Lightning Tantrum

HINT Create a word picture of what the audience will hear or see for each structural element.

4 **Short Response** Describe the sounds, actions, and setting you would use if you were putting on this play. Use script details as support.

_____

_____

_____

_____

_____

_____

_____

_____

Check Your Writing

☐ Did you read the prompt carefully?

☐ Did you put the prompt in your own words?

☐ Did you use the best evidence from the text to support your ideas?

☐ Are your ideas clearly organized?

☐ Did you write in clear and complete sentences?

☐ Did you check your spelling and punctuation?

▶ **Read**

The Endless Tale

by Augusta Stevenson, *Children's Classics in Dramatic Form*

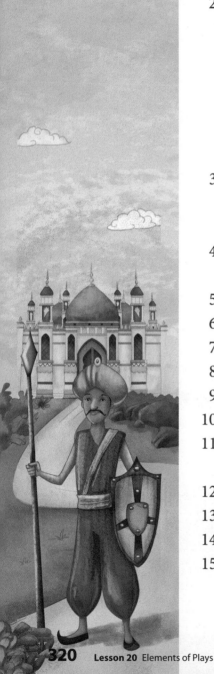

WORDS TO KNOW
As you read, look inside, around, and beyond these words to figure out what they mean.

• **interrupt**
• **seize**

1 *Setting*
TIME: *a long time ago*
PLACE: *the King's palace*

2 *Cast of Characters*
KING
PRINCESS
FIRST STORYTELLER
SECOND STORYTELLER
LORDS and LADIES
GUARDS

3 [*The* KING *sits on a cushion in the great hall. The* PRINCESS *sits on a cushion by him. In front of them sits the* FIRST STORYTELLER. *The* LORDS *and* LADIES *sit nearby.*]

4 FIRST STORYTELLER: "Then the prince married the princess and they were happy forever and ever."

5 [*There is a pause.*]

6 KING: Go on!

7 [*The* STORYTELLER *hangs his head.*]

8 KING: Go on, I say!

9 FIRST STORYTELLER: That is all, your Majesty.

10 KING: [*outraged*] All!

11 FIRST STORYTELLER: The prince married the princess. There is nothing more to tell.

12 KING: I cannot bear so short a story!

13 PRINCESS: Why, father, for three months we have listened to it!

14 KING: 'Tis short, I say! I bid you make it longer, sir!

15 FIRST STORYTELLER: I cannot, Sire. The prince married the princess. There is nothing—

16 KING: Throw him out of the palace, guards! Cut off his head!

17 [GUARDS *seize the* STORYTELLER.]

18 PRINCESS: Father!

19 LORDS: Your Majesty!

20 LADIES: Sire!

21 PRINCESS: Spare his life!

22 FIRST STORYTELLER: Let me keep my head, Sire!

23 KING: Why should you keep it? You do not use it.

24 FIRST STORYTELLER: For three months I have used it, Sire!

25 KING: Your story is too short, I say! Away with him, guards! Away!

26 [GUARDS *take out the* FIRST STORYTELLER.]

27 KING: Bid another storyteller come!

28 [A GUARD *admits the* SECOND STORYTELLER, *who bows before the* KING *and* PRINCESS.]

29 KING: Sir, hear me. You must tell a story that will last forever.

30 SECOND STORYTELLER: I hear, O King!

31 KING: If you can do this, you shall marry my daughter and be king after me.

32 SECOND STORYTELLER: I hear, O King!

33 KING: If you fail, you shall lose your head. Begin! And remember, the story must go on forever. Now again I say, begin!

34 SECOND STORYTELLER: "Once upon a time a certain king seized upon all the corn in his country. He had it stored in a strong granary. Then came a swarm of locusts over the land. Soon they found a crack in the south side of the granary. Now the crack was just large enough for one locust to pass through at a time. So one locust went in and carried away a grain of corn. Then another locust went in and carried away a grain of corn. Then another locust went in and carried away a grain of corn. Then—"

35 KING [*interrupting*]: Yes, yes! Now go on with the story.

36 SECOND STORYTELLER: The story shall go on, O King! "Then another locust went in and carried away another grain of corn. Then another locust—"

37 KING [*interrupting*]: I tell you to go on with the story!

38 SECOND STORYTELLER: I obey, great King. "Then another locust went in and carried away another grain of corn. Then another—"

39 KING: The story! The story, I tell you!

40 SECOND STORYTELLER: This is the story, O King! "Then another locust went in and carried away another grain of corn. Then—"

41 KING: I cannot stand it! How long will it take the locusts to carry away all the grain?

42 SECOND STORYTELLER: One thousand years, O King! "Then another locust went in and—"

43 KING: Stop! Stop! Take my daughter! Be king after me! Be king now! Anything to stop the locusts!

44 [*The lights go out. The curtain falls. The play is over.*]

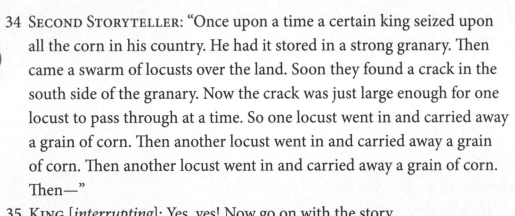

▶ **Think** Use what you learned from reading the drama to respond to the following questions.

1 Which **two** features below are found only in a script for a play and would not be found in a story?

    A descriptions provided by a narrator

    B events that tell what happens

    C stage directions

    D dialogue between characters

    E cast of characters

    F description of the setting

2 The following question has two parts. First, answer Part A. Then answer Part B.

Part A

Read the sentence from line 14.

    KING: I <u>bid</u> you make it longer, sir!

What does the word <u>bid</u> mean as it is used in this sentence?

    A offer

    B provide

    C request

    D answer

Part B

Which detail from the story provides the **best** clue for the meaning of <u>bid</u>?

    A "There is nothing more to tell."

    B "I cannot bear so short a story!"

    C "That is all, your Majesty."

    D "I cannot, Sire."

3 Which of the statements below **best** describes why the script provided this detail in line 7?

[*The* STORYTELLER *hangs his head.*]

A to let the audience know that the storyteller is tired

B to let the audience know the storyteller's neck is sore

C to let the audience know the storyteller is finished with his story

D to let the audience know the storyteller is ashamed

4 The following question has two parts. First, answer Part A. Then answer Part B.

Part A

What does the writer do by adding the stage direction in line 35?

KING [*interrupting*]: Yes, yes! Now go on with the story.

A She shows that the King is not interested in the story.

B She shows that the Second Storyteller is speaking quietly.

C She shows that the King is impatient to hear what happens next.

D She shows that the Second Storyteller is about to have his head cut off.

Part B

Underline **two** sentences from the lines below that **best** support your answer in Part A.

SECOND STORYTELLER: This is the story, O King! "Then another locust went in and carried away another grain of corn. Then—"

KING: I cannot stand it! How long will it take the locusts to carry away all the grain?

SECOND STORYTELLER: One thousand years, O King! "Then another locust went in and—"

Write

5 **Short Response** Describe how you think this play should be
performed. In your description, tell which three characters are the
most important to the action and how they should perform their
parts.

_____

_____

_____

_____

_____

_____

_____

 Learning Target

**In this lesson, you learned about the purpose of different parts
of a play. Now, write about how you developed ways of talking
and writing about plays.**

LAFS.4.RL.2.5 Explain major differences between poems, drama, and prose, and refer to the structural elements of poems (e.g., verse, rhythm, meter) and drama (e.g., casts of characters, settings, descriptions, dialogue, stage directions) when writing or speaking about a text.

Lesson 21
Comparing Poems, Plays, and Prose

Learning Target

Comparing and contrasting the features of poems, drama, and prose will help you write and speak about the main differences between them.

▶ **Read** The three major forms of literature—poetry, **drama**, and **prose**—all make use of distinctive **structural elements**, or special features. Their shapes alone make the literature forms easy to tell apart.

These forms of literature differ in other ways. A poem often packs deep thoughts and feelings into a few words. A drama is written to be performed onstage. And for prose—novels and short stories—a narrator reveals the characters' thoughts, feelings, and actions. Each form of literature has its own features, so reading it is a unique experience!

Study the sheets of paper below. Can you use the text shapes and word clues to identify each form of literature?

Jack and the Beanstalk

Once upon a time,

And everyone lived happily ever after—except ～～～！

The Star

Twinkle, ～～～ star,
～～～ are,
Up ～～～ so high,
～～～ the sky!
～～～ star,
～～～ are!

The Three Little Pigs

WOLF: ～～～～～

PIG ONE: ～～～～～
～～～

WOLF: ～～～～～

PIG TWO: ～～～～～
～～～～

PIG ONE: ～～～～～
～～～

WOLF: ～～～!!

▶ **Think** What have you learned about the ways poems, drama, and prose differ? In the chart below, describe each element. Then mark an X in the box where the element is frequently found.

Element	Description	Poem	Drama	Prose
setting	Time or place something happens			
dialogue				
cast of characters				
stage directions				
description				
chapters				
stanza				
narrator				

▶ **Talk** Share your charts. Did you mark the same elements? What are some other differences between poetry, drama, and prose?

◉ **Academic Talk**
Use these words and phrases to talk about the text.
- **drama**
- **prose**
- **structural elements**

Read

Angie's Solo

by Lars Gary

1   My sister Angie's glee club was about to perform for their annual show, and the auditorium was packed. I was incredibly nervous because Angie would be singing her first solo in front of an audience, and I really wanted her to do well.

2   At last, the glee club members filed onstage and began singing the first song on the program. Too soon it came time for Angie to sing. Although she seemed tense and was probably trembling inside, I could tell Angie put her heart into it and sang away. But I also knew what she sounded like when she practiced—and tonight's performance was far from perfect. In fact, Angie sounded flat several times. Still, the crowd started cheering even before she had finished.

3   I almost dreaded seeing Angie after the show. Should I be honest about her performance? After all, I knew Angie was extremely sensitive and hated any form of criticism. I didn't want to hurt her feelings, so what should I tell her?

4   "Brian!" she called when she saw me. "What did you think of my solo?"

5   I didn't hesitate for a moment. "It was really beautiful! You should be proud of yourself," I replied. When I saw her beaming, I knew at that moment how right I was to think that the truth is sometimes wrong.

At the Concert

by Lars Gary

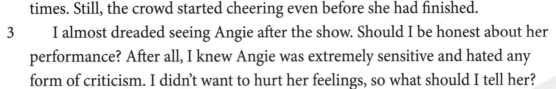

When my sister sang her solo,
I thought it sounded awfully flat.
But I didn't want to hurt her feelings,
So I could hardly tell her that.

5   So later when she asked me
What I thought about her song,
I told her, *It was beautiful,*
Because that night the truth felt wrong.

Close Reader Habits

Reread the story and poem. **Underline** details the story provides that the poem does not.

Explore   **What are the similarities and differences between the ways the two pieces of literature tell the same story?**

Ask yourself: What elements make this form of literature different from the other forms?

Think

1 Complete the chart below by writing Xs in the boxes next to details that appear in the poem, the prose, or both. Some details may have been used in both.

Details	Poem	Prose
The night of his sister's solo (setting)		
Dialogue between two characters		
Rhyming words that help describe events		
Ideas grouped as stanzas		
Thoughts and feelings of the narrator		
Ideas grouped as paragraphs		

2 What are **two** details you learn about the sister's performance in **both** the story and the poem? Write them in the box below.

Talk

3 The story and poem use different structural elements to tell about the concert. Describe the similarities and differences between what you learn about it from the story and the poem. Make a list of your ideas.

HINT How are the feelings of the narrator revealed in each passage?

 ### Write

4 **Short Response** Compare and contrast the different ways the story and poem describe the same event. Include text evidence in your response. Use the space provided on page 334 to write your response.

> Read

The Sound of Money

based on a Turkish folktale

1 *Cast of Characters*: A Traveler, *an* Innkeeper, *the* Town Judge

2 *Setting: Outside a country inn in Turkey, a very long time ago*

3 [*A poor* Traveler *stops outside a country inn. The* Innkeeper *stands outside, cooking a large pot of soup over an open fire.*]

4 Traveler [*leans over the pot to smell the soup*]: Oh, I am so hungry. And this soup smells so delicious!

5 Innkeeper [*angrily grabbing the* Traveler's *arm*]: Hey, what do you think you're doing, stealing my soup? Why, you rascal!

6 Traveler: But sir, I took no soup. I was only smelling the steam from the pot.

7 [*Just then the* Town Judge *walks onto stage. He stops to listen to the* Innkeeper *and the* Traveler.]

8 Innkeeper: I do not give my soup away. You must pay me, this minute. I demand money!

9 Traveler [*pulls out his pockets to show they are empty*]: But I have no money. Not a cent, for I am a poor man.

10 Town Judge: Ah, but I do! [*He reaches into his pocket and pulls out a handful of coins.*]

11 Innkeeper: I don't care whose money it is, as long as I get paid for my soup!

12 Town Judge: And I know just the price you deserve. [*He jingles the handful of coins in front of the* Innkeeper.] For the smell of soup, you receive only the sound of the money.

Close Reader Habits

How does the drama tell you about the characters' actions? **Circle** details that tell the characters how to act.

The SOUND of MONEY

1   A beggar was given a piece of bread, but nothing to put on it. Hoping to get something to go with his bread, he went to a nearby inn and asked for a handout. The innkeeper turned him away with nothing, but the beggar sneaked into the kitchen where he saw a large pot of soup cooking over the fire. He held his piece of bread over the steaming pot, hoping to thus capture a bit of flavor from the good-smelling vapor. Suddenly the innkeeper seized him by the arm and angrily accused him of stealing soup.

2   "I took no soup," said the beggar. "I was only smelling the vapor."

3   "Then you must pay for the smell," answered the innkeeper. The poor beggar had no money, so the angry innkeeper dragged him before the qadi.[1]

4   Now Nasreddin Hodja was at that time serving as qadi, and he heard the innkeeper's complaint and the beggar's explanation.

5   "So you demand payment for the smell of your soup?" summarized the Hodja after the hearing.

6   "Yes!" insisted the innkeeper.

7   "Then I myself will pay you," said the Hodja, "and I will pay for the smell of your soup with the sound of money."

8   Thus saying, the Hodja drew two coins from his pocket, rang them together loudly, put them back into his pocket, and sent the beggar and the innkeeper each on his own way.

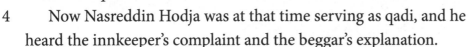

[1] **qadi:** judge

Close Reader Habits

How does the story tell you about the setting? **Circle** the words that tell you where the action occurs.

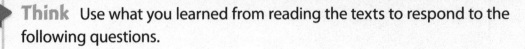

▶ **Think** Use what you learned from reading the texts to respond to the following questions.

1 Which statement **best** describes one difference between how the writers describe the setting in the drama and in the story?

   A The writer of the drama describes the setting first. The writer of the story has to describe the setting quickly using stage directions.

   B The writer of the drama describes the setting early in the play. The writer of the story describes the setting as different story details are told.

   C The writer of the drama describes the setting at the end of the play. The writer of the story describes the setting first so the story makes sense.

   D The writer of the drama describes the setting at the end of the play. The writer of the story also waits until the end to describe the setting.

2 Which statements **best** explain how readers learn about the innkeepers' accusations against the traveler and the beggar? Pick **two** choices, one from the drama and one from the folktale.

   A In the drama, the dialogue provides the details.

   B In the drama, the stage directions supply the details.

   C In the drama, the narrator's dialogue provides the details.

   D In the folktale, the stanza supplies the details.

   E In the folktale, the dialogue provides the details.

   F In the folktale, the narrator's description supplies the details.

3 What elements in the drama tell the Innkeeper, the Traveler, and the Town Judge how to act and what to say?

   A stage directions and dialogue

   B dialogue and setting

   C rhythm and dialogue

   D dialogue, meter, and stanzas

4 This question has two parts. Answer Part A. Then answer Part B.

Part A

What is one way in which the drama and the folktale are alike?

> **A** The thoughts of some characters are written out.
>
> **B** Stage directions explain the action.
>
> **C** A cast of characters is provided.
>
> **D** Dialogue is used to help tell the story.

Ask yourself: What elements make this form of literature different from the other forms?

Part B

What evidence from the end of the drama and the folktale **best** supports the answer to Part A? Write the similar details in the boxes.

Drama	Folktale

Talk

5 Compare and contrast how you learn about the characters in the drama and the story. Use the chart on page 335 to organize your thoughts.

 Write

6 **Short Response** Compare and contrast how you learn about the characters in the drama and the story. Use the information in your chart for help. Include at least **two** details from each passage to support your response. Use the space provided on page 335 to write your response.

HINT Compare and contrast how the story and the drama show what the characters say and feel.

Write Use the space below to write your answer to the question on page 329.

Angie's Solo   **At the Concert**

4 **Short Response** Compare and contrast the different ways the story and poem describe the same event. Include text evidence in your response.

_____

_____

_____

_____

_____

_____

_____

_____

_____

_____

Don't forget to check your writing.

Check Your Writing

☐ Did you read the prompt carefully?

☐ Did you put the prompt in your own words?

☐ Did you use the best evidence from the text to support your ideas?

☐ Are your ideas clearly organized?

☐ Did you write in clear and complete sentences?

☐ Did you check your spelling and punctuation?

The Sound of Money

5 **Use the chart below to organize your ideas about the story and play.**

Story Details	Both	Play Details

 Write **Use the space below to write your answer to the question on page 333.**

6 **Short Response** Compare and contrast how you learn about the characters in the drama and the story. Use the information in your chart for help. Include at least **two** details from each passage to support your response.

> **HINT** Compare and contrast how the story and the drama show what the characters say and feel.

_____

_____

_____

_____

_____

_____

_____

▶ **Read**

The Talker

based on the short story by Ari Washington

WORDS TO KNOW

As you read, look inside, around, and beyond these words to figure out what they mean.

• **obviously**

• **serious**

CAST OF CHARACTERS
CLARISSE .... a 6th-grade student
MOTHER .... Clarisse's mother

1   *Setting: A bare stage with a kitchen table, four chairs, and a refrigerator.* MOTHER *and* CLARISSE *are at the table.* MOTHER *is reading a magazine.* CLARISSE *is talking on a phone.*

2   CLARISSE [*into the phone*]: Mary, I'm not kidding! He was great, and now the whole school knows my brother can really dance!

3   MOTHER: Clarisse, it's 7:15. You need to get off the phone and get busy on your homework!

4   CLARISSE [*putting her hand over the phone*]: Mama, I was just telling Mary about Jerome winning the dance contest, and—

5   MOTHER: You can tell her all about it at school tomorrow, but tonight is not the time.

6   CLARISSE [*rolling her eyes and sighing*]: See you tomorrow, Mary. [*hangs up*]

7   MOTHER [*shaking her head*]: Clarisse, all you do all day is talk, talk, talk! Why do I constantly have to remind you to get to work? When are you going to figure out it's the right thing to do?

8   CLARISSE: But Mom, talking isn't so bad, you know. Why, just today at school—

9   MOTHER [*flipping through her magazine, clearly annoyed*]: I mean, really, Clarisse. All that talking is no recipe for success. Nobody ever got anywhere by just talking.

10 CLARISSE: But that's what I'm trying to tell you! Just today—

11 MOTHER [*worried*]: You know, one of these days, you're going to wake up with no skills and have to go to a boring job every day that you hate. That's not right. Don't you want a rewarding career?

12 CLARISSE: Like as a radio talk-show host?

13 MOTHER [*finally looking up from her magazine*]: What?

14 CLARISSE: I've been trying to tell you. The Communications Club at school is starting a real radio station, and every Tuesday they're going to broadcast a live talk show after school, called "Talk Time." So guess who they invited to host it? The biggest little talker you know—me!

15 MOTHER [*laughing*]: Wow! That's great! [*Reaches across to give* CLARISSE *a high-five.*] But you're still going to get serious about your homework. There's no talking your way out of this.

16 [CLARISSE *groans, puts her head down on the table. Mother smiles, obviously proud. Curtain.*]

Genre: Realistic Fiction

The Talker

by Ari Washington

WORDS TO KNOW
As you read, look inside, around, and beyond these words to figure out what they mean.

- **discipline**
- **situation**

1   "MARY, I'm not kidding," Clarisse giggled into the phone. "He was great, and now the whole school knows my brother can dance!"

2   "Clarisse, it's already 7:15. You need to get off the phone and get busy on your homework! You've got a pile of work right next to you on the kitchen table. This is no time to be talking to friends."

3   "Mama, I was just telling Mary about Jerome winning the dance contest," Clarisse said in a wounded tone. "And—"

4   "You can tell her all about it at school tomorrow, but tonight is not the time. I will get up from this chair and take away your phone if I have to."

5   "See you tomorrow, Mary," Clarisse said, sighing.

6   Turning back to her magazine, Clarisse's mother sighed and furrowed her brow. Why did she have to remind Clarisse to quit talking and get down to work? How would things turn out for her if she didn't start getting better grades? All day and night she did nothing but talk, talk, talk. That wasn't a recipe for success.

7   It wasn't a matter of intelligence: Clarisse was as smart as any straight-A student. No, it was a matter of discipline. At this rate, Clarisse would probably wake up one day with no skills and discover herself stuck in a boring job. How would she talk her way out of that kind of unrewarding situation?

8   "Mama," Clarisse announced just then, "I was so excited about Jerome winning the dance contest that I forgot to tell you what else happened today! The Communications Club at school is starting a real AM radio station, and every Tuesday they're going to broadcast a live talk show after school, called 'Talk Time.' So guess who they invited to host it? The biggest little talker you know . . . me!"

Think Use what you learned from reading the texts to respond to the following questions.

1 If the story or drama were presented as a poem, how would it most likely be different?

    A   It wouldn't have verses.

    B   It would have more characters.

    C   It wouldn't have stanzas.

    D   It would have rhythm.

2 Underline **two** details from the story and play excerpts below that provide the reader with details about the mother's actions.

From the story	From the play
6 Turning back to her magazine, Clarisse's mother sighed and furrowed her brow. Why did she have to remind Clarisse to quit talking and get down to work? How would things turn out for her if she didn't start getting better grades? All day and night she did nothing but talk, talk, talk. That wasn't a recipe for success.	7 MOTHER [*shaking her head*]: Clarisse, all you do all day is talk, talk, talk! Why do I constantly have to remind you to get to work? When are you going to figure out it's the right thing to do? 8 CLARISSE: But Mom, talking isn't so bad, you know. Why, just today at school— 9 MOTHER [*flipping through her magazine, clearly annoyed*]: I mean, really, Clarisse. All that talking is no recipe for success.

3 Which statement **best** describes how the story and drama differ?

    A   The story writer uses stage directions to tell about the setting.

    B   The story writer uses stanzas to organize separate ideas.

    C   The drama writer uses stage directions to tell the setting.

    D   The drama writer uses stage directions to organize ideas.

4 Read the sentence from the story "The Talker."

> The <u>Communications</u> Club at school is starting a real AM radio station, and every Tuesday they're going to broadcast a live talk show after school, called "Talk Time."

Which phrase **best** states the meaning of <u>communications</u>?

    A means of passing along information

    B people involved in repairing electronics

    C organization engaged in sending letters

    D classmates taking part in a popular social club

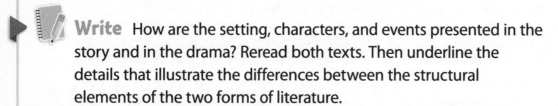

Write How are the setting, characters, and events presented in the story and in the drama? Reread both texts. Then underline the details that illustrate the differences between the structural elements of the two forms of literature.

5 **Plan Your Response** What structural elements are present in the story? What elements appear in the drama? Use a chart to organize your thoughts before you start writing.

6 **Write an Extended Response** Using evidence from both texts, compare and contrast the way each form of literature presents the setting, characters, and events through its structural elements.

_____

_____

_____

_____

_____

_____

_____

_____

_____

_____

_____

_____

_____

_____

_____

_____

_____

 Learning Target

In this lesson, you've compared and contrasted different structural elements in poems, drama, and prose. Explain the understanding you've developed about how to write and speak about these three forms of literature.

_____

_____

_____

_____

Read the story. Then answer the questions that follow.

The Escape

a story by John Martin

1   I picked at the lock of the prison cell I shared with Kasper. I almost had it, I was sure. We didn't have much time before the prince's guards returned to drag the two of us before Prince Robert.

2   The only light in the stone dungeon came from two foul-smelling torches on the walls. My friend Kasper lay groaning on the cold damp floor by my feet.

3   "What a foolish thing we've done," Kasper said, "Did we do the right thing, Carl, trying to help that old couple?"

4   "The prince's men were stealing the last of their food," I said. "We had to try and help them."

5   "The pair of us, with our shovels and hoes, we weren't much of a match for those thugs and their swords, were we?" Kasper said, laughing. "But we put up a good fight!" He let out a sharp moan. "Oh, Carl, my leg is so terribly painful!"

6   "We've got to get you help," I said. "The monks at the monastery will know what to do. But first, we must escape." I picked at the lock a moment longer, then smiled as I pushed the creaking door open.

7   "I can barely stand, let alone walk," Kasper said. "You might make it by yourself, but you won't have a chance if you are burdened with me."

8   I stood in silence, thinking our predicament over. *What Kasper said may very well be true. But more than likely, he would not survive here.*

9   "To escape alone would be no escape at all," I said firmly. "I would be a prisoner, trapped and wandering in the labyrinth of my mind if I left my courageous friend behind."

10   I raised Kasper up, and then, with a grunt of effort, lifted him onto my shoulders. Together we escaped as one into the frosty, moonlit night.

▶ Think

1 What does the word <u>labyrinth</u> mean as it is used in paragraph 9?

    A castle

    B forest

    C maze

    D city

2 Underline **one** word in the excerpt from "The Escape" that means "weighed down."

> "We've got to get you help," I said. "The monks at the monastery will know what to do. But first, we must escape." I picked at the lock a moment longer, then smiled as I pushed the creaking door open.

> "I can barely stand, let alone walk," Kasper said. "You might make it by yourself, but you won't have a chance if you are burdened with me."

> I stood in silence, thinking our predicament over. *What Kasper said may very well be true. But more than likely, he would not survive here.*

3 The sentence below is from paragraph 6 of the story.

> I picked at the lock a moment longer, then smiled as I pushed the creaking door open.

What element in the text of a play would **most likely** give this information to the reader?

    A stage directions

    B dialogue

    C setting

    D cast of characters

4 How would the story be different if it were told from Kasper's point of view?

    A The reader would feel sad about Kasper's time in prison.

    B The reader would know Kasper's inner thoughts instead of Carl's.

    C The reader would know how Kasper's injury happened.

    D The reader would understand more about Carl's feelings than Kasper's.

▶ **Read**

Read the poem. Then answer the questions that follow.

The Escape

a poem by John Martin

Two strong and brave men were locked in a cell
    For fighting the Prince and his menacing men.
One man was injured, the other stayed well,
    But both swore they'd rise up and do it again.

The well man, he picked at the lock of the door,
    And then faced a choice—leave his sick friend behind?
The well man, he knew that would lead ever more
    To making a cage of his own guilty mind.

▶ **Think**

5 What is the meaning of <u>guilty</u> as it is used in the last line of the poem?

    A troubled

    B excited

    C curious

    D honest

6 **Short Response** Both the story and the poem of "The Escape" tell how Carl and Kasper came to be in prison. Compare how the story and the poem present this event. Refer to at least **one** feature of a story and **one** feature of a poem in your answer.

_____

_____

_____

_____

_____

7 This question has two parts. First, answer Part A. Then answer Part B.

Part A
Which statement correctly describes both the story and the poem?

    A   The story and the poem both have first-person narrators.

    B   The story and the poem both have third-person narrators.

    C   The story has a first-person narrator, and the poem has a third-person narrator.

    D   The story has a third-person narrator, and the poem has a first-person narrator.

Part B
Which sentence from the story **best** supports the answer to Part A?

    A   "The only light in the stone dungeon came from two foul-smelling torches on the walls."

    B   "'I can barely stand, let alone walk,' Kasper said."

    C   _"What Kasper said may very well be true. But more than likely, he would not survive here."_

    D   "I raised Kasper up, and then, with a grunt of effort, lifted him onto my shoulders."

Read

Read the play. Then answer the questions that follow.

THE ESCAPE

a play by John Martin

Characters
CARL .... A prisoner
KASPER .... A prisoner

(*Setting: The dark, underground prison in an evil prince's castle, a long time ago.*)

(*Curtain opens on a torch-lit, stone dungeon. Two prisoners, CARL and KASPER, can be seen behind bars. CARL is reaching through the bars, working on a lock. KASPER lies on the floor.*)

KASPER: What a foolish thing we've done, to land ourselves here, in the prince's dungeon. Did we do the right thing, Carl, trying to help that old couple?

CARL: The prince's men were stealing the last of their food. Those poor people are already near starving, and almost everything they grow goes to the castle. We had to try and help them.

KASPER: The two of us, with our shovels and hoes, we weren't much of a match for armed guards, were we? But we put up a fight! (*He groans and holds his leg.*) Oh, but I am hurt bad!

CARL: Your leg will heal, but we've got to get you help. The monks at the monastery will know what to do. But first, we must escape. (*He picks at the lock some more.*) I think I've almost got it. There! (*He pulls the lock off and opens their cell door. He steps out and looks both ways.*)

KASPER: (*pulls himself up from the floor, groaning*) Carl, you must go alone. I can barely stand, let alone walk. You can make it on your own, but you won't have a chance with me.

CARL: (*thinking*) What you say may be true. If I escaped, I might get a message to King Halberd. If he hears what the Prince and his men have been doing, his people might help you. He's a good man, and nothing like his wicked son.

KASPER: Then go, Carl. Leave while you can. Run!

CARL: (*reaching for the door, then stopping and straightening his back*) I can't do this without you, Kasper. To escape alone would be no escape at all. I'd be a prisoner in the labyrinth of my mind if I left you, my brave friend, behind.

[CARL *stoops and lifts* KASPER *onto his shoulders. They exit the stage. The lights go down on the open cell door.*]

► Think

8 Read the following sentence from the play.

He's a good man, and nothing like his <u>wicked</u> son.

What does the word <u>wicked</u> mean as it is used in the sentence?

A childish

B evil

C dangerous

D foolish

9 This question has two parts. First, answer Part A. Then answer Part B.

Part A
Which statement **best** describes a key difference between the story and the drama?

   A   Only the drama tells that Carl considered leaving without Kasper.

   B   Only the drama uses dialogue to move the plot forward.

   C   Only the story describes that the setting is an underground dungeon.

   D   Only the story explains what the characters did to end up in prison.

Part B
Which sentence **best** supports the answer to Part A?

   A   "I picked at the lock of the prison cell I shared with Kasper." (story)

   B   "I stood in silence, thinking our predicament over." (story)

   C   "CARL: The prince's men were stealing the last of their food." (drama)

   D   "CARL [*reaching for the door, then stopping and straightening his back*]: I can't do this without you, Kasper." (drama)

10 Compare how the three texts tell about the same escape.

Complete the chart by drawing Xs in the boxes next to the statements that describe the story, the play, and the poem. A statement may be used for one, two, or all three of the texts.

Statement	Story	Play	Poem
The men's actions are conveyed through stage directions.			
The action is set in a prison cell.			
The main characters are named.			
The characters speak their own words.			
There is first-person narration.			
There is third-person narration.			

Write

11 **Extended Response** The table below contains parts of the story, the poem, and the play. These parts show Carl reaching his decision to take Kasper with him.

From the Story	From the Poem	From the Play
I stood in silence, thinking our predicament over. *What Kasper said may very well be true. But more than likely, he would not survive here.*	And then faced a choice— leave his sick friend behind? The well man, he knew that would lead ever more To making a cage of his own guilty mind.	CARL [*reaching for the door, then stopping and straightening his back*]: I can't do this without you, Kasper.

> Compare how the story, the poem, and the play show Carl's decision. Why does each selection show Carl's decision in such different ways? Use details from each selection to support your answer.
>
> In your answer, be sure to include
> - what features the story, the poem, and the play use to show the decision
> - why the story, the poem, and the play show the decision in the way they do
> - details from **each** selection to support your answer

Check your writing for correct spelling, grammar, capitalization, and punctuation.

_____

_____

_____

_____

_____

_____

_____

UNIT 5

Integration of Knowledge and Ideas in Informational Text

How are good readers like smart shoppers? Smart shoppers look for facts before they buy a product. For example, imagine you want new sneakers. As a smart shopper, you would look at a magazine or website to see the new styles. You'd find out what others think about the best sneakers. Then, you'd go to a store and ask the salespeople what they think. Finally, you'd try on more than one pair to see how they feel and look. In the same way, when good readers need to learn about a topic, they gather **knowledge** and **ideas** from different sources. They identify an author's points and figure out if those points are well supported. They put together, or **integrate**, facts from those sources to fully understand a topic.

In this unit, you'll read information in visual displays to help you better understand a text. You'll learn how an author uses reasons and evidence to support a point. You'll read and combine information from two sources about a topic. Good readers, like smart shoppers, do a lot of work—but what you get at the end is totally worth it.

✓ Self Check

Before starting this unit, check off the skills you know below. As you complete each lesson, see how many more skills you can check off!

I can:	Before this unit	After this unit
read and understand information presented in charts, graphs, diagrams, and time lines.	☐	☐
explain how the information in charts, graphs, diagrams, and time lines helps me better understand a text.	☐	☐
explain how authors use reasons and evidence to support their points.	☐	☐
combine information from two texts when writing about a single topic.	☐	☐

page 362

page 370

page 377

page 386

page 392

 **Introduction**

LAFS.4.RI.3.7 Interpret information presented visually, orally, or quantitatively (e.g., in charts, graphs, diagrams, time lines . . .) and explain how the information contributes to an understanding of the text in which it appears.

Lesson 22
Interpreting Visual Information

Learning Target

By figuring out information that is shown in charts or other visuals, you will gain a clearer understanding of a topic in an informational text.

▶ **Read** While reading informational texts, you often see photos, **diagrams,** and **time lines**. These **visuals** explain ideas about a topic that words alone cannot. You also might see **graphs** with **quantitative** information in the form of numbers or other data.

If you come across a special text feature, figure out its purpose. Ask yourself: What information does it give? How does it work together with text details to add to your understanding of the topic?

Read the text, and study the bar graph. Figure out how the graph helps you understand the text.

A few months ago, I helped my science teacher set up a fish tank. The tank has three types of fish. We put in just two of the largest type of fish and many of the smaller types of fish. The tank is large enough to follow this rule: Each fish needs about one gallon of water to be healthy.

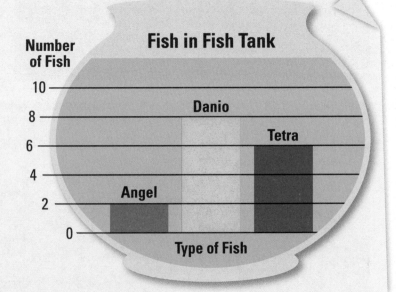

▶ **Think**   Were you able to **interpret**, or figure out, the information
in the text and graph? From the details, you should have a good
idea of how many fish are in the tank and what kinds of fish live in
it. Use the passage and the graph to fill in the chart below.

What the Text Says	What the Graph Shows
"The tank has three types of fish."	

▶ **Talk**   Compare the information in your charts. What inference can you
draw about the minimum number of gallons the tank should hold? Use
information from the text and the graph. Draw a picture of the fish in
the tank to help you answer.

 **Academic Talk**
Use these words to talk about the text.

- **diagrams**   • **time lines**   • **visuals**   • **graphs**
- **quantitative**   • **interpret**

Features of the Ocean Floor
by Connie Rather

1   Picture this: You're in a submarine right next to a continent. Looking down, you see a part of the ocean floor called the **continental shelf**. Now, head out to sea. The ocean floor drops away to form the **continental slope**. You might pass through a range of **seamounts**, or volcanoes rising from the ocean floor. In time, you'll reach the **abyssal plain**, a dark realm with deep valleys called **trenches**. Finally, you might encounter long, snakelike **ocean ridges** that rise from the ocean floor. They connect to form a long chain of underwater mountains around the planet.

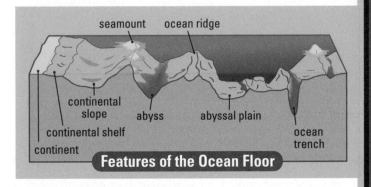
Features of the Ocean Floor

2   The deepest ocean trench in the world is the Mariana Trench in the Pacific. It is one of the most difficult places to reach on Earth. It is so deep that if Mount Everest, one of the tallest mountains in the world, were picked up and put at the bottom of the trench, the mountain would still be covered with water!

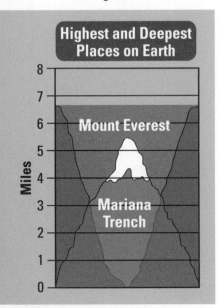

Close Reader Habits

Study the diagrams as you reread the text. **Circle** the title of each diagram. Think of how the title connects the diagram to the text.

Explore How do the text and diagrams work together to provide information about the ocean floor?

Think

> Look for information, data, or details in the diagrams that the text does not provide.

1 Use information about the abyssal plain and the Mariana Trench to complete the chart below. Identify what you learned from the text and what you learned from each diagram.

What the Text Says	What the Diagram Shows
abyssal plain	"Features of the Ocean Floor"
Mariana Trench	"Highest and Deepest Places on Earth"

Talk

2 Share your chart with a partner. What information came from the text, the "Features of the Ocean Floor" diagram, and the "Highest and Deepest Places on Earth" graph? Why do you think the author presented certain information visually rather than in words?

Write

3 **Short Response** How do the diagram, graph, and text work together to give you information about the Mariana Trench? Use evidence from each to support your response. Use the space provided on page 360 to write your response.

> **HINT** Make sure to clearly state where your evidence comes from, the text or a diagram.

Going DOWN, DOWN, DOWN

by Justin Oh

1   The ocean has three main zones. These zones are distinguished by the amount of sunlight they receive.

2   In the sunlight zone, the sun's rays penetrate from the surface to a depth of 650 feet. The light lets plants grow here, and these plants provide food for animals. Here you will find sea mammals and schools of fish.

3   The twilight zone stretches from 650 feet to 3,300 feet below the ocean surface. There is almost no sunlight, so no plants grow. Animals that live here wait for dead plants and animals to drift down from the sunlit zone. The animals here have ways of surviving difficult conditions. Many can produce their own light, which helps them search for food.

4   Below 3,300 feet, the midnight zone lies in complete darkness. There is very little food, the water is cold, and the water pressure is enormous. Some animals at this level are soft, so the pressure doesn't affect them as much. Many are blind or have no eyes, but they can feel the smallest movement of food that might brush up against them.

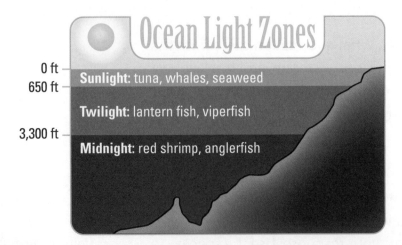

Ocean Light Zones

0 ft
650 ft
Sunlight: tuna, whales, seaweed

Twilight: lantern fish, viperfish

3,300 ft
Midnight: red shrimp, anglerfish

Close Reader Habits

What do you learn about the zones from the text? From the diagram? Reread the article. **Underline** details shared by the text and diagram.

Think Use what you learned from reading the science article to respond to the following questions.

1 This question has two parts. Answer Part A. Then answer Part B.

> Visuals often help you "see" what is explained in a science text. Think about how the visuals support the topic.

Part A
Which ocean animals listed in the diagram are most likely to live among creatures that have soft bodies and no eyes?

- **A** red shrimp and anglerfish
- **B** viperfish and lantern fish
- **C** tuna and whales
- **D** red shrimp and tuna

Part B
Circle **one** detail in the diagram on page 358 that supports the answer to Part A.

2 Which fact about the twilight zone is given in both the passage and the diagram? Write it on the lines.

_____

_____

Talk

3 Describe at least one type of information you can find in the diagram that the passage does not give you. How does the diagram help you better understand the differences in the three zones?

 Write

4 **Short Response** Compare and contrast information about the ocean zones that is provided by the text and the diagram. Use at least **one** detail from both the passage and the diagram to support your response. Use the space provided on page 361 to write your answer.

> **HINT** Reread the text for details that explain what is shown in the diagram.

 Write **Use the space below to write your answer to the question on page 357.**

Features of the
Ocean Floor

HINT Make sure to clearly state where your evidence comes from, the text or a diagram.

3 **Short Response** How do the diagram, graph, and text work together to give you information about the Mariana Trench? Use evidence from each to support your response.

_____

_____

_____

_____

_____

_____

_____

_____

Don't forget to check your writing.

Write Use the space below to write your answer to the question on page 359.

Going DOWN, DOWN, DOWN

4 **Short Response** Compare and contrast information about the ocean zones that is provided by the text and the diagram. Use at least **one** detail from both the passage and the diagram to support your response.

> **HINT** Reread the text for details that explain what is shown in the diagram.

_____

_____

_____

_____

_____

_____

_____

Check Your Writing

☐ Did you read the prompt carefully?

☐ Did you put the prompt in your own words?

☐ Did you use the best evidence from the text to support your ideas?

☐ Are your ideas clearly organized?

☐ Did you write in clear and complete sentences?

☐ Did you check your spelling and punctuation?

> **Read**

VOYAGE to the Bottom of the SEA

by Martine Costi

WORDS TO KNOW

As you read, look inside, around, and beyond these words to figure out what they mean.

- descent
- emerge
- released

1   On January 23, 1960, six-foot waves rocked the surface seven miles above the Mariana Trench in the Pacific Ocean. Carefully, Jacques Piccard and Donald Walsh rowed a small rubber boat toward the *Trieste*. This craft would soon take them almost seven miles down to the deepest part of the ocean's floor.

2   No one had ever explored the Mariana Trench before. It was so deep that the weight of the miles of water above it would crush most crafts. The *Trieste* was built to withstand such pressure, however, so the men inside should be safe on their underwater journey. During the descent, the men on the *Trieste* would communicate by radio with the surface.

3   Shortly after 8:00 A.M., Piccard and Walsh sat jammed in the *Trieste's* observation gondola. The space was so small that they could barely move, but they were ready. Water from the ocean filled the water ballast tanks. Slowly, the *Trieste* began traveling down to the trench.

4   At 340 feet, Piccard released gasoline from the tanks, letting water fill them instead. Water weighs more than gasoline, so this made the craft sink farther into the darkness.

5   An hour later and a mile farther down, the men saw plankton. These are tiny ocean creatures that glow in specks of yellowish green. Two hours later, they were more than five miles down, and there was no sign of life.

6   A little past noon, they were about a half-mile from the bottom. Then they heard a small explosion. Tension flooded the observation gondola, but nothing seemed wrong, so they agreed to keep going. Just before one o'clock, they reached the bottom of the Mariana Trench. They had landed where no other human had ever been.

7   They flashed lights and saw a flat, white fish about a foot long that Piccard described as a sole. Little red shrimp swam in front of their window. Both discoveries were groundbreaking. Now humans knew that animals lived on the deepest part of the ocean floor.

Diagram of *Trieste*

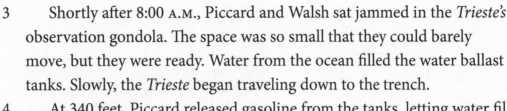

Propellers

Vent

Gasoline tanks

Water ballast tanks

entrance tunnel

Floodlamps

Lead ballast chamber

Window

Lead ballast chamber

Guide rope

Observation gondola

— 50 feet —

8   Then the men turned on an inside light. Piccard spotted the cause of the earlier noise—it was a cracked window. Now he became more worried about their safety. Piccard released 800 pounds of lead pellets from the ballast chamber. Releasing this weight caused the *Trieste* to move upwards. Piccard and Walsh could hear people speaking on the radio, but for some reason no one could hear them speaking back.

9   At 5:00 P.M., the *Trieste* emerged. No one had heard Piccard on the wireless for hours, so the people above did not know what to expect. The crews on both ships watched breathlessly for movement from the *Trieste*. They waited for fifteen long minutes. Then suddenly, the two men emerged unharmed. They had traveled to the deepest part of the ocean and made history.

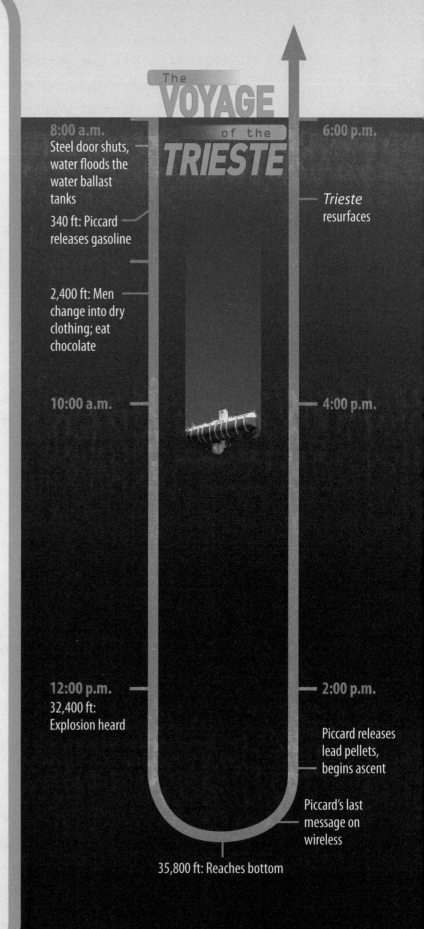

The VOYAGE of the TRIESTE

8:00 a.m.
Steel door shuts, water floods the water ballast tanks

340 ft: Piccard releases gasoline

2,400 ft: Men change into dry clothing; eat chocolate

10:00 a.m.

12:00 p.m.
32,400 ft: Explosion heard

35,800 ft: Reaches bottom

6:00 p.m.
Trieste resurfaces

4:00 p.m.

2:00 p.m.

Piccard releases lead pellets, begins ascent

Piccard's last message on wireless

▶ **Think** Use what you learned from reading the science article to respond to the following questions.

1 From the text, you could infer that the voyage of the *Trieste* was a dangerous research project. Which **two** details from the time line **best** support this inference?

    A 8:30 A.M.—340 ft: Piccard releases gasoline

    B 9:15 A.M.—2,400 ft: Men change into dry clothing . . .

    C 12:00 P.M.—32,400 ft: Explosion heard

    D 1:00 P.M.—35,800 ft: Reaches bottom

    E 1:15 P.M.—Piccard's last message on wireless

    F 5:00 P.M.—*Trieste* resurfaces

2 This question has two parts. First, answer Part A. Then answer Part B.

Part A
Which detail from the diagram of the *Trieste* is supported by the text?

    A A small window in the observation gondola allowed the crew to see outside the *Trieste*.

    B The observation gondola of the *Trieste* was large enough to fit several crew members comfortably.

    C The flood lamps were too far away for the crew members of the *Trieste* to see outside.

    D The propellers allowed the crew of the *Trieste* to steer the craft underwater.

Part B
Underline **two** sentences from the text that support your answer in Part A.

They . . . saw a flat, white fish about a foot long that Piccard described as a sole. Little red shrimp swam in front of their window. Both discoveries were groundbreaking. Now humans knew that animals lived on the deepest part of the ocean floor.

3 In paragraph 7, what is the meaning of the word <u>groundbreaking</u>?

    A underground

    B underneath the ocean

    C new and important

    D very destructive

4 The box below includes details about the voyage of the *Trieste*.

> **Details**
>
> • The designers of the *Trieste* only meant for it to be used one time.
>
> • Releasing lead pellets helped the craft rise to the surface of the ocean.
>
> • After entering the *Trieste*, the crew changed into dry clothes and had a snack.
>
> • The crew saw shrimp at the bottom of the Mariana Trench.
>
> • Gasoline powered the *Trieste's* motor as it pushed the craft to the ocean floor.

Complete the chart by using details from the box. Write **one** detail that only appears in the text, **one** detail that only appears in a visual, and **one** detail that appears in both the text and in a visual.

What the Text Says	What a Visual Shows	What the Text Says and a Visual Shows

Write

5 **Short Response** How did the diagram and the time line support the details in the passage? Explain how these visuals added to the text information. Describe **one** example of a fact you learned from the "Diagram of the *Trieste*" that was not in the passage. Describe **one** example of a fact you learned from the time line "Voyage of the *Trieste*" that was not in the passage.

_____

_____

_____

_____

_____

_____

_____

Learning Target

In this lesson, you interpreted information that was presented in images, charts, graphs, and other visuals. Explain how this information gave you a deeper understanding of the text topic.

_____

_____

_____

_____

LAFS.4.RI.3.8 Explain how an author uses reasons and evidence to support particular points in a text.

Lesson 23
Explaining an Author's Reasons and Evidence

Learning Target

Explaining how authors use reasons and evidence to support their points about a topic will help you better understand what you read.

▶ **Read** Some authors write to get you to agree with their way of thinking about a topic. To **persuade** you, authors provide **points**, or ideas, to explain their thinking.

- Authors back up their points with good **reasons** telling why their ideas might be true.

- Authors support each reason with **evidence**, or facts and examples that explain more.

Good reasons and evidence are what make the authors' points convincing.

Look at the cartoons below that take place on a space station in 2450. Think about how each child asks for a dog.

Which child do you think is more likely to convince his or her parents that a dog is a good idea?

▶ **Think**   What have you learned about how authors use reasons and evidence to support a point? Think about which child is most likely to get a dog and why. Complete the chart below to show the child's point, reasons, and evidence.

What does the child think? (The Point)	Why does the child think this way? (Reason)	How do details support the child's thinking? (Evidence)

▶ **Talk**   Share your chart with a partner.

- Did you identify the same point?
- What reasons did each of you include? Do they make sense?
- What evidence was used to support each reason?

◎ **Academic Talk**
Use these words to talk about the text.

- **persuade**
- **reasons**
- **points**
- **evidence**

Read

Should We Explore Space? Absolutely!

by Marc Lucas

1   Exploring space is one of the most important things the United States can do. But why? For one reason, the work of getting people and machines into space leads to new technologies. Some of these new technologies then become available to everyone and improve their lives. Do you need examples? Then try these: Because of the space program of the 1960s and 1970s, we have digital clocks, laser surgery, and instant foods. And these new technologies have broader effects on society. They help create new businesses, which then make new jobs, a richer population, and a stronger economy.

2   But there is a second and more important reason for exploring space, and it has nothing to do with money. It's called the need to discover. Human beings are naturally curious. We want to know what's out there. If it's at the top of a mountain, or across a river, or at the bottom of the sea, we want to see it and touch it.

3   Humans are also competitive—we want to be both the first and the best at what we do. When the Soviet Union put the first human in space in 1961, Americans didn't just sit and watch. The United States surged ahead with a space program and eight years later put the first person on the Moon.

Close Reader Habits

Circle the author's main point. Then **underline** three reasons the author provides to support his point.

Explore | What is the author's point, and what reasons and evidence does he provide to support his thinking?

> A *reason* answers a question that begins with *why*. *Evidence* is a fact or example that explains the reason.

▶ Think

1 Complete the chart below by identifying the author's point, reasons, and evidence.

What does the author think? (The Point)	Why does the author think this way? (Reason)	How do details support the author's thinking? (Evidence)

▶ Talk

2 What point does the author make about space exploration? What are the reasons and evidence he gives for what he thinks? Discuss the text details given to support the author's point.

▶ Write

3 **Short Response** Explain the author's point about space exploration and the reasons he gives for his thinking. Include details the author provides as evidence to support his reasons. Use the space provided on page 374 to write your response.

> **HINT** Look for evidence, or facts and examples, that supports the reasons you underlined.

Should We Settle the Moon?

by Jo Newbold

1   Whenever people say "Let's shoot for the Moon!" they mean that anything is possible. So, when people think of space exploration, a colony on the Moon seems like the next step. The views from the Moon would be spectacular, and being a "Moontonian" would be exciting. But is it feasible?

2   Let's start with the Moon's surface, which is not an easy place for life to thrive. There is little atmosphere, so all air would have to be brought from Earth. The lack of atmosphere causes temperatures to vary greatly, from 232°F during the day to –315°F at night. And then there's the radiation. Without a thick, Earth-like atmosphere to filter the sun's rays, radiation would sicken any colonists.

3   And what about water? True, there is ice below the Moon's surface. If astronauts can mine that ice, they can melt it and use it to make oxygen and rocket fuel. But if the ice is unreachable, all water would have to be carted up to the Moon—a cumbersome and unworkable task.

4   But the biggest obstacle to living on the Moon is the regolith. Regolith is a layer of fine stone dust. It covers almost the entire surface and sticks to everything. It can gum up a spacesuit, jam an engine, and ruin machines. Worst of all, if we couldn't find a way to keep it out of the colony, it would destroy the lungs of everyone living there.

5   So, will we ever have a Moon colony? Never say never, but today our technology does not make the idea practical.

Close Reader Habits

What reasons support the author's point? **Circle** three reasons the author gives to support her point.

▶ **Think** Use what you learned from reading the essay to respond to the following questions.

1 This question has two parts. Answer Part A. Then answer Part B.

A title with a question in it is a clue to the author's point. Finding answers will help you identify reasons and evidence.

Part A
Which statement below provides a reason the author uses in paragraph 2 to support her main point about settling the Moon?

    A Regolith can destroy the lungs of humans living there.

    B The Moon's surface is a dangerous environment for life.

    C Temperatures vary because of the lack of atmosphere.

    D Radiation from the sun's rays is likely to make colonists ill.

Part B
Underline **three** pieces of evidence in paragraph 2 of "Should We Settle the Moon?" that support your answer in Part A.

2 What evidence does the author give to support her line of reasoning about regolith? Write **two** pieces of evidence in the box below.

▶ **Talk**

3 What point does the author make about settling the Moon? What reasons and evidence does she provide as support? Use the chart on page 375 to organize your ideas.

▶ **Write**

4 **Short Response** Describe the reasons and evidence the author provides to support her point about a Moon settlement. Include at least **three** details from the text to support your response. Use the space provided on page 375 to write your response.

HINT Think about the reasons the author gives to prove her point.

Write Use the space below to write your answer to the question on page 371.

Should We Explore Space? Absolutely!

3 **Short Response** Explain the author's point about space exploration and the reasons he gives for his thinking. Include details the author provides as evidence to support his reasons.

> **HINT** Look for evidence, or facts and examples, that supports the reasons you underlined.

_____

_____

_____

_____

_____

_____

_____

_____

_____

_____

Don't forget to check your writing.

Check Your Writing

- ☐ Did you read the prompt carefully?
- ☐ Did you put the prompt in your own words?
- ☐ Did you use the best evidence from the text to support your ideas?
- ☐ Are your ideas clearly organized?
- ☐ Did you write in clear and complete sentences?
- ☐ Did you check your spelling and punctuation?

Should We Settle the Moon?

3 **Use the chart below to organize your ideas.**

What does the author think? (The Point)	Why does the author think this way? (Reason)	How do details support the author's thinking? (Evidence)

✏️ **Write** **Use the space below to write your answer to the question on page 373.**

4 **Short Response** Describe the reasons and evidence the author provides to support her point about a Moon settlement. Include at least **three** details from the text to support your response.

> **HINT** Think about the reasons the author gives to prove her point.

_____

_____

_____

_____

_____

_____

▶ **Read**

WORDS TO KNOW
As you read, look inside, around, and beyond these words to figure out what they mean.

- **encounter**
- **relay**
- **resources**

1   Far away, on the rocky surface of the planet Mars, a small but powerful robot called a rover moves dutifully along. Back and forth and up and down the robot roams. It scans the planet. It also sends valuable information back to scientists on Earth at the National Aeronautics and Space Administration (NASA). The scientists have big goals for this rover, which they have named *Curiosity*. They hope it will tell them whether life has existed on Mars, what the planet's environment is like, and whether humans will ever be able to explore it. But the missions to Mars come at a high price—*Curiosity* alone cost 2.5 billion dollars to build and send. Some people question whether that money might be better spent here on Earth. Should the exploration of Mars continue, despite the staggering cost?

ALL IN FAVOR

2   Scientists and others who support space exploration believe that the rovers may one day tell us if life ever existed on Mars. This would be the first evidence of life elsewhere in our universe. Second, the rovers can study the climate and geology of Mars. They relay information about how it has changed over time. This kind of information would help us learn whether any of the planet's resources can help us here on Earth. It may also help scientists understand features of our own planet. Third, scientists want to learn about the planet's environment. They hope to prepare for human exploration.

THE PARTS OF A MARS ROVER

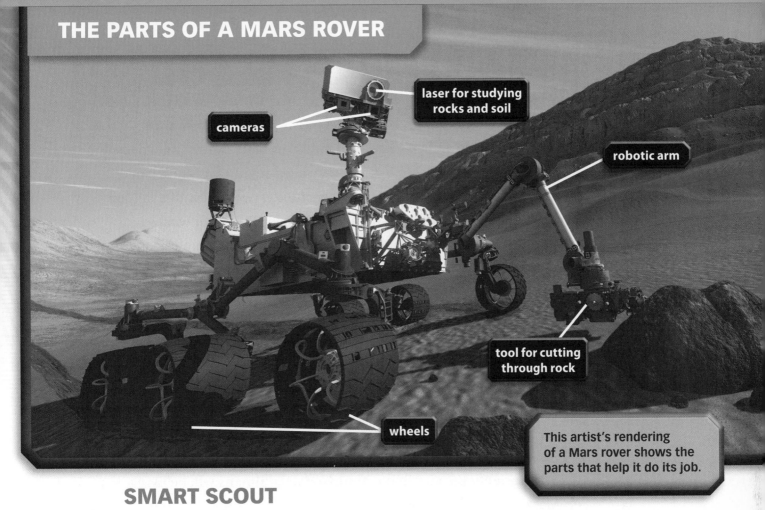

cameras

laser for studying rocks and soil

robotic arm

tool for cutting through rock

wheels

This artist's rendering of a Mars rover shows the parts that help it do its job.

SMART SCOUT

3   Supporters of Mars exploration also point out that, as a vehicle, *Curiosity* can do much more than a science station that's fixed in one place. *Curiosity* moves—or roves—across the surface of Mars, collecting information as it goes. Its "eyes" are 17 cameras that can see and analyze the landscape. The rover's "feet" are its wheels. Those wheels roll over obstacles as high as 2.5 feet. The robot's "ears" hear commands relayed from NASA. *Curiosity* also has a laser that can analyze the chemicals in soil and rocks.

4   With all that equipment, *Curiosity* can send NASA a steady stream of data about the surface of Mars. That makes NASA scientists very happy.

WHAT *CURIOSITY* CAN TEACH US

5   There are many good reasons to explore Mars. It's hard to put a value on discovering new knowledge, and the rovers are providing plenty of that. *Curiosity* already has made valuable discoveries. During its first 100 days on Mars, the rover detected water in the planet's soil. Why is that important? Scientists believe that water is a crucial clue to the existence of life on Mars or other planets. This life could take the form of tiny microbes. Finding evidence of life on Mars—even if it is just microbes—would be a big deal to scientists.

HIDDEN VALUE

6   Although they were enormously expensive, *Curiosity* and the rovers that came before it may give NASA scientists more value than the scientists expected. When *Curiosity* landed on Mars, scientists expected it to work for two years. However, it may keep roving for much longer. Scientists predicted that *Spirit* and *Opportunity*, two rovers that landed on Mars in 2004, would work for about 90 days. But *Spirit* worked for six years before it got stuck in sand. *Opportunity* is still going strong. *Curiosity* might keep going for a long time, too, as long as it doesn't get stuck or encounter other problems.

7   Furthermore, NASA points out that *Curiosity* and the other rovers have helped the U.S. economy by creating jobs. More than 7,000 people in 31 states have worked on the *Curiosity* mission. And *Curiosity* may help the economy in another way, too. It may turn up precious minerals and energy resources on Mars that we could mine to use on Earth.

THE FUTURE

8   Some scientists claim that within 40 years, humans will be living on Mars. They call it a "foregone conclusion," or a sure thing. If that's true, then robot missions like *Curiosity* are important stepping-stones to that future. Even if that never happens, the Mars rovers may provide knowledge that is key to understanding our own universe.

This look back at a Martian dune was taken by one of *Curiosity*'s cameras. The wheel tracks are about nine feet apart.

Think Use what you learned from reading the science article to respond to the following questions.

1 This question has two parts. First, answer Part A. Then answer Part B.

Part A
Which statement gives a reason that supports the author's point about Mars rovers?

   A A science station has a lot of capabilities.

   B Vehicles like *Curiosity* are well-suited for exploring Mars.

   C Mars rovers must be able to collect data and send it to Earth.

   D *Curiosity* has human-like traits that will help people travel to Mars.

Part B
Underline the evidence that **best** supports your answer in Part A.

Supporters of Mars exploration also point out that, as a vehicle, *Curiosity* can do much more than a science station that's fixed in one place. *Curiosity* moves—or roves—across the surface of Mars, collecting information as it goes. Its "eyes" are 17 cameras that can see and analyze the landscape. The rover's "feet" are its wheels. Those wheels roll over obstacles as high as 2.5 feet. The robot's "ears" hear commands relayed from NASA.

2 Read the sentence from the passage.

   Should the <u>exploration</u> of Mars continue, despite the staggering cost?

What does the suffix *-ation* mean in the word <u>exploration</u>?

   A state of

   B result of

   C result of

   D process of

3 Which detail is a reason that **best** supports the author's main point?

    A "Some scientists claim that within 40 years, humans will be living on Mars. "

    B "*Curiosity* also has a laser that can analyze the chemicals in soil and rocks."

    C "During its first 100 days on Mars, the rover detected water in the planet's soil."

    D "Mars rovers may provide knowledge that is key to understanding our own universe."

4 In paragraphs 6 and 7, the author explains more about exploring Mars. What reasons and evidence are provided to support the author's point? Complete the chart by drawing Xs in the boxes. Identify which statement describes a reason and which describe evidence that supports the reason.

Statement	Reason	Evidence
Mars rovers may turn up new energy sources to use on Earth.		
Curiosity and other rovers have worked much longer than expected.		
The rover missions provide additional benefits.		
Curiosity and other rovers help the economy because they create jobs.		

5 What reasons do supporters of space exploration give to explain why sending rovers to Mars is important? Choose **three** reasons.

    A They can learn how to prepare for people to go to Mars.

    B They can find ways to use money and resources to build new rovers.

    C They can stream data from Mars back to Earth on a regular basis.

    D They can use knowledge of changes on Mars to understand our planet.

    E They can search for evidence of life beyond Earth.

Write

6 **Short Response** What point is the author making about exploring Mars? Describe the author's point and how he supports this point with reasons and evidence from the text.

_____

_____

_____

_____

_____

_____

_____

_____

 Learning Target

In this lesson, you learned to identify the reasons and evidence authors use to support their points about a topic. Explain how this skill can help you better understand the ideas in texts you read.

_____

_____

_____

 **Introduction**

LAFS.4.RI.3.9 Integrate information from two texts on the same topic in order to write or speak about the subject knowledgeably.

Lesson 24
Integrating Information from Two Sources

Combining information from two texts on the same topic will help you better understand the topic as well as write and speak about it.

▶ **Read** To write or speak about a topic, you must often combine, or **integrate**, information from two or more sources. First, look in different texts for main ideas and key details that answer questions about a topic. Then combine the information in an organized way to write or speak **knowledgeably**, or like an expert, about your **topic**.

Imagine you are reporting on mound builders. How would you integrate the information from the two sources below?

No one is sure who built the Serpent Mound in Ohio. 10 feet wide and 4 feet high in some places, the snakelike ridge of soil winds along the ground for over 1300 feet.

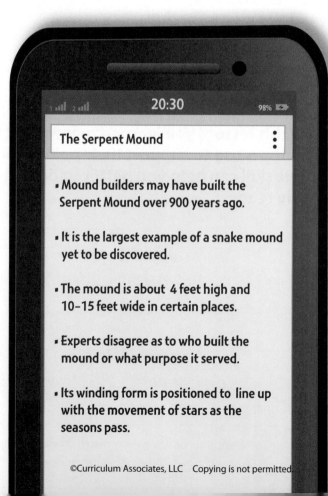

20:30   98%

The Serpent Mound   ⋮

- Mound builders may have built the Serpent Mound over 900 years ago.

- It is the largest example of a snake mound yet to be discovered.

- The mound is about 4 feet high and 10–15 feet wide in certain places.

- Experts disagree as to who built the mound or what purpose it served.

- Its winding form is positioned to line up with the movement of stars as the seasons pass.

▶ **Think** Complete the chart with details from each source.
Then write a short paragraph to integrate information about the
Serpent Mound.

TOPIC: _____

Questions	Answers	
	Photo: Serpent Mound	Website: The Serpent Mound
What does the mound look like?		
Who built the mound?		
How big is it?		
When was it built?		
Why was it built?		

Paragraph: _____

_____

_____

_____

_____

▶ **Talk** Share your chart and paragraph with a partner. Did you agree
about the answers? What did each of you include in your descriptions?

 Academic Talk
Use these words to talk about the text.
- **integrate**   - **knowledgeably**   - **topic**

Henry Hudson

adapted from Edward R. Shaw, Explorers and Discoverers

1   Henry Hudson was one of the best sea captains in all England. He loved the ocean, and he did not know the word "fear."

2   In 1607 a company of London merchants sent him to look for a northwest passage to China. If such a passage could be found, the journey to China would be much shorter than by the overland route then used. It would take less time to sail around the Earth near the pole than to sail around the Earth near the equator. Besides, everyone who had attempted to reach China by sailing west had reached, instead, that long coast of the New World. . . . [Only] one opening had ever been found. The route through this opening, the Strait of Magellan, had been . . . too long for use in commerce. So traders were trying hard to find a northwest passage.

 # The Coming of the Dutch

by John McMaster, from A Brief History of the United States

[In 1609 there came to the New World] a little Dutch ship called the *Half-Moon.* [A Dutch company] had . . . sent Captain Henry Hudson in her to seek a northeasterly passage to China. Driven back by ice in his attempt to sail north of Europe, Hudson turned westward. He came at last to Delaware Bay. Up this the *Half-Moon* went a little way, but, grounding on the shoals, Hudson turned about. [He] followed the coast northward, and sailed up the river now called by his name. He went as far as the site of Albany. Then, finding that the Hudson was not a passage through the continent, he returned to Europe.

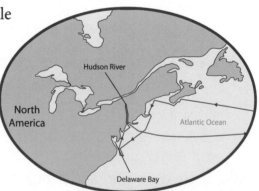

Close Reader Habits

Underline words and phrases in both passages that tell you the purpose of Hudson's missions.

Explore **How does the information in both passages add to your understanding of Hudson's missions and discoveries?**

Asking *who, what, when, why,* and *how* questions will help you identify important information in each passage.

▶ **Think**

1 Answer the questions below to identify key details about Henry Hudson's missions. Combine details from both passages. Also identify the source you used by writing (S1) for the first passage and (S2) for the second passage.

What was the purpose of each of Hudson's missions?

_____

_____

_____

_____

Was either of Henry Hudson's missions to find a new route a success? Explain, using supporting details.

_____

_____

_____

_____

▶ **Talk**

2 Which details from each source helped you understand Hudson's missions? Describe how you would present the details to help others understand the information. Organize your questions and details in a chart like the one on page 383.

 ▶ **Write**

HINT Choose the best way to structure your writing to explain a series of events.

3 **Short Response** Describe Henry Hudson's missions and discoveries. Include details from both texts in your response. Use the space provided on page 390 to write your response.

Read

A DESERT OF ICE

by Tam Tohuko

Only emperor penguins are able to lay eggs and raise chicks in Antarctica's harsh winter conditions.

1   Of the seven continents, Antarctica is most unlike the other six. This land mass is about 1.5 times the size of the United States, but there are no permanent human residents there. This is due to the continent's inhospitable climate. Home of the South Pole, Antarctica is the coldest, driest, and windiest place on Earth.

2   A thick ice sheet almost completely covers the continent. The ice varies in thickness from place to place, but on average it is about one mile thick. If all the ice in Antarctica were to melt, oceans worldwide would rise by about 200 feet.

3   During its warmest month, January, the continent's average high temperature is about 18 degrees below zero. Scientists recorded a cruel 129 degrees below zero in 1983. The sun shines continuously from mid-September to mid-March. Then it disappears for the other half of the year. Few creatures can survive the extreme winter cold.

4   We normally think of deserts as hot, sandy places. Yet Antarctica is a desert, too. In the middle of the continent, only about 2 inches of moisture (usually in the form of snow) fall each year. Even the Sahara desert receives more rain. The coasts of Antarctica receive more precipitation, but only an 8-inch-per-year average.

5   Despite its dryness, the continent has colossal blizzards. Mighty winds lift snow from the ground and whip it around in huge white swirls. Winds can reach up to 200 miles per hour. (Winds this strong would destroy most buildings.) Antarctica's climate makes it a forbidding place for most living things.

Close Reader Habits

Why does the author say Antarctica is most unlike all the other continents? **Underline** sentences that support this idea.

ANTARCTICA'S LIFE

by Morgan Minier

1   Antarctica has an extremely harsh climate. This continent is colder, drier, and windier than anyplace else on our planet. As a result, far fewer plants and animals live there than on any of the other six continents.

2   Besides the emperor penguin, the only creatures that live on land in Antarctica year-round are a handful of insects. The largest of these bugs is the midge. It is a wingless insect that looks like a small fly. Tiny ticks also live in Antarctica. They feed on sea birds such as penguins. These year-round dwellers become inactive in the cold winter months. They awake when daylight arrives and the air warms.

3   Although they do not live on land all year, several marine animals do make their homes in Antarctica. Because its interior climate is so harsh, most animals live along the coast. These creatures include penguins, other sea birds, seals, and whales. Most share a trait that allows them to handle the sub-zero temperatures. Their bodies have special feathers or thick layers of blubber (fat) that insulate them. Even so, many come ashore just to bear and raise their young. Only the seas provide these creatures with enough food and shelter to survive.

4   There are no trees or bushes in Antarctica. The continent has only two kinds of flowering plants. The ice-covered land mass does support over 800 forms of fungi and lichen.

5   In recent years, scientists have discovered that microscopic life forms live in lakes beneath Antarctica's ice sheets. About 4,000 microbe species live in Lake Whillans, which is located beneath 2,625 feet of ice. Identifying these microbes has given scientists hope that life can exist on planets that seem as desolate as Antarctica.

Close Reader Habits

Look for details in the article that tell about the author's main idea. **Underline** details that help support the main idea.

▶ **Think** Use what you learned from reading the science articles to respond to the following questions.

1 Complete the chart below by filling in details from each source that answer the questions about Antarctica.

Questions	Answers	
	"A Desert of Ice"	**"Antarctica's Life"**
What is Antarctica's climate like?		
What kinds of animal life can be found in Antarctica?		
What kinds of plant life can be found in Antarctica?		

2 Antarctica has an extreme climate. Underline **two** sentences from each passage that support this idea.

"A Desert of Ice"	"Antarctica's Life"
Of the seven continents, Antarctica is most unlike the other six. This land mass is about 1.5 times the size of the United States, but there are no permanent human residents there. This is due to the continent's inhospitable climate. Home of the South Pole, Antarctica is the coldest, driest, and windiest place on Earth.	These creatures include penguins, other sea birds, seals, and whales. Most share a trait that allows them to handle the sub-zero temperatures. Their bodies have special feathers or thick layers of blubber (fat) that insulates them. Even so, many come ashore just to bear and raise their young. Only the seas provide these creatures with enough food and shelter to survive.

©Curriculum Associates, LLC   Copying is not permitted.

3 This question has two parts. Answer Part A. Then answer Part B.

Part A
Which statement about Antarctica is **best** supported by both passages?

Authors of science articles often focus on one area of a topic. Consider what topic the passages share.

  A   Antarctica is home to over 4,000 species of microbes.

  B   Antarctica is the coldest and driest continent on Earth.

  C   Antarctica has several species of marine animals.

  D   Antarctica is sunny from September to mid-March.

Part B
Which **two** paragraphs, one from each article, **best** support the answer to Part A?

  A   Paragraph 1 in "Desert of Ice"

  B   Paragraph 2 in "Desert of Ice"

  C   Paragraph 4 in "Desert of Ice"

  D   Paragraph 1 in "Antarctica's Life"

  E   Paragraph 3 in "Antarctica's Life"

  F   Paragraph 5 in "Antarctica's Life"

▶ **Talk**

4 Using details from both passages, describe how animals living in Antarctica survive the climate. Use the chart on page 391 to organize your thoughts.

 ▶ **Write**

5 **Short Response** Use the information from both passages and your chart to describe how animals survive in Antarctica. Include at least **two** details from each text to support your response. Use the space provided on page 391 to write your response.

HINT Think about which details from each source answer questions about the topic.

Write Use the space below to write your answer to the question on page 385.

Henry Hudson
The Coming of the Dutch

> **HINT** Choose the best way to structure your writing to explain a series of events.

3 **Short Response** Describe Henry Hudson's missions and discoveries. Include details from both texts in your response.

_____

_____

_____

_____

_____

_____

_____

Check Your Writing

Don't forget to check your writing.

☐ Did you read the prompt carefully?

☐ Did you put the prompt in your own words?

☐ Did you use the best evidence from the text to support your ideas?

☐ Are your ideas clearly organized?

☐ Did you write in clear and complete sentences?

☐ Did you check your spelling and punctuation?

A **DESERT** OF **ICE**   ANTARCTICA'S **LIFE**

4 **Use the chart below to organize your ideas.**

Questions	Answers	
	"A Desert of Ice"	**"Antarctica's Life"**

Write **Use the space below to write your answer to the question on page 389.**

5 **Short Response** Use the information from both passages and your chart to describe how animals survive in Antarctica. Include at least **two** details from each text to support your response.

> **HINT** Think about which details from each source answer questions about the topic.

_____

_____

_____

_____

_____

_____

_____

> Read

A Short History of EASTER ISLAND

BY MONIQUE JENKINS

1   Easter Island is one of the most remote, inhabited islands in the world. It is in the Pacific Ocean about 3,780 kilometers west of South America. It was formed by three volcanoes, which are now extinct. As far as inhabited islands go, Easter Island is quite small. It measures just 101 square kilometers, which is the size of San Francisco.

2   Scientists believe that the island was settled between 1,200 and 1,600 years ago by Polynesians. They called the island Rapa Nui. These first inhabitants, called the Rapanui, flourished. Scientists believe that as many as 7,000 people once lived on the tiny island. The earliest inhabitants moved tons of volcanic rock and used it to carve the enormous statues that look out over the island's landscape.

3   Rapa Nui remained isolated from other humans for hundreds of years. Then in 1722, a Dutch captain, Jacob Roggeveen, discovered it. His ship arrived on Easter Sunday, so he named the island "Easter Island." He estimated that 2,000 to 3,000 people lived there. Fifty-two years later, Captain James Cook came to Easter Island. He counted about 600 people living in misery. Clearly, something had gone terribly wrong. Beginning in 1864, Christian missionaries arrived on the island. They found a society whose members were constantly at war with each other. The population on Easter Island continued to decline.

4   Finally, the South American country Chile laid claim to Easter Island. In 1966, the island was made open to tourists. Finally, in 1995, it became a UNESCO World Heritage Site. This means that governments around the world help to protect the island so that future generations of people can visit and enjoy it. Today Easter Island has about 4,000 inhabitants. Some of them are descended from the Rapanui people.

Genre: History Article

Easter Island's DECLINE

by Erik Lehman

1   More than 1,000 years ago, a civilization thrived on Easter Island. The island's rich soil yielded harvests of sweet potatoes, and the inhabitants (called the Rapanui) ate chickens they raised. The Rapanui had a lot of spare time, and they used it to carve huge stone statues, called *moai*. The average moai was 4 meters tall. The larger ones measured more than 30 meters tall and weighed 80 tons. The island boasts 600 of these mysterious figures.

2   Part of the mystery is how these people moved the statues around the island. Sixty years ago, a man named Thor Heyerdahl sought to explain it. He did an experiment and showed how people could have placed the statues on huge logs. Then they rolled the heavy weights long distances atop the logs. He proved this process would have worked.

3   Logs come from trees, but the Easter Island of today is almost completely treeless. Where did the trees go? Scientists concluded that the Rapanui cut down most of the trees and used them to move the statues. As the forests disappeared, so did the soil. Without trees on the island to prevent erosion, rainwater washed away the fertile earth, destroying the farmland. With fewer crops, people became hungry and fought over the food that was available. The island's population plummeted from a peak of 7,000 to just a few hundred.

4   Today Easter Island is still treeless, but its population has grown. Now the people who live there welcome tourists who visit the grand statues and spend money. Ironically, the statues that indirectly led to Easter Island's fall are now helping to heal it.

WORDS TO KNOW

As you read, look inside, around, and beyond these words to figure out what they mean.

• **inhabitants**

• **fertile**

▶ **Think** Use what you learned from the history articles to respond to the following questions.

1 Read these sentences from "A Short History of Easter Island."

> Fifty years later, Captain James Cook came to Easter Island. He counted about 600 people living in misery. Clearly, something had gone terribly wrong.

Which statement **best** explains the misery Captain Cook found?

A Thor Heyerdahl showed how the statues were moved.

B The volcanic rock made the soil bad for farming.

C The Rapanui ruined farmland by cutting down trees.

D The population declined to just a few hundred people.

2 Underline **one** word in the excerpt from "Easter Island's Decline" that means "to fall quickly."

> . . . [Rainwater] washed away the fertile earth, destroying the farmland. With fewer crops, people became hungry and fought over the food that was available. The island's population plummeted from a peak of 7,000 to just a few hundred.

3 The time line below shows some events described in "A Short History of Easter Island." Write **two** details from "Easter Island's Decline" to complete the time line.

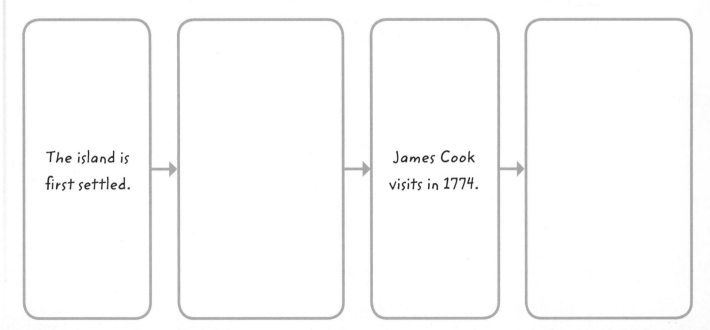

The island is first settled. → → James Cook visits in 1774. →

4 Reread paragraph 4 from "A Short History of Easter Island." Which **two** sentences from "Easter Island's Decline" **best** explain how becoming a World Heritage Site affected the people of Easter Island?

    A "The island's rich soil yielded harvests of sweet potatoes, and the inhabitants . . . ate chickens they raised." (paragraph 1)

    B "The Rapanui had a lot of spare time, and they used it to carve huge stone statues, called *moai*." (paragraph 1)

    C "Logs come from trees, but the Easter Island of today is almost completely treeless." (paragraph 3)

    D "Now the people who live there welcome tourists who visit the grand statues and spend money." (paragraph 4)

    E "Ironically, the statues that indirectly led to Easter Island's fall are now helping to heal it." (paragraph 4)

 Write

Easter Island went through great changes between Jacob Roggeveen's visit in 1722 and 1966, when tourists began to visit. Combine information from both passages to explain a possible cause of one change.

5 **Plan Your Response** Identify one change and supporting details from each passage. Use a chart to organize your thoughts.

6 **Write an Extended Response** Use your chart and details from the text to describe one change and its possible causes. Include at least **two** details from each text in your response.

_____

_____

_____

_____

_____

_____

_____

_____

_____

_____

_____

_____

_____

_____

_____

_____

_____

_____

 ## Learning Target

In this lesson, you learned to integrate information from two sources on the same topic. Explain how integrating information helps you better speak and write about the topic.

_____

_____

_____

_____

▶ **Read**

Read the science article. Then answer the questions that follow.

The **Layers** of Earth's Atmosphere

by Tawni Walker

1   Earth is surrounded by invisible gases that form a thin protective blanket that we call the atmosphere. It contains the oxygen we breathe. It also holds other important gases such as nitrogen, carbon dioxide, water vapor, and ozone.

2   Our atmosphere lets us breathe, but it is important for several other reasons. It burns and destroys meteors headed toward Earth's surface. It keeps our planet from having extreme temperature changes. Without this protective blanket, we would have hot days and freezing nights. One part of Earth's atmosphere, called the ozone layer, protects us from the Sun's harmful rays.

Earth's Atmosphere

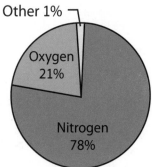

Other 1%
Oxygen 21%
Nitrogen 78%

3   The atmosphere is divided vertically into four layers based on temperature: the troposphere, the stratosphere, the mesosphere, and the thermosphere.

Prefix	Prefix Meaning
Tropo–	change
Strato–	layer
Meso–	middle
Thermo–	heat

Troposphere

4   The **troposphere** begins at Earth's surface and extends up to 12 miles (20 km) high. This is the layer of the atmosphere in which we live. Almost all weather occurs in this region.

5   If you were to walk from the bottom of a mountain to its top, you would notice the air getting thinner and the temperature dropping. This is the general pattern from the bottom to the top of the troposphere. At Earth's surface, the average temperature is around 62°F (17°C). At the top of the troposphere, the average temperature is around –60°F (–51°C).

Stratosphere

6   The **stratosphere** starts at the top of the troposphere. It then rises to about 31 miles (50 km) above Earth's surface. From the bottom to the top, the temperature increases from an average of –60°F (–51°C) to 5°F (–15°C). The stratosphere holds 19 percent of the atmosphere's gases.

Mesosphere

7   The **mesosphere** begins at the top of the stratosphere. It climbs to about 56 miles (90 km) above Earth's surface. From bottom to the top, the temperature decreases from about 5°F (–15°C) to as low as –184°F (–120°C). The air keeps getting thinner and thinner. However, gases in the mesosphere are still thick enough to create friction when meteors enter the atmosphere, slowing them down as they hurtle toward Earth. This causes the meteors to burn up, leaving fiery trails in the night sky.

Thermosphere

8   Above the mesosphere is the **thermosphere**. This layer rises up to 375 miles (600 km) above Earth. The temperature shoots up, reaching as high as 3,600°F (2,000°C) near the top. The gases of the thermosphere are much thinner than those in the mesosphere.

9   The next time you look up at the sky, remember this: You are at the very bottom of the lowest layer of a vast ocean of gas that rises hundreds of miles above the clouds.

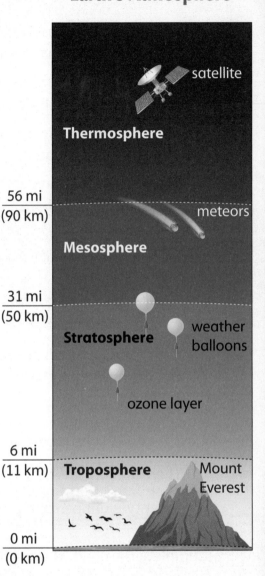

The Layers of Earth's Atmosphere

satellite

Thermosphere

56 mi (90 km)

meteors

Mesosphere

31 mi (50 km)

Stratosphere

weather balloons

ozone layer

6 mi (11 km)

Troposphere

Mount Everest

0 mi (0 km)

▶ **Think**

1. How does the circle graph help the reader understand the information in paragraph 1 of "The Layers of Earth's Atmosphere"?

    A It shows that carbon dioxide, water vapor, and ozone make up less than 1% of Earth's atmosphere.

    B It shows that more than 90% of Earth's atmosphere is made up of water vapor and oxygen.

    C It shows that oxygen, nitrogen, and water vapor make up just 90% of Earth's atmosphere.

    D It shows that gases like carbon dioxide, oxygen, and nitrogen are only a tiny fraction of Earth's atmosphere.

2. The box below contains information about our atmosphere.

Details

- The ozone layer is located in the stratosphere.

- *Strato-* means "layer."

- The ozone layer protects us from the Sun's dangerous rays.

- There are four layers of Earth's atmosphere.

- Seventy-eight percent of Earth's atmosphere is made of nitrogen.

Complete the chart by using information from the box. Write **one** detail that appears only in the text, **one** detail that only appears only in the diagram, and **one** detail that appears in both the text and the diagram.

What the Text Says	What the Diagram Shows	What the Text Says and the Diagram Shows

3 Read this sentence from paragraph 7 of "Layers of Earth's Atmosphere."

> From bottom to the top, the temperature <u>decreases</u> from about 5°F (-15°C) to as low as -184°F (-120°C).

The word <u>decreases</u> uses the prefix *de-*, which means "down" or "away from." Using this information and context clues, choose the **best** definition of <u>decrease</u> as it is used in this sentence.

    A   to grow larger in size

    B   to get smaller in number

    C   to become warmer

    D   to change suddenly

4 **Short Response** The author of "The Layers of Earth's Atmosphere" concludes that we are are "at the very bottom of . . . a vast ocean of gas." What reasons does the author give to support this conclusion? Include at least two supporting details from the text in your response.

_____

_____

_____

_____

_____

_____

_____

_____

_____

_____

▶ **Read**

Read the science article. Then answer the questions that follow.

Air Works for Me

from *The Courage to Soar*, National
Aeronautics and Space Administration

1   Would you be surprised to learn that we live at the bottom of
an ocean? It is an ocean of air. Probably because we can't see it,
we take the air around us for granted. We only feel or notice air
when the wind blows, so why pay any attention to it?

2   We all know that air is necessary for life. Animals need the
oxygen in air, and plants need the carbon dioxide that air
contains. Air is important to us in countless other ways, too.
It dries our clothes and vacuums our floors; it lifts kites and
airplanes. In air conditioners and heaters, it cools us down and
warms us up. We ride on it, and we can even sleep on it (think of
air mattresses). As you explore all the ways air works for you, you
may be amazed.

Air Is Pushy

3   Air is matter: it takes up space and it has mass. Because air has
mass, Earth's gravity attracts it and gives it weight. And because
it has weight, it presses on things—it exerts pressure. Think about
it: you have mass—your body is made up of millions of molecules.
That means Earth's gravity gives you weight; because you have
weight, you exert pressure. Right now, you are probably sitting on
a chair, a desk, or the floor. Therefore, you are exerting pressure

on the chair, the desk, or the floor. Wherever you walk, wherever you sit, wherever you lie down, you exert pressure because you have weight.

4   The pressure, or push, caused by air is called air pressure. Air pressure is a very strong force. It can make a hot air balloon rise into the sky, it can crush a can, and it can hold water in a glass that is upside down. To prove this to yourself, try the following experiment.

Is This Magic?

5   Fill a plastic cup half-full of water. Take some of the water and rub it along the rim of the cup to make a good seal. Lay an index card on top. Lay your hand on the index card and turn the cup upside down. Take your hand away. The air pressure will hold the water in the cup!

6   Since we are sitting at the bottom of an ocean of air, the air is always pressing on us. Air pressure changes as you go higher or lower in the atmosphere. As you travel higher in the sky, air pressure goes down. This is because the higher you go, the less air there is pressing down on you from above.

7   Picture yourself at the bottom of the ocean of air, where all of the air above you is pushing down on your body. Now, picture yourself at the summit of Mount Everest, the highest mountain in the world. There is far less air above you, so there is far less pressure on you.

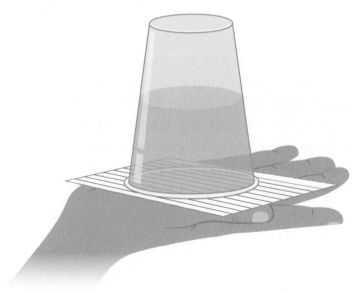

▶ Think

5   Read these sentences from paragraph 2 of "Air Works for Me."

> We all know that air is <u>necessary</u> for life. Animals need the oxygen in air, and plants need the carbon dioxide that air contains. Air is important to us in countless other ways, too.

Using context clues, choose the best definition of <u>necessary</u> as it is used in this sentence.

    A   helpful

    B   harmful

    C   needed

    D   wanted

6   This question has two parts. First, answer Part A. Then answer Part B.

Part A

What point does the author of "Air Works for Me" make about air?

    A   It can be used in magic tricks.

    B   It has both mass and weight.

    C   We need not pay attention to it.

    D   It is important to us in many ways.

Part B

Read paragraph 3 from "Air Works for Me." Underline **three** sentences that **best** support the point in Part A.

> Air is matter: it takes up space and it has mass. Because air has mass, Earth's gravity attracts it and gives it weight. And because it has weight, it presses on things—it exerts pressure. Think about it: you have mass—your body is made up of millions of molecules. That means Earth's gravity gives you weight; because you have weight, you exert pressure. Right now, you are probably sitting on a chair, a desk, or the floor. Therefore, you are exerting pressure on the chair, the desk, or the floor. Wherever you walk, wherever you sit, wherever you lie down, you exert pressure because you have weight.

7 The box below contains details about the experiment discussed in "Air Works for Me."

Details

- You should use a plastic cup half-full of water.

- Using too little water could weaken the seal.

- Turn the cup upside down after placing the index card.

- The cup should balance on the center of your hand.

- The experiment is a fun way to learn about water pressure.

Complete the chart by using details from the box. Write **one** detail that only appears in the text, **one** detail that only appears in the drawing, and **one** detail that appears in both the text and in the drawing.

What the Text Says	What the Diagram Shows	What the Text Says and the Diagram Shows

8 **Short Response** Write a paragraph that answers the following questions:

- What is the troposphere?

- What are two qualities of the troposphere that living things need to survive?

_____

_____

_____

_____

_____

Write

9 **Extended Response** The Earth's atmosphere is an invisible ocean of air. But not all of the parts of this ocean are the same. How are the upper layers of the atmosphere different from the bottom layer? Use details from **both** passages to support your answer.

In your answer, be sure to
- tell what the bottom layer of the atmosphere is like
- tell how the upper layers of the atmosphere differ from the bottom layer
- use details from both passages to support your answer

Check your writing for correct spelling, grammar, capitalization, and punctuation.

_____

_____

_____

_____

_____

_____

_____

_____

_____

_____

_____

_____

_____

_____

Integration of Knowledge and Ideas in Literature

Have you ever had this experience? You start reading a story that begins something like this: "Long, long ago, when the earth was very new, the animals had no fire." You to think to yourself, "Oh no! I've read this before." But as you read on, you realize it's not the same story at all. The topic of the tale is the same—how fire and light were brought to earth—but the characters and events are different from the other story you read. This experience often happens to readers because literature has many topics and patterns that appear again and again. The more you read such stories, the more **knowledge** and **ideas** you gain from and about them. You can then **integrate** (put together) what you learn to understand the stories of people from around the world.

In this unit, you'll compare and contrast stories that have similar topics. You'll compare and contrast stories that have similar patterns of events. So, when you begin to read a story and you think, "Oh no! I've read this before," don't close that book. You might be in for a welcome surprise.

✔ Self Check

Before starting this unit, check off the skills you know below. As you complete each lesson, see how many more skills you can check off!

I can:	Before this unit	After this unit
compare and contrast the topics of stories, myths, and literature from various cultures.	☐	☐
compare and contrast the themes of stories, myths, and literature from various cultures.	☐	☐
compare and contrast patterns of events in stories, myths, and literature from various cultures.	☐	☐

page 417

page 422

page 424

page 434

page 435

page 448

page 441

page 446

👥 **Introduction**

LAFS.4.RL.3.7 Make connections between the text of a story or drama and a visual or oral presentation of the text, identifying where each version reflects specific descriptions and directions in the text.

Media Feature
Connecting Presentations of a Text

Learning Target

Connecting the experience of reading a story or drama to hearing it or seeing it performed will help you gain a better understanding of the story.

▶ **Read** Hearing a story or watching a play is different from reading it. Instead of imagining a setting or story events, narrators, actors, and others have made those decisions for you. They interpret how the setting should look or how characters should act and sound.

Often, story details are changed or features such as music and sound effects are added. But you can have fun when you find ways to connect a written text with its spoken or staged performance.

Read this excerpt from *Robin Hood and the Mournful Knight* to yourself. Then read it out loud. How do the two reading experiences compare?

WILL SCARLET: Look! [*pointing*] I've never seen a knight in such rags! What ails him, I wonder?

[*Enter the KNIGHT. He looks weary and mournful. He wears fine clothes, but they are old, torn, and dirty.*]

ROBIN HOOD: Welcome, gentle knight. I am Robin Hood. Will you not dine with us? . . .

KNIGHT: Thank heavens for generous fellows like you! I have not tasted a bite for days. . . .

▶ **Think** Reread the script of *William Tell* on page 110. In the chart below, tell how you learned about the story details. Then listen carefully to the recording of the same drama, and complete the last column of the chart.

	Script	Recording
Setting		
Characters		
Events		

▶ **Talk** Compare and contrast the written and recorded versions of the drama. Then figure out the reason behind each difference.

Learning Target

In this lesson, you've compared hearing dramas to reading their written forms. Explain how the connections will help you better understand how literature can be experienced.

_____

_____

_____

LAFS.4.RL.3.9 Compare and contrast the treatment of similar themes and topics (e.g., opposition of good and evil) . . . in . . . traditional literature from different cultures.

Lesson 25
Comparing Topics and Themes in Stories

Learning Target

Comparing and contrasting similar themes and topics in stories from different parts of the world will help you better understand the stories and the people who tell them.

▶ **Read** Comparing and contrasting stories can help you make connections between **topics**, characters, events, and **themes** in **traditional literature**. These stories were originally passed down by word of mouth and were written down much later.

Traditional stories often share the same topic. For example, the **opposition**, or struggle, between good and evil is a common topic. The theme of a story is its message or lesson, which is told through the characters and events as the story unfolds.

Below are two stories with the same topic. Read each story and decide how they are similar and different.

The Jealous Bluebird

Rabbit and Mouse were best friends. But Bluebird, who was jealous, tried to separate them. "I will grant you each one wish," said Bluebird.

"I wish to travel to a faraway land," Rabbit said. Bluebird granted the wish, noting with a smirk that Rabbit did not wish he could also return.

But Mouse was not fooled. "I wish that my friend will always find his way home." And Bluebird had no choice but to grant this wish, too.

The Sad Frog

Once there lived a frog who wished she could fly. So she asked a heron to teach her. "Flying is easy," said the heron. "Just flap your wings like this." And the heron flew away before the frog could say, "But I have no wings."

The frog hopped away sadly, wishing for wings she could never have. She didn't realize that a snake near a rock had heard everything and was wishing he could hop as gracefully as the frog.

▶ **Think**   To identify the topic of a story, ask yourself, "What is this story about?" To identify the theme of a story, ask yourself, "What is this story trying to teach me?" Use the chart below to compare and contrast the characters, events, and themes of the stories you read.

"The Jealous Bluebird"	"The Sad Frog"
Topic What can happen when wishes are made	
Characters	**Characters**
Events	**Events**
Theme	**Theme**

▶ **Talk**   Share your chart with a partner. Were your events and themes similar or different? How did comparing and contrasting the characters, events, and themes help you better understand the stories?

 Academic Talk
Use these words and phrases to talk about the text.

- **theme**
- **topic**
- **opposition**
- **traditional literature**

The Flask of Oil an Indian folktale

A poor man received the gift of a large and valuable flask of oil from a kind and wealthy neighbor. Delighted, the poor man carefully put it onto the top shelf in his home. One evening, as he was gazing at it, he said, "If I should sell it, I could buy five sheep. Every year I should have lambs. If I sold the lambs, I would be rich enough to marry and perhaps have a son. And what a fine boy he would be! But if he should disobey me"—and he raised the staff in his hand—"I should punish him thus!" So saying, he swung the staff, knocking the flask off the shelf so that the oil ran over him from head to foot.

The Peasant and the Cucumbers
by Leo Tolstoy

A peasant once went to the gardener's to steal cucumbers. He crept up to the cucumbers and thought, "I will carry off a bag of cucumbers, which I will sell; with the money I will buy a hen. The hen will lay eggs, hatch them, and raise a lot of chicks. I will feed the chicks and sell them; then I will buy me a young sow, and she will bear a lot of pigs. I will sell the pigs and buy me a mare; the mare will foal me some colts. I will raise the colts and sell them. I will buy me a house and start a garden. In the garden I will sow cucumbers and will not let them be stolen but will keep a sharp watch on them. I will hire watchmen and put them in the cucumber patch, while I myself will come on them, unawares, and shout, 'Oh, there, keep a sharp lookout!'" And this he shouted as loud as he could. The watchmen heard it, and they rushed out and beat the peasant.

Close Reader Habits

As you read, **underline** important characters and events in each story that help you identify its topic and theme.

Explore | **How are the topics and themes of the two tales similar? How are they different?**

Think

Compare and contrast what the characters learn at the end of each story.

1 Compare and contrast the two stories by completing the chart below.

"The Flask of Oil"	"The Peasant and the Cucumbers"
Topic	
Characters	Characters
Events	Events
Theme	

Talk

2 Discuss your charts, and star any details you decide are similar in each story. Then discuss the lesson you learned from the men's experiences.

 ## Write

3 **Short Response** Compare and contrast the way the events in the two stories develop similar themes. Use text evidence in your response. Use the space provided on page 420 to write your response.

HINT In what way are the men's dreams in the two stories alike?

Juvadi and the Princess
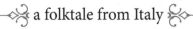
a folktale from Italy

1   Many, many years ago, as Juvadi the village fool strolled by the castle, he noticed a beautiful princess standing near a window. Upon hearing her lovely laugh, Juvadi whispered, "May you fall in love with me!" As usually occurs, the princess fell in love with him immediately.

2   Learning of their feelings, the ancient king became terribly embarrassed. He consulted his advisors, saying, "My daughter is in love with a fool. You are wise, so tell me how I should punish this shame!"

3   "Put them both into a wooden barrel and roll it over a cliff," they answered. "Then you will never see them again." At once the king commanded it to be done.

4   As the barrel rolled along, Juvadi cried, "Let me out—I'll reward you with figs and raisins!" So saying, he threw handfuls of the luscious fruit out a hole in the barrel. Then coming to a level spot, the barrel stopped rolling. Juvadi broke it open, and the pair clambered out.

5   Coincidentally, a nearby frog saw this, and she laughed so hard that a wart on her neck disappeared. Happy to carry less weight, the frog called to Juvadi, "What is your wish? I can do anything and everything. Allow me to do something amazing for you."

6   Quickly Juvadi replied, "We wish to be married, but we have no place to live. Kindly build us a humble cottage."

7   Just as quickly the frog responded, "Watch as I turn this pebble into a palace, with all the comforts of the world." Suddenly, a sparkling palace appeared out of thin air, and Juvadi and the princess entered it through its glittering gates.

8   The princess loved Juvadi, but she also knew him very well. "Soon," she said, "I will indeed marry you. But first we must find a wish that will drive out your stupidity."

9   Juvadi just grinned, because he loved her more than ever.

Close Reader Habits

What is each story about? Reread both stories, and **underline** the details that help you understand each story's topic.

Hans and the Princess

a folktale from Germany

1   A king wished to know whom his daughter would marry. He sent his favorite dog to find her future husband. The dog dragged back Hans, the stupid village fool.

2   The embarrassed king put the princess and Hans in a casket and set them out to sea. The princess cried out, "You horrible fool. How is it that you are my future husband?"

3   "I wished for it," said Hans. "All my wishes come true."

4   "If that is so," she said, "then wish us something to eat." So Hans wished for a plate of potatoes, which she devoured.

5   Hans then said, "I wish for a grand ship." They appeared on a proud vessel, fully crewed and forging back to land.

6   Upon reaching shore, Hans declared, "Here there shall be a castle, and within it shall dwell the princess and her handsome, intelligent husband." Upon saying this, a castle appeared, and Hans became handsome and smart. The princess and Hans fell in love, married, and lived happily.

7   Years later, the princess' father was out riding and stumbled upon the castle. The king did not recognize his daughter, but she knew him. She treated him well, but before he left, she hid a golden cup in his pocket. The princess then accused him of having stolen the cup.

8   The king protested that he did not know how the cup had come into his pocket. The princess said, "Do you see, now, how it feels to be treated unfairly?" She revealed herself as his daughter and forgave him. The king, overjoyed, named the princess and Hans as his heirs. Upon the king's death, Hans and the princess became king and queen.

Close Reader Habits

What is the theme in each story? For each folktale, **circle** at least two words or phrases that tell something about each story's message.

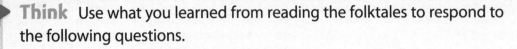

Think Use what you learned from reading the folktales to respond to the following questions.

1. Which of the following statements is a theme expressed by both folktales?

   A Putting your trust in a fool is a bad idea.

   B Love can overcome unexpected challenges.

   C Children should listen to the wisdom of their parents.

   D Hard work is what helps even fools succeed.

2. Choose the statement that **best** tells how the king's actions in each folktale contribute to the theme.

   A He asked the fool to treat the princess like royalty.

   B He ordered the fool to build a castle for his daughter.

   C He demanded that the fool become handsome and intelligent.

   D He created the problem that the fool had to handle.

3. Which theme is developed in "Hans and the Princess" but not in "Juvadi and the Princess"?

   A It is important to treat people fairly.

   B Parents should teach their children lessons.

   C Children should forgive their parents.

   D Doing things for other people is a good idea.

4. Reread paragraph 8 of "Hans and the Princess." Find the sentence that describes the lesson the princess wanted to teach the king, and write it in the box below.

5 Compare the story events that help develop the theme in "Juvadi and the Princess" with those in "Hans and the Princess." Draw Xs in the boxes next to details from each folktale. Some events appear in both tales.

Story Events	"Juvadi and the Princess"	"Hans and the Princess"
A frog helps a fool.		
A fool marries a princess.		
A king is embarrassed.		
A golden cup is found in a pocket.		
A fool rescues a princess.		
A princess and a fool live happily ever after.		

Many details in the stories are similar, but "Hans and the Princess" has a different ending. Think about how "Hans and the Princess" provides an additional theme.

 Talk

6 Explain the similarities and differences in themes between "Juvadi and the Princess" and "Hans and the Princess." Also describe how the characters learned lessons about life. Use a chart to organize your thoughts.

Write

7 **Short Response** Use the information in your chart to compare and contrast the similarities and differences between the topics and themes in the two folktales. Use at least **two** details from **each** tale to support your response. Use the space provided on page 421 to write your response.

HINT Choose the best way to structure your ideas to show similarities and differences.

Write **Use the space below to write your answer to the question on page 415.**

The Flask of Oil
The Peasant and the Cucumbers

3 **Short Response** Compare and contrast the way the events in the two stories develop similar themes. Use text evidence in your response.

> **HINT** In what way are the men's dreams in the two stories alike?

_____

_____

_____

_____

_____

_____

_____

_____

> Don't forget to check your writing.

Write Use the space below to write your answer to the question on page 419.

Juvadi and the Princess

7 **Short Response** Use the information in your chart to compare and contrast the similarities and differences between the topics and themes in the two folktales. Use at least **two** details from **each** tale to support your response.

> **HINT** Choose the best way to structure your ideas to show similarities and differences.

_____

_____

_____

_____

_____

_____

_____

_____

_____

Check Your Writing

☐ Did you read the prompt carefully?

☐ Did you put the prompt in your own words?

☐ Did you use the best evidence from the text to support your ideas?

☐ Are your ideas clearly organized?

☐ Did you write in clear and complete sentences?

☐ Did you check your spelling and punctuation?

The Two-Headed Weaver

a tale from *The Panchatantra*

1   In a certain place there lived a weaver by the name of Mantharaka, which means "the simpleton." One day, while weaving cloth, the wooden pieces on his loom broke. He took an ax and set forth to find some wood. He found a large sissoo tree at the ocean's shore, and said aloud, "Now this is a large tree. If I fell it, I will have wood enough for all my weaving tools."

2   Having thus thought it through, he raised his ax to begin cutting. However, a spirit lived in this tree, and he said, "Listen! This tree is my home. . . ."

3   The weaver said, "Then what am I to do? If I don't find a good tree, then my family will starve. You will have to go somewhere else. I am going to cut it down."

4   The spirit answered, "Listen, I am at your service. Ask whatever you would like, but spare this tree!"

5   The weaver said, "If that is what you want then I will go home and ask my friend and my wife, and when I return, you must give me what I ask for."

6   The spirit promised, and the weaver, beside himself with joy, returned home. Upon his arrival in his city he saw his friend, the barber, and said, "Friend, I have gained control over a spirit. Tell me what I should demand from him!"

7   The barber said, "My dear friend, if that is so then you should demand a kingdom. You could be king, and I would be your prime minister. . . ."

8   The weaver spoke, "Friend, so be it! But let us also ask my wife."

9   Having said this, he went quickly to his wife and said to her, "Dear one, today I have gained control over a spirit who will grant me one wish. Hence I have come to ask for your advice. Tell me, what should I ask for? My friend the barber thinks that I should request a kingdom."

10   She answered, "Oh, son of your excellence . . . . a king's life is an unending procession of annoyances. He must constantly worry about friendships, animosities, wars, servants, defense alliances, and duplicity. . . . Never envy the life of a king."

11   The weaver said, "You are right. But what should I ask for?"

12   She answered, "You can now work on only one piece of cloth at a time. That is barely enough to pay for the necessities. You should ask for another pair of arms and a second head so that you can work on two pieces of cloth at once, one in front of you, and one behind you. . . ."

13   After hearing this he spoke with joy, "Good, you faithful wife! You have spoken well, and I will do what you say. That is my decision."

14   With that he went to the spirit and let his will be known, "Listen, if you want to fulfill my wish, then give me another pair of arms and another head."

15   He had barely spoken before he was two-headed and four-armed. Rejoicing, he returned home, but the people there thought that he was a demon and beat him with sticks and stones, until he fell over dead. . . .

THE RIDICULOUS WISHES

by Charles Perrault,
Old Time Stories Told by Master Charles Perrault

WORDS TO KNOW

As you read, look inside, around, and beyond these words to figure out what they mean.

- impatience
- former

1   There was once a poor woodcutter who, tired of his hard life . . . declared that in all his days heaven had not granted even one of his wishes. One day in the woods, as the woodcutter was complaining of his unhappy lot, Jupiter appeared before him, his thunderbolts in his hands. . . .

2   "Have no fear," said Jupiter. "I have heard your complaints and I have come to show you how unfairly you judge me. Now listen! I am king of all the world and I promise to grant your first three wishes, no matter what they may be. . . ."

3   With these words, Jupiter returned to his heavens and the happy woodcutter, taking up his bundle of sticks, hurried to his home. "This is an important matter," he said to himself. "I certainly must have my wife's advice."

4 "Hey, Fanchon," he shouted, as he entered his cottage. "Light us up a good fire. We are rich for the rest of our lives. All we have to do is to make three wishes!"

5 With this, he told his wife what had happened, whereupon she in her imagination began to form a thousand plans. "Blaise, my dear, let us not spoil anything by our impatience. We must think things over very carefully. Let us put off our first wish until tomorrow. Let us sleep on it."

6 "I think you are right," said he. . . . Relaxing, he leaned back in his chair before the fire. "To match such a fine blaze," he said, "I wish we had a measure of sausage. It would go very well indeed!"

7 Scarcely had he spoken these words when his wife, to her great astonishment, saw a long link of sausage moving over to them like a snake from the chimney corner. She cried out in alarm, but realizing at once that this was the result of the wish which her foolish husband had made, she began to . . . scold him angrily. "When you might," she said, "have a kingdom, with gold, pearls, rubies, diamonds, fine clothes; and all you wish for is a sausage!"

8   "Alas," her husband replied. "I was wrong, I made a very bad choice. I admit my mistake. Next time I will do better."

9   "Yes! Yes!" said his wife . . . "To make such a choice as you did, you must be a donkey."

10   At this the husband became very angry. . . . "A curse on this and all sausages. I wish that it was hanging from the end of your nose!"

11   The wish was heard at once . . . and the sausage fastened itself on her nose. Fanchon had once been pretty, and—to tell the truth—this ornament did not have a very pleasing effect. . . .

12   "With my remaining wish I could very well still make myself a king," he said to himself. "But we must think of the queen, too, and her unhappiness if she were to sit on the throne with her new yard-long nose. She must decide which she wants, to be a queen with that nose or a woodcutter's wife and an ordinary person."

13   Whereupon his wife agreed that they had no choice. She would never have the riches and diamonds and fine clothes she had dreamed of, but she would be herself again if the last wish would free her from the frightful sausage on her nose.

14   And so the woodcutter did not change his lot. He did not become a king. His purse was not filled with gold. He was only too glad to use his remaining wish in restoring his poor wife to her former state.

▶ **Think** Use what you learned from reading the folktales to respond to the following questions.

1 Which sentence **best** describes the theme that the two folktales share?

   A If you work hard, you will be ready for luck when it comes.

   B People can overcome unexpected challenges.

   C Having riches does not always make people happy.

   D People should think before they speak or act.

2 Underline **one** sentence from **each** passage that develops this topic:
   A person's wishes end up making trouble.

from "The Two-Headed Weaver"	from "The Ridiculous Wishes"
With that he went to the spirit and let his will be known, "Listen, if you want to fulfill my wish, then give me another pair of arms and another head." He had barely spoken before he was two-headed and four-armed. Rejoicing, he returned home, but the people there thought that he was a demon and beat him with sticks and stones, until he fell over dead. . . .	"Yes! Yes!" said his wife . . . "To make such a choice as you did, you must be a donkey." At this the husband became very angry. . . . "A curse on this and all sausages. I wish that it was hanging from the end of your nose!" The wish was heard at once . . . and the sausage fastened itself on her nose. Fanchon had once been pretty, and—to tell the truth—this ornament did not have a very pleasing effect. . . .

3 The sentences below are from paragraph 10 of "The Two-Headed Weaver." Underline the word that means "feel jealous of."

   " . . . a king's life is an unending procession of annoyances. He must constantly worry about friendships, animosities, wars, servants, defense alliances . . . . Never envy the life of a king."

4 Which of the following describes an important difference between "The Two-Headed Weaver" and "The Ridiculous Wishes"?

    A "The Two-Headed Weaver" teaches that friends and family are a good source of advice. "The Ridiculous Wishes" teaches that people should trust themselves before listening to others.

    B "The Two-Headed Weaver" teaches that accepting who you are can make you happy. "The Ridiculous Wishes" teaches that it is important to keep changing and improving.

    C "The Two-Headed Weaver" teaches that people who change their lives can face problems. "The Ridiculous Wishes" teaches that people who accept their lives can be happy.

    D "The Two-Headed Weaver" teaches that beauty matters more than riches. "The Ridiculous Wishes" teaches that riches matter more than beauty.

 **Write**

The tales "The Two-Headed Weaver" and "Ridiculous Wishes" have important similarities and differences. Write a response that compares and contrasts the topics and themes in the two folktales.

5 **Plan Your Response** How are the topics, events, characters, and themes in both tales similar? How are they different? Use a chart like the one on page 415 to collect your thoughts before you write.

6 **Write an Extended Response** Use evidence from both texts and information from your chart to compare and contrast how each folktale develops its topic and theme.

_____

_____

_____

_____

_____

_____

_____

_____

_____

_____

_____

_____

_____

_____

 Learning Target

In this lesson, you compared and contrasted stories that share a topic or theme. Explain how this helped you develop a deeper understanding of traditional literature.

_____

_____

_____

_____

 **Introduction**

LAFS.4.RL.3.9 Compare and contrast the treatment of similar ... patterns of events (e.g., the quest) in stories, myths, and traditional literature from different cultures.

Lesson 26
Comparing Patterns of Events in Stories

Noting similarities and differences among events in various stories and myths will help you understand stories told in many parts of the world.

▶ **Read** Traditional stories come from different parts of the world, but many share similar **patterns of events**, or the likely or expected ways things happen.

One kind of story that follows a pattern is a **quest**. In a quest, a character goes on a journey to reach a certain goal, often to help other people. **Myths** that explain human behavior or ancient beliefs about nature also may share similar patterns. By comparing story events and outcomes, you will gain a better understanding of the tales you read.

As you look at the cartoons below, think about the story each one tells. How is the pattern of events similar and different?

The villagers are tired of Tall Boy's constant bragging.

The villagers are hoping she'll bring warmth back to the world.

▶ **Think**   What have you learned about the patterns of events in stories? What are the similarities and differences in the events in each cartoon? Complete the *Patterns of Events Chart* below to tell what happens.

	Story About a Boy	Story About a Girl
Order of Events		
Beginning		
Middle		
End	The villagers become angry at Tall Boy's foolish ways.	

▶ **Talk**   Share your chart with a partner.

- What events did each of you list for the beginning, middle, and end of each story? Which are similar?
- How do the patterns of events compare to each other?

⊚ **Academic Talk**
Use these words and phrases to talk about the text.
- **patterns of events**   • **quest**   • **myth**

▶ **Read**

TARA AND THE SUN

BY EMMA ROUNDTREE

1   For many years, the Clan had faced hardship after hardship. The rivers had dried up, and the once plentiful herds had moved away. Worst of all, the air had become much colder. The people feared they would freeze to death, alone amidst a cold and ruined Earth.

2   Tara could bear to see her people suffer no longer, so she braved the dangers of the Mountain. After many days of climbing, she reached the top and called forth the Sun.

3   "Should my people die," she told the Sun angrily, "you shall have no one to shine upon. No one will be left to care about you, and you'll fade away, friendless and alone."

4   The Sun mulled this over and arrived at a decision. "Very well," he answered. "Here, take this small piece of me."

5   Tara returned to the Clan with the piece of Sun. Slowly, the air warmed, the herds returned, and the rivers began to flow once again.

Lonely MOON

by Luna Merison

1   Long ago, a young boy noticed a glowing white stone and picked it up. The moment his fingers touched the stone, the boy could hear Moon speaking to him. "I am terribly lonely," said Moon. "I offer this part of myself to you so that, with it, we may talk." The boy and Moon became good friends, and they shared many secrets.

2   As time passed, however, the Earth grew cold, and soon, all was frozen. Moon realized that he had caused the problem; the Moon-stone was harming the world. Sorrowfully, Moon lowered himself to Earth, gathered back the piece of himself, and returned to his lonely existence in the heavens. And, in due time, the Earth warmed once more.

Close Reader Habits

Underline the events that are similar in each story. Also write brief notes to tell *when* they occur.

Explore **How are the patterns of events similar and different in the two folktales?**

Think

> Use a chart to help you compare and contrast the events in each story. Then you can look for patterns of events.

1 In "Tara and the Sun," Tara is on a quest. Identify story details that show the pattern of events of a quest. Then summarize Tara's quest.

_____

_____

_____

_____

_____

2 What are some ways that "Lonely Moon" is different from Tara's story? Describe three or more of these differences.

_____

_____

_____

_____

_____

_____

Talk

3 The characters in both stories get a piece of a heavenly body. Compare what happens when Tara gets a piece of the Sun with what happens when the boy gets a piece of the Moon. Use a chart to organize your ideas.

Write

> **HINT** Is the boy in "Lonely Moon" also on a quest? Think of how your answer affects your response.

4 **Short Response** Describe the similarities and differences in the patterns of events in "Tara and the Sun" and "Lonely Moon." Include details from both stories in your response. Use the space provided on page 438 to write your response.

Genre: Folktale

The Monkeys and the MOON

a Tibetan folktale,
from *Tibetan Tales Derived from Indian Sources*

1   In long-past times there lived a band of monkeys in a forest. As they rambled about, they saw the reflection of the moon in a well, and the leader of the band said, "O friends, the moon has fallen into the well. The world is now without a moon. Ought not we to draw it out?"

2   The monkeys said, "Good; we will draw it out."

3   So they began to hold counsel as to how they were to draw it out. Some of them said, "Do not you know? The monkeys must form a chain, and so draw the moon out."

4   So they formed a chain, the first monkey hanging on to the branch of a tree, and the second to the first monkey's tail, and a third one in its turn to the tail of the second one. When in this way they were all hanging on to one another, the branch began to bend a good deal. The water became troubled, the reflection of the moon disappeared, the branch broke, and all the monkeys fell into the well and were disagreeably damaged.

5   A deity uttered this verse, "When the foolish have a foolish leader, they all go to ruin, like the monkeys which wanted to draw the moon up from the well."

> **Close Reader Habits**
>
> Why do the monkeys fall into the well? **Underline** important events that lead up to that story event.

The King's Fire Dogs

a Korean folktale,
retold by Mary Hoffman
in *Sun, Moon, and Stars*

1   Heaven contains just as many countries as the Earth does. There is one called Land of Darkness where there is a king who keeps huge, fierce dogs called fire dogs. This king is always trying to think of ways to bring more light to his country.

2   One day, he called the biggest and most ferocious of his fire dogs and told it to go and bring him the sun. Off loped the dog and tried to seize the sun in his jaws. But the sun was so hot that it burned the dog's mouth. He snapped at it again and again but could not hold on. He had to go back to his master with his tail between his legs.

3   The king summoned his next biggest dog. He sent it to steal the moon for him, thinking that the moon wouldn't be as hot as the sun. But the second dog fared no better than the first. The moon was so cold that when he tried to bite it, the moon froze the dog's tongue to his mouth and made his teeth sing with pain. Hard as he tried, he could not hang on to the moon and had to spit it out. He too slunk back to the king.

4   Still, the king of darkness never gives up hope. Every now and then he sends one of his fire dogs to try and steal the sun or the moon. You can see the bite marks whenever there's an eclipse.

Close Reader Habits

How does the king try to steal the sun and moon? Why? **Underline** events that help you answer these questions.

▶ **Think** Use what you learned from reading the stories to respond to the following questions.

1 Complete the chart by drawing Xs in the boxes next to the statements that describe events in "The Monkeys and the Moon," "The King's Fire Dogs," or both tales.

Statement	"The Monkeys and the Moon"	"The King's Fire Dogs"
A leader wants to bring more light to his land.		
A leader wants to rescue the moon.		
A leader sends out a dog to bring back the moon.		
Characters reach out to touch the moon.		
A character cannot hold on to the moon.		
A character never gives up hope of capturing the moon.		
The characters never reach their goal.		
The characters agree to work together on a solution to a problem.		
Some characters leave marks showing that they are still trying to reach their goal.		

2 Which statement below **best** describes a pattern of events that is true of both passages?

    A To avoid hurting themselves, the characters give up on their plans.

    B The characters capture the moon to bring more light to their countries.

    C Though trying to be helpful, the characters make unwise decisions.

    D Because they don't listen carefully to orders, the characters make mistakes.

3 Read this saying from paragraph 5 of "The Monkeys and the Moon."

When the foolish have a foolish leader, they all go to ruin . . . .

Which **two** statements, one describing details from "The Monkeys and the Moon" and one describing details from "The King's Fire Dogs," explain what the saying means?

To compare and contrast these stories, mark details showing similar and different patterns of events.

    A   The characters are hurt because they obey impossible orders.

    B   The characters agree to bring more light into the world.

    C   The characters never learn their lesson and still give advice.

    D   The characters wrongly conclude that a problem exists and fail to fix it.

    E   The characters try to reach for a thing that keeps disappearing.

    F   The characters decide to follow their leader on a hard and dangerous journey.

▶ **Talk**

4 Compare and contrast the patterns of events in both stories. What are the leaders like? What happens when the other characters help their leaders? How do earlier events influence the story outcomes? Use the Patterns of Events Chart on page 439 to list important story details and to organize your thinking.

▶ **Write**

5 **Short Response** Use the information in your chart to compare and contrast the patterns of events in both folktales. Include details from both tales to support your response. Use the space provided on page 439 to write your response.

HINT Look for details that show how the patterns of events are similar or different.

▶ **Write** **Use the space below to write your answer to the question on page 433.**

TARA AND THE SUN

Lonely MOON

4 **Short Response** Describe the similarities and differences in the patterns of events in "Tara and the Sun" and "Lonely Moon." Include details from both stories in your response.

> **HINT** Is the boy in "Lonely Moon" also on a quest? Think of how your answer affects your response.

_____

_____

_____

_____

_____

_____

_____

Check Your Writing

Don't forget to check your writing.

☐ Did you read the prompt carefully?

☐ Did you put the prompt in your own words?

☐ Did you use the best evidence from the text to support your ideas?

☐ Are your ideas clearly organized?

☐ Did you write in clear and complete sentences?

☐ Did you check your spelling and punctuation?

4 Use the Patterns of Events Chart below to organize your ideas.

Order of Events	"The Monkeys and the Moon"	"The King's Fire Dogs"
Beginning		
Middle		
End		

Write Use the space below to write your answer to the question on page 437.

5 **Short Response** Use the information in your chart to compare and contrast the patterns of events in both folktales. Include details from both tales to support your response.

> **HINT** Look for details that show how the patterns of events are similar or different.

_____

_____

_____

_____

_____

_____

WORDS TO KNOW
As you read, look inside, around, and beyond these words to figure out what they mean.

- **pity**
- **stationed**
- **pursue**

How MAUI Snared the SUN

from *Hawaiian Folk Tales: A Collection of Native Legends*

1 Maui was the son of Hina-lau-ae and Hina, and they dwelt at a place called Makalia, above Kahakuloa, on West Maui. Now, his mother Hina made *kapas*. And as she spread them out to dry, the days were so short that she was put to great trouble and labor in hanging them out and taking them in day after day until they were dry.

2 Maui, seeing this, was filled with pity for her. The days were so short that, no sooner had she got her kapas all spread out to dry, than the Sun went down, and she had to take them in again. So he determined to make the Sun go slower.

3 He first went to Wailohi, in Hamakua, on East Maui, to observe the motions of the Sun. There he saw that it rose toward Hana. He then went up on Haleakala, and saw that the Sun in its course came directly over that mountain.

4 He then went home again, and after a few days went to a place called Paeloko, at Waihee. He cut down all the cocoanut-trees, and gathered the fibre of the cocoanut husks in great quantity. This he manufactured into strong cord.

5 One Moemoe, seeing this, said tauntingly to him: "You will never catch the Sun. You are an idle nobody."

6   Maui answered: "When I conquer my enemy, and my desire is attained, I will be your death."

7   So he went up Haleakala again, taking his cord with him. And when the Sun arose above where he was stationed, he prepared a noose of the cord. Casting it, he snared one of the Sun's larger beams and broke it off. And thus he snared and broke off, one after another, all the strong rays of the Sun.

8   Then shouted he exultingly: "You are my captive, and now I will kill you for going so swiftly."

9   And the Sun said: "Let me live, and you shall see me go more slowly hereafter. Behold, have you not broken off all my strong legs, and left me only the weak ones?"

10   So the agreement was made, and Maui permitted the Sun to pursue its course. And from that time on it went more slowly; and that is the reason why the days are longer at one season of the year than at another.

How Crow Brought DAYLIGHT

adapted from an Inuit folktale

WORDS TO KNOW
As you read, look inside, around, and beyond these words to figure out what they mean.

- **efficiently**
- **exhausted**

1   Long ago when the world was young, the Inuit knew nothing about daylight. They lived and hunted under the stars of the northern darkness and thought nothing of it. Crow, however, had traveled far and wide and had seen daylight for himself. He told the Inuit about the light he saw at the horizon and how it made the earth glow with warmth and brilliance. The people began to think how wonderful it would be to have light. They could hunt more efficiently and gaze upon each other without need of a fire. The village elders begged Crow to find the daylight and bring it to them.

2   Crow agreed to make the journey south, flying endless hours until he reached a village where the sky turned bright with colors soft and wondrous. Crow saw a man who looked like the village chief and followed him home. Through an open window, Crow spied a ball glowing like a jewel resting in a corner. He knew the ball must be daylight. Waiting until the man went out again, Crow flew through the window, grabbed the ball, and flew away.

3   Crow's journey back north was long and even more tiring because he had to hold the ball in his beak. By the time he reached the Inuit village, he was exhausted from his journey. Crow looked like a spark of light as he flew closer, flapping his wings as hard as he could. But Crow could not hold the ball any longer. It fell to the ground and exploded into a brilliant light, chasing away the night. The sky became a bright blue. The shadowed mountains took on color and form.

4   As the people screamed in delight, Crow warned them that the daylight would not last forever. "It must rest every six months to regain its strength," he explained.

5   So, from that day until this, the Inuit have lived half a year in darkness and the other half in light. And they always treat Crow kindly, for it was he who first brought them daylight.

▶ **Think** Use what you learned from reading the stories to respond to the following questions.

1 The box below contains events from both stories.

> He flies south, finds a ball of daylight, and brings it to the Inuit.
>
> The people beg him to bring daylight to them.
>
> The Sun does not shine long enough. He decides to slow it down.
>
> He had traveled far and wide and had seen daylight.
>
> The Sun promises to shine longer. He is successful.
>
> One Moemoe warns him not to capture the Sun.
>
> The ball gives the people daylight. He is successful.
>
> He makes a cord, captures the Sun, and threatens to kill it.

In the chart, write details about similar story events in the appropriate column. You will not use every detail.

	"How Maui Snared the Sun"	"How Crow Brought Daylight"
Beginning		
Middle		
End		

2 Read the first sentence in paragraph 2 from "How Crow Brought Daylight." What does the suffix -*less* mean in the word <u>endless</u>?

    A full of

    B similar to

    C without

    D in a state of

3 Which **two** statements below **best** describe story details that are true of both passages?

    A   A character makes a secret agreement with the Sun.

    B   A character has never seen daylight before.

    C   A character wants to help improve the lives of others.

    D   A character captures sunlight for his own benefit.

    E   A character goes on a quest to get daylight.

    F   A character steals light from other characters.

4 Which statement below **best** describes **one** difference between "How Maui Snared the Sun" and "How Crow Brought Daylight"?

    A   Maui causes the Sun to stay. Crow makes the daylight go away.

    B   Maui uses cord to slow the Sun. Crow carries a ball of daylight.

    C   Maui tries to help only himself. Crow tries to help others.

    D   Maui does not have to travel. Crow travels a long way.

▶ Write

"How Maui Snared the Sun" and "How Crow Brought Daylight" were told by people in different places, yet the tales share many similarities. Reread the stories. Find events that make them similar and different.

5 **Plan Your Response**   Identify **two** similarities between the stories and at least **one** difference. Use a chart to organize your thoughts.

6 **Write an Extended Response**   Use your chart and details from both tales to describe similarities and differences in the patterns of events of "How Maui Snared the Sun" and "How Crow Brought Daylight."

_____

_____

_____

_____

_____

_____

_____

_____

_____

_____

_____

_____

_____

 Learning Target

**Now you've learned how to compare and contrast patterns of
events in different stories and myths. Explain how this skill
helped you better understand the stories you read.**

▶ **Read**

Read the folktales. Then answer the questions that follow.

The Old Couple and the Crane

a Japanese folktale

1   In Japan some winters ago, an elderly couple lived a modest life on the edge of a forest. One snowy morning, the old man went to the forest to cut firewood. In the forest, he encountered a beautiful crane trapped in a hunter's trap. Out of pity, the old man used his axe to free the crane.

2   That evening, the old man and his wife heard a knock at the door. A beautiful young woman stood on their doorstep.

3   "The snow is falling too heavily and I cannot make it to town," the young woman said. "Will you kindly let me stay here for the night?"

4   The elderly couple did not have much, but they were kind souls. They welcomed the young woman into their home, shared their dinner, and gave her a warm room in which to sleep.

5   The next morning, the snow was still falling. The elderly couple awoke and found that the young woman had prepared food and cleaned their home. She took care of them and made them very happy. Eventually, the young woman asked if she could stay with the couple forever and live as their daughter. They happily agreed.

6   One day, the young woman asked the elderly woman to go to town and buy some simple cotton yarn so she could weave some cloth. When the elderly woman returned with the yarn, the young woman said, "I am going to weave the most beautiful cloth you've ever seen and give it to you to sell. While I weave, you must never enter this room or watch me work." With that, she closed the door.

7   For three days and three nights, the young woman did not emerge from her room. When she did, she held the most beautiful cloth the couple had ever seen. "Take this to market, sell it, and buy more yarn. Keep the rest of the profits for yourself," the young woman said.

8   The cloth quickly earned a reputation in town as being beautiful and strong, and selling it brought the couple great fortune. After selling the cloth, the elderly woman would buy more yarn and bring it to the young woman.

9   The third time the young woman shut herself in the room to weave, the elderly woman grew curious. How was the young woman making simple yarn into something so beautiful? Unable to contain her curiosity, the elderly woman peeked inside the room.

10   She discovered a crane sitting in front of the loom, plucking its own feathers and weaving them into the cloth with the yarn. The once beautiful bird had plucked so many of its feathers that it looked tattered and worn. The feathers made the cloth glimmer like the night sky. When the crane saw the elderly woman spying, she transformed back into the young woman.

11   "I intended to stay with you forever as your daughter as thanks for saving my life," the crane woman said with sadness in her voice. "But I cannot stay now that you know my true self." And with that, she became a bird once more and flew out the window, leaving the elderly couple with only a half-woven cloth and two hearts full of regret.

▶ **Read**

Kileken,
Orphan Boy of the Sky

a Masai folktale

1   Many years ago in Kenya, a solitary old man lived in a tiny hut. His back always ached, and he struggled to tend to all his cattle and complete his chores each day. On one particularly difficult morning, the old man raised his arms to the sun and begged for assistance.

2   The next morning, a strong young boy appeared at the old man's hut.

3   "Call me Kileken," the strange boy said to the old man. "I am an orphan looking for a home. Will you allow me to look after your cattle in exchange for shelter and a soft bed?"

4   The old man enthusiastically agreed.

5   "There is only one condition," Kileken said. "I will only work in the morning and the evening, and you must never watch me work."

6   The old man thought this suspicious, but he desperately needed the help and so he agreed.

7   Despite his curiosity, the old man remained in his hut the next morning and did not peer out to see if the orphan boy had completed the promised chores. At noon, after the morning

expired, the old man inspected his cattle. To his surprise and delight, he discovered a herd of lowing, well-fed cattle. Kileken had finished his work in record time and left the cattle contented.

8   The days and weeks passed, and Kileken's help quickly made the old man rich. The cattle grew fat and earned a high price at market. The old man now spent his days resting his sore feet and back, which were tired from years of hard work.

9   Yet while the cattle grew fat and blissful, the old man grew greedy and curious. How could Kileken possibly do so much work with such speed? He suspected that Kileken was using magic. If so, the old man reasoned, then he could force Kileken to use more magic to earn more money.

10   Each afternoon, the old man approached Kileken and asked to observe him the next morning. He claimed that he wanted to brag of Kileken's strength to the men of the village, but Kileken continued to insist his work would cease if he were watched.

11   The old man's curiosity and greed grew too strong. He thought the orphan boy was bluffing and had nowhere else to go, and so one morning, the old man rose with the sun. He hid himself behind a wide baobab tree within sight of the herd and waited until he saw Kileken approaching. When the orphan boy started to feed the cattle, his arms moved so quickly that the old man only saw a blur.

12   Then, suddenly, Kileken stopped and spun around to face the old man. Disappointment flickered in his face. Without a word and in a blinding flash, Kileken turned into a beam of light and shot up into the sky. The old man saw the light take its place in the sky next to the sun. Kileken was gone.

13   Unable to appreciate a gift from the gods, the old man was left poor and alone once more. As soon as the orphan boy left, the cattle grew skinny and the old man's new wealth disappeared. And each morning when he dragged himself outside to take care of his cattle, he saw the star that once was Kileken, watching but never again helping.

▶ Think

1 Which statement is true about only **one** of the tales?

    A Events in the story could not happen in real life.

    B Spying on someone leads to regret and suffering.

    C A desire for wealth makes someone break a promise.

    D The story's setting determines what happens at the end.

2 "Alone, without anyone else" is the dictionary definition for a word used in the following paragraph from "Kileken, Orphan Boy of the Sky." **Underline** the word in the paragraph that matches this definition.

> Many years ago in Kenya, a solitary old man lived in a tiny hut. His back always ached, and he struggled to tend to all his cattle and complete his chores each day. On one particularly difficult morning, the old man raised his arms to the sun and begged for assistance.

3 Compare the story events that help develop the theme in "Kileken, Orphan Boy of the Sky" with those in "The Old Couple and the Crane." Draw Xs in the boxes next to details from each folktale. Some events appear in both tales.

Story Events	"The Old Couple and the Crane"	"Kileken, Orphan Boy of the Sky"
An older person begs for help.		
A helpful young person appears.		
The young person weaves beautiful cloth.		
The young person works hard.		
An older person betrays a trust.		
The young person disappears in a flash of light.		

4 **Short Response** The main characters in both "Kileken, Orphan Boy of the Sky" and "The Old Couple and the Crane" have a secret they try to protect. How are their secrets alike? How are they different? Include details from **both** stories to support your response.

_____

_____

_____

_____

_____

_____

_____

_____

_____

_____

_____

_____

_____

_____

5 Which statement **best** describes how the young people in both stories feel about leaving the older people?

    A   They are sorry they must leave.

    B   They are angry at the older people.

    C   They are eager to go back to their normal lives.

    D   They are exhausted from having to work so hard.

6 Read the following sentence from "The Old Couple and the Crane." Then choose the **best** definition for the word <u>modest</u>.

> In Japan some winters ago, an elderly couple lived a <u>modest</u> life on the edge of a forest.

    A advanced in years

    B generous to a fault

    C wanting more than you have

    D having limited wealth

7 This question has two parts. First, answer Part A. Then answer Part B.

Part A
Which statement **best** describes a theme in both stories?

    A Good deeds are rewarded.

    B Money can't buy happiness.

    C It is better to accept good fortune than to question it.

    D People should not depend on magic to make them happy.

Part B
Which two sentences from the texts **best** support the answer to Part A?

    A "Out of pity, the old man used his axe to free the crane." ("The Old Couple and the Crane")

    B "He suspected that Kileken was using magic." ("Kileken, Orphan Boy of the Sky")

    C "Unable to appreciate a gift from the gods, the old man was left poor and alone once more." ("Kileken, Orphan Boy of the Sky")

    D "Eventually, the young woman asked if she could stay with the couple forever and live as their daughter." ("The Old Couple and the Crane")

    E "Each afternoon, the old man approached Kileken and asked to observe him the next morning." ("Kileken, Orphan Boy of the Sky")

    F "And with that, she became a bird once more and flew out the window, leaving the elderly couple with only a half-woven cloth and two hearts full of regret." ("The Old Couple and the Crane")

8 The box below contains events from both stories.

> A young helper cooks and cleans.
>
> An old woman spies on a young helper.
>
> The young helper flies out the window.
>
> An old man wants more wealth.
>
> A young helper tends to a herd of cattle.
>
> The young helper returns to the sky.
>
> An old man's prayers are answered.
>
> A young helper weaves beautiful cloth.
>
> An old man performs an act of kindness.

In the chart, write details about similar story events in the appropriate column. You will not use every detail.

	"Kileken, Orphan Boy of the Sky"	"The Old Couple and the Crane"
Why magical help is granted		
How magic is used		
How the story ends		

Write

9 **Extended Response** "Kileken, Orphan Boy of the Sky" and "The Old Couple and the Crane" are traditional stories from different cultures. How are these stories alike? How are they different?

In your answer, be sure to
- describe how the stories treat similar themes and topics
- explain how the patterns of events are alike and different
- use details from both stories in your answer

Check your writing for correct spelling, grammar, capitalization, and punctuation.

_____

_____

_____

_____

_____

_____

_____

_____

_____

_____

_____

_____

_____

_____

_____

_____

Glossary of Words to Know

access *n.* permission to enter or use: *My sister refused to give me access to her bedroom.*

advance *v.* to move something forward: *The photographer advanced the film by clicking a button on her camera.*

annoyance *n.* something that causes bother or irritation: *The mosquitoes were an annoyance on our camping trip.*

atmosphere *n.* layers of air that surround Earth: *Meteors usually burn up in the atmosphere before reaching Earth.*

baffled *adj.* confused: *Ray was baffled by the tough math problem.*

brilliant *adj.* very bright: *The fireworks looked brilliant against the dark night sky.*

certainly *adv.* without doubt: *The rain will certainly ruin the picnic.*

charity *n.* giving money or items to people in need: *Marnie donated old clothes as an act of charity.*

conduct *n.* behavior: *The hockey player got in trouble for his rude conduct toward the other team.*

constant *adv.* happening all the time: *The constant ticking of the clock annoyed Annabel.*

conversation *n.* a discussion between two or more people: *Jamie and her parents had a conversation during dinner.*

convinced *adj.* sure that something is true: *Al was convinced he would win the contest.*

cooperate *v.* to do what is asked: *Linda cooperated with her mother by eating the vegetables.*

courtesy *n.* politeness: *Will showed courtesy when he opened the door for Mrs. Walters.*

current *adj.* happening now: *Olivia reads the newspaper every morning to keep up with current events.*

decline *v.* to grow smaller in amount: *The number of sweaters at the store is declining because sweaters are on sale this week.*

demonstration *n.* a public display: *People gathered to watch demonstrations of how to use the new computers.*

descent *n.* the act of going down: *The trail to the lake follows a steep descent.*

determine *v.* to decide and set out to do something: *I determined that I would study hard and pass the test.*

Glossary of Words to Know

discipline *n.* good behavior and hard work: *The runner showed his* **discipline** *by running even though it was raining.*

disobedient *adj.* not following orders or rules: *The trainer scolded the* **disobedient** *puppy.*

dissolve *v.* to become part of a liquid: *The sugar* **dissolved** *in the cup of tea.*

efficiently *adv.* in a way that is successful without wasting time or resources: *My grandmother* **efficiently** *chopped all the vegetables for the soup.*

emerge *v.* to come out or appear from a hidden place: *I love to watch my turtle* **emerge** *from its shell.*

encounter *v.* to meet up with or happen upon: *We'll get there in two hours if we don't* **encounter** *any traffic.*

endangered *adj.* very rare and at risk of dying out: *The blue whale is considered* **endangered** *because there are not many left in the world.*

establish *v.* to bring into being: *The city* **established** *new parking laws in the downtown area.*

eternal *adj.* everlasting: *The sun will rise and set everyday as part of an* **eternal** *process.*

exhausted *adj.* very tired: *After mowing the big lawn, Damien was* **exhausted**.

fertile *adj.* able to produce many plants: *The farmer planted his crops in the* **fertile** *soil.*

flourish *v.* to grow or live successfully: *If we get lots of sunlight and rain this year, our garden will* **flourish**.

folly *n.* a foolish act: *Having a real dog onstage during the play turned into a* **folly** *when it ran into the audience.*

foreign *adj.* unfamiliar; coming from a different place: *Greg did not understand the movie because the actors spoke in a* **foreign** *language.*

former *adj.* related to the past: *Our* **former** *house was closer to the park than where we live now.*

function *n.* a task or purpose: *The* **function** *of the pipe was to bring in clean water.*

genuine *adj.* real or authentic: *The stone in the ring was a* **genuine** *diamond.*

grudge *v.* to do something unwillingly: *Marcia was so busy that she began to* **grudge** *babysitting her sister.*

Glossary of Words to Know

hinged *v.* connected by a movable joint: *The gate was **hinged** to the fence.*

immediately *adv.* without delay: *The fire fighters jumped into the fire truck **immediately** after hearing the alarm.*

immortal *adj.* living forever: *The Greek gods were said to be **immortal** because they could never die.*

immune *adj.* protected from disease: *Because the children had already had chicken pox, they were **immune** from getting it again.*

impatience *n.* unwillingness to wait for something: *Charles tapped his foot in **impatience** as I tried to answer his question.*

inhabitant *n.* a person who lives in a certain place: *The mayor gave a speech to the **inhabitants** of the town.*

innocent *adj.* not capable of causing harm: *Everyone is scared of my big dog, but he is sweet and **innocent**.*

interrupt *v.* to say something while someone else is talking: *Sara's mother told her it was rude to **interrupt** her brother.*

introduce *v.* to use for the first time: *The chef **introduced** hot pepper to her recipe to make the chili even spicier.*

isolated *adj.* far away from other people: *My uncle lives alone on an **isolated** island.*

launch *v.* to send an object, such as a spacecraft, into the air: *Eric decided to **launch** the paper airplane toward his sister.*

lure *n.* an object used to tempt or attract: *My dad caught a big fish with his new **lure**.*

mournful *adj.* very sad: *Chris and Laura looked **mournful** when they heard that their grandmother was ill.*

myriad *adj.* very many: *There are **myriad** ways of combining different colors.*

native *adj.* relating to place of birth or origin: *The panda's **native** country is China.*

necessities *n.* everything needed: *We packed the **necessities** for a picnic: food, lemonade, a blanket, and sunscreen.*

Glossary of Words to Know

obviously *adv.* in a clear or plain way: *Enrico and his dog played until they were both **obviously** tired.*

pardon *v.* to forgive: *Please **pardon** me for disrupting the class, but could you point me to the cafeteria?*

particle *n.* one very small part: *Ron used a cloth to wipe every **particle** of dust off of the bookcase.*

pinnacle *n.* a tall, steep, pointed formation: *The tall, narrow building is shaped like a **pinnacle**.*

pity *n.* a feeling of being sorry for someone: *When I broke my arm, my teacher felt **pity** for me and gave me extra time on the test.*

produce *v.* to make or cause to be made: *The company **produced** a new type of cell phone.*

project *v.* to use light to cause an image to appear on a surface: *The artist was known for **projecting** her pictures on the walls of buildings.*

propose *v.* to suggest: *John **proposed** that the team should get new uniforms.*

pursue *v.* to follow or go along: *The travelers **pursued** a trail west to the ocean.*

recent *adj.* happening not very far in the past: *The back porch was a **recent** addition to the house.*

regulate *v.* to control with rules or laws: *The government **regulated** the development of the new fruit so people would know it was safe to eat.*

relay *v.* to pass along: *Can you **relay** this message to your teacher?*

release *v.* to let go or stop holding something: *Mrs. Kwon **released** her son's hand after they crossed the street.*

remote *adj.* far away: *The **remote** cabin is at the top of a mountain.*

resources *n.* natural features that enhance human life: *The United States has many **resources** such as water, farmland, and coal.*

restore *v.* to bring back or return: *The technical expert was able to **restore** the lost file.*

revolutionize *v.* to change completely: *The invention of the assembly line helped to **revolutionize** the automobile industry.*

role *n.* a part to play: *Marta played the **role** of leader and kept the group on task.*

Glossary of Words to Know

seize *v.* to grab with force: *The fan reached out to* ***seize*** *the fly ball.*

series *n.* a set or group: *Dana read every book in the* ***series*** *about the teenage detective.*

serious *adj.* interested and dedicated: *The mountain climber was* ***serious*** *about her training.*

service *n.* the act of helping or doing work for someone: *You can ask the waiter for more water because his job is to be of* ***service***.

situation *n.* everything that affects a person at a certain time or place: *The Civil War was a dangerous* ***situation*** *for Americans.*

station *v.* to stay in one place for a long time: *Whenever the letter carrier came, the dog was* ***stationed*** *at the window.*

stern *adj.* serious: *The librarian looked at us with a* ***stern*** *expression when we made too much noise.*

summit *n.* the top or highest point: *David paused at the* ***summit*** *of the hill to catch his breath after his climb.*

supplement *n.* a dose of vitamins or minerals taken as an extra part of a healthy diet: *Debbie takes vitamins and calcium* ***supplements*** *every day.*

tread *v.* to walk: *Kylie* ***treads*** *along the shore of the lake.*

victim *n.* a person who is hurt by something: *The* ***victim*** *of the tornado lost her home.*

Language Handbook

Table of Contents

Relative Pronouns and Adverbs

LAFS.4.L.1.1b: Use relative pronouns (*who, whose, whom, which, that*) and relative adverbs (*where, when, why*).

Introduction

A **clause** is a group of words with a subject and a predicate. Some sentences include a **dependent clause**, which depends on, or gives more information about, the main clause. A dependent clause cannot stand alone as a sentence.

main clause	dependent clause
[Some restaurants offer meals]	[that come from different countries.]

- The **pronouns** *who, whose, whom, which,* and *that* can introduce a dependent clause. Use *who, whose,* and *whom* when talking about people. Use *that* and *which* when talking about things or places.

  Many immigrants have a recipe **that** they brought from another country.

  The recipe might have come from relatives **who** lived long ago.

- The **adverbs** *where, when,* and *why* can also introduce a dependent clause.

  When Gina's parents lived in Italy, they owned restaurants.

Guided Practice

Underline the dependent clause in each sentence. Circle the pronoun or adverb that introduces the clause.

HINT A dependent clause can come at the beginning, middle, or end of a sentence.

1. Chinese restaurants are popular in San Francisco, where many Chinese Americans live.

2. People who live in the Northeast can enjoy wonderful Italian restaurants.

3. Tex-Mex, which became popular in the 1950s, is a blend of Mexican and American food.

4. Now I understand why there are so many Tex-Mex restaurants in the Southwest.

5. When I go out to eat, I love to try new foods.

6. My friend Kanti, whose family is from India, took me to a great Indian restaurant.

Independent Practice

For numbers 1 and 2, which word in each sentence introduces a dependent clause?

1 San Francisco is one place where you will find Chinese hot pot dishes.

A one

B you

C where

D find

2 Chicken, pork, and fish are just some of the ingredients that might go into the hot pot.

A that

B are

C might

D just

For numbers 3 and 4, which group of words in each sentence is a dependent clause?

3 I have a good friend whose family comes from China.

A a good friend whose

B I have a good friend

C family comes from China

D whose family comes from China

4 When I eat at his house, his mother serves hot pot dishes.

A his mother serves hot pot dishes

B serves hot pot dishes

C When I eat at his house, his mother

D When I eat at his house

Progressive Verb Tenses

LAFS.4.L.1.1c: Form and use the progressive (e.g., *I was walking; I am walking; I will be walking*) verb tenses.

Introduction The tense of a verb helps tell when something is happening. The **progressive tenses** show action that continues, or is ongoing. They combine a form of the helping verb *be* with a main verb that ends in *-ing*.

> helping verb   main verb
> She [is] [walking] in the woods today.

- **Present Progressive Tense:** To show continuing action in the present, use the present tense of *be*. Use *am* with the pronoun *I*. Use *is* with *he, she, it,* and singular nouns. Use *are* with *we, you, they,* and plural nouns.

> I **am walking** with a friend. The sun **is shining**. We **are strolling**.

- **Past Progressive Tense:** To show continuing action in the past, use the past tense of *be*. Use *was* with *I, he, she, it,* and singular nouns. Use *were* with *we, you, they,* and plural nouns.

> She **was walking** here yesterday. The birds **were chirping**.

- **Future Progressive Tense:** To show continuing action in the future, use the future tense of *be*.

> I **will be coming** back tomorrow.

Guided Practice Write the correct form of the verb in parentheses ( ) to show continuing action in each sentence.

HINT Look for time words and phrases, such as *yesterday, now,* and *next week,* to know when the action takes place.

1 Our scout troop _____ on a hike next week. (go)

2 I _____ last night to get ready for the trip. (pack)

3 Right now, I _____ about the weather forecast. (wonder)

4 At the moment, it _____ and very cold! (rain)

Independent Practice

For numbers 1–5, which words should replace the underlined part of the sentence to make it correct?

1 Yesterday, we will be hiking to the top of a mountain.

   A was hiking

   B are hiking

   C were hiking

   D is hiking

2 At first, I are struggling with my heavy backpack.

   A is struggling

   B was struggling

   C were struggling

   D will be struggling

3 When we reached the top, my back am aching.

   A were aching

   B will be aching

   C are aching

   D was aching

4 Right now, I is feeling sore but proud.

   A are feeling

   B were feeling

   C am feeling

   D will be feeling

5 Tomorrow, my troop were taking an even longer hike.

   A will be taking

   B am taking

   C was taking

   D are taking

Lesson 3
Modal Auxiliaries

LAFS.4.L.1.1d: Use modal auxiliaries (e.g., *can, may, must*) to convey various conditions.

Introduction
You know that a **helping verb** works with a main verb, or the verb that names a specific action or state of being. The helping verb and main verb create a *verb phrase*. Helping verbs can also be called **auxiliary verbs**. One special group of helping verbs includes the following: *can, could, will, would, might, may, must,* and *should*.

| helping verb | main verb | | helping verb | main verb |

You [should] [exercise] regularly. Sports [can] [improve] your health.

- These special helping verbs show different conditions, or meanings.

Helping Verb	Meaning	Example
can	"able to"	I can play softball today.
could	"able to" or "possibly"	I could play later.
will	"definitely, in the future"	I will play softball later.
would	"under a certain condition"	I would be on your team.
might	"possibly, now or in the future"	I might play Monday.
may	"possibly" or "allowed to"	You may play if you wish.
must	"definitely need to"	We must practice hard.
should	"expect to" or "need to"	We should win the game.

Guided Practice
Circle the helping verb in each sentence. Underline the main verb that goes with the helping verb.

HINT The word *not* is an adverb. It is *not* a helping verb. But it can come between a helping verb and a main verb to make the sentence negative.

1. People must play softball according to certain rules.
2. A team should have nine players on the field.
3. In slow-pitch softball, there might be one more player.
4. Teams may play from three to seven innings.
5. A tied score can push the game into extra innings.
6. With the creation of softball, people could play year-round.
7. Baseball players would enjoy softball in the off-season.
8. In summer 2016, softball will not be an Olympic sport.

👤 Independent Practice

Read the paragraph. The writer would like to replace the underlined phrases. Which verb phrase best replaces the underlined portion of each sentence in numbers 1–4?

People <u>are able to enjoy</u> softball all year round. Most players <u>are usually</u> between the ages of eight and seventy. Many schools have softball teams, but so do many businesses. Companies <u>often have</u> softball teams. Businesses play against other teams for fun or to raise money for charities. Most people <u>definitely agree</u> that the game is great fun.

---

1 People <u>are able to enjoy</u> softball all year round.

  A must enjoy

  B should enjoy

  C will enjoy

  D can enjoy

2 Most players <u>are usually</u> between the ages of eight and seventy.

  A will not be

  B must be

  C may be

  D would be

3 Companies <u>often have</u> softball teams.

  A must have

  B should not have

  C could have

  D may not have

4 Most people <u>definitely agree</u> that the game is great fun.

  A will agree

  B could agree

  C must agree

  D should not agree

Order of Adjectives

LAFS.4.L.1.1e: Order adjectives within sentences according to conventional patterns (e.g., *a small red bag* rather than *a red small bag*).

Introduction

An **adjective** is a word that describes a noun or a pronoun. Some adjectives describe by telling what kind or how many.

- Sometimes more than one adjective describes a noun or a pronoun.

  > We saw **three interesting wooden** statues at the museum.

- Notice how the adjective *three* comes before *interesting* and *wooden*. When you use more than one adjective, it is important to place them in a certain order. Put the different kinds of adjectives in the order shown in this chart, going from left to right.

Number	Opinion	Size	Shape	Color	Material
three	pretty	huge	oval	green	leather
several	cute	tall	round	yellow	plastic

- Look at this example.

  >   **two huge square**
  > There are ~~square two huge~~ murals near the exit.

Guided Practice

Read each sentence. Then write the underlined adjectives in the correct order.

HINT When you use more than one adjective before a noun, say the sentence aloud. If it doesn't sound right, look at the chart to see if you've put the adjectives in the correct order.

1 The museum has <u>metal beautiful blue</u> vases on display.

_____

2 <u>Round one crystal</u> vase comes from India.

_____

3 I see <u>tiny wonderful many</u> paintings on that wall.

_____

4 That painting includes <u>brick several tall</u> buildings.

_____

Independent Practice

For numbers 1–5, choose the answer that has the underlined adjectives in the correct order.

1 A This artist created <u>square small green</u> paintings.

 B This artist created <u>green square small</u> paintings.

 C This artist created <u>square green small</u> paintings.

 D This artist created <u>small square green</u> paintings.

2 A She also drew <u>graceful some gray</u> birds.

 B She also drew <u>graceful gray some</u> birds.

 C She also drew <u>some gray graceful</u> birds.

 D She also drew <u>some graceful gray</u> birds.

3 A That watercolor has <u>beautiful blue wavy</u> lines.

 B That watercolor has <u>wavy beautiful blue</u> lines.

 C That watercolor has <u>beautiful wavy blue</u> lines.

 D That watercolor has <u>wavy blue beautiful</u> lines.

4 A I love the <u>two silver small</u> teapots in this picture.

 B I love the <u>silver two small</u> teapots in this picture.

 C I love the <u>two small silver</u> teapots in this picture.

 D I love the <u>small two silver</u> teapots in this picture.

5 A Did you notice the <u>red long silk</u> tablecloth?

 B Did you notice the <u>long red silk</u> tablecloth?

 C Did you notice the <u>silk red long</u> tablecloth?

 D Did you notice the <u>red silk long</u> tablecloth?

Lesson 5
Prepositions and Prepositional Phrases

LAFS.4.L.1.1f: Form and use prepositional phrases.

Introduction A **preposition** is a word that shows the relationship between other words in a sentence. Words such as *about, after, at, behind, by, during, for, in, on,* and *under* are prepositions.

- A **prepositional phrase** includes a preposition, a noun or pronoun that is the object of the preposition, and any words in between.

preposition	object of preposition

Myka looked [at] the large [tree].

- A prepositional phrase can describe a noun or a verb. It sometimes describes by telling *how, when, where,* or *what kind.*

Examples	What They Tell
Myka and Lily *went* outside **after** lunch.	*when* they went
They *sat* **under** the oak tree.	*where* they sat
It was a good *spot* **for** a tree house.	*what kind* of spot
Lily showed Myka a *book* **about** tree houses.	*what kind* of book
They *could build* a tree house **by** themselves.	*how* they could build

Guided Practice Underline each prepositional phrase, and circle the preposition. Then finish the last two sentences by adding a prepositional phrase to each.

HINT
A prepositional phrase can come at the beginning, in the middle, or at the end of a sentence.

1 The tall oak tree was behind the house.

2 Myka and Lily would build their tree house in its branches.

3 During dinner, they discussed different ideas.

4 "Should we draw our plans after school?" Myka asked.

5 Their dad could buy wood and nails _____.

6 Myka and Lily decided to start building _____

_____.

Independent Practice

For numbers 1–3, identify the prepositional phrase in each sentence.

1 The girls used solid wood planks for the tree house floor.

    A used solid wood

    B planks for

    C The girls used

    D for the tree house floor

2 Lily made a small window in one wall.

    A one wall

    B Lily made

    C in one wall

    D a small window

3 Myka put curtains over the window.

    A over the window

    B put curtains

    C Myka put

    D the window

For numbers 4 and 5, what does the underlined prepositional phrase tell?

4 Myka and Lily hung a "Members Only" sign <u>on the door</u>.

    A when they hung the sign

    B where they hung the sign

    C what kind of sign they hung

    D how they hung the sign

5 Then the girls had a discussion <u>about safety rules</u>.

    A what kind of discussion

    B when the discussion took place

    C where the discussion took place

    D how the discussion started

Complete Sentences and Fragments

LAFS.4.L.1.1g: Produce complete sentences, recognizing and correcting inappropriate fragments....

👥 Introduction A **sentence** is a group of words that tells a complete thought.

- A **complete sentence** has a subject and a predicate. The **subject** tells whom or what the sentence is about. The **predicate** tells what the subject does or is.

subject	predicate
[Nick and his friends]	[listen to jazz music.]

- A **sentence fragment** is a group of words that is written as a sentence, but it does not tell a complete thought. It does not have a subject and a predicate. When you write, be sure your sentences are complete!

Sentence Fragments	Complete Sentences
Played the trumpet.	Two friends played the trumpet.
My brother and sister.	My brother and sister are in a band.

👥 Guided Practice

Read each group of words. Write *S* if it is a sentence or *F* if it is a fragment. Then write each fragment correctly as a complete sentence.

> **HINT** The subject of a sentence will always have a noun or pronoun. The predicate will always have a verb.

1 Jazz all over the world. _____

_____

2 In the early 1900s, jazz became popular. _____

_____

3 Was very different from other music at the time. _____

_____

4 Big bands played a kind of jazz called swing. _____

_____

5 Dancing to swing. _____

_____

Independent Practice

For numbers 1 and 2, which group of words is a complete sentence?

1 **A** Louis Armstrong influenced other musicians.

    B Louis Armstrong, one of the greatest jazz musicians.

    C Was one of the greatest jazz musicians of all time.

    D Was a huge influence on jazz music in general.

2 **A** His music also exciting for dancing.

    B Because his music was so happy and lively.

    C Danced and listened to his upbeat music.

    D People loved to dance to his music.

For numbers 3 and 4, which choice changes the fragment into a complete sentence?

3 Developed a new way of playing.

    A Developed a new way of playing jazz music.

    B Developed a new way of playing his trumpet.

    C In the 1920s, developed a new way of playing.

    D Louis Armstrong developed a new way of playing.

4 Armstrong's jazz style.

    A Becoming famous, Armstrong's jazz style.

    B Armstrong's jazz style became famous.

    C Famous over the years, Armstrong's jazz style.

    D Armstrong's jazz style famous for years.

Lesson 7
Run-on Sentences

LAFS.4.L.1.1g: Produce complete sentences, recognizing and correcting inappropriate . . . run-ons.

Introduction You know that a **sentence** is a group of words that tells a complete thought. A **run-on sentence** is two or more sentences that run together with a comma between them or with no punctuation at all.

> **Run-on:** Julia is always helping other people she hardly has time for herself.
>
> **Run-on:** She tutors kids after school, she volunteers at a food pantry on weekends.

- One way to fix a run-on sentence is to split it into two sentences.

> **Correct:** Julia is always helping other people. She hardly has time for herself.

- Another way to fix a run-on sentence is to use a conjunction, such as *and*, *but*, *so*, *because*, or *while*, to join the two thoughts.

> **Correct:** She tutors kids after school, and she volunteers at a food pantry on weekends.

Guided Practice

Read each sentence. Write *R* for run-on sentence or *C* for correct. Fix the run-on sentences by adding a conjunction or by dividing the thoughts into two sentences.

HINT When you use the conjunction *and*, *or*, *so*, or *but* to combine two sentences, put a comma before the conjunction. Do not use a comma before the conjunction *because*.

1 My friends and I want to have a party for Julia's birthday. _____

_____

2 We hope to keep it a surprise, we will have to be careful. _____

_____

_____

3 The party will be at Stella's house her parents will help. _____

_____

_____

4 Stella will invite Julia over for a nice lunch that day. _____

_____

Independent Practice

For numbers 1 and 2, which choice is a run-on sentence?

1 **A** My friends and I admire Julia, but we worry about how busy she is.

   B She doesn't have time for sports or movies.

   C Donica and I decided that we could help Julia, we could take turns tutoring after school.

   D I could tutor on Tuesdays, and Donica could tutor on Thursdays.

2 **A** Julia could still tutor on Mondays, there is no tutoring on Fridays.

   B Julia needs a break so she can have more time to see friends.

   C Donica and I will talk to Julia and ask for her opinion.

   D We know that she enjoys her volunteer work, and we don't want her to stop doing it.

For numbers 3 and 4, what is the best way to fix each run-on sentence?

3 Julia agreed to our plan she was happy to have the help.

   A Julia agreed to our plan, she, was happy to have the help.

   B Julia agreed to our plan. She was happy to have the help.

   C Julia agreed to our plan, she was happy to have the help.

   D Julia agreed to our plan, She was happy to have the help.

4 I enjoyed tutoring I decided to sign up for more days.

   A I enjoyed tutoring, I decided to sign up for more days.

   B I enjoyed tutoring but, I decided to sign up for more days.

   C I enjoyed tutoring, so I decided to sign up for more days.

   D I enjoyed tutoring and, I decided to sign up for more days.

Commonly Confused Words

LAFS.4.L.1.1h: Correctly use frequently confused words (e.g., to, too, two; there, their).

👥 Introduction

Homophones are words that sound alike but have different meanings and spellings. Homophones are easy to confuse because they sound the same!

- Watch out for the homophones *two*, *too*, and *to* in your writing. The homophones *there*, *their*, and *they're* are also easy to confuse.

Word	Meaning	Example
two	"a number"	Kira is excited about two things.
too	"also"	She loves swimming, but she loves writing, too.
to	"in a certain direction"	She goes to the pool almost every day.
there	"in that place"	The swim team practices there.
their	"belonging to them"	They try to improve their speed.
they're	"contraction for *they are*"	Next week they're having a big meet.

- Learn the spellings and meanings of these homophones, too!

no	"opposite of *yes*"		right	"correct" or "opposite of *left*"
know	"to be aware of"		write	"to put down on paper"

it's	"contraction for *it is*"		would	"under a certain condition"
its	"belonging to *it*"		wood	"part of a tree"

hours	"units of time"		new	"opposite of *old*"
ours	"belonging to *us*"		knew	"past tense of *know*"

👥 Guided Practice

Circle the correct homophone in parentheses ( ).

HINT If you're not sure which spelling to use for a homophone, check the different spellings and their meanings in a dictionary.

1 Not many people (know, no) how fast Kira is.

2 They (wood, would) not want to compete against her if they did!

3 She has a (knew, new) coach who is helping her train.

4 He thinks (it's, its) possible for her to be on the Olympic team.

5 Kira is working hard to prove him (write, right).

6 (Their, There, They're) goal is for Kira to beat her own time.

Independent Practice

For numbers 1–5, in which sentences are the underlined homophones spelled correctly?

1 **A** Kira spends at least <u>two hours</u> at the pool every day.

   B Kira spends at least <u>too hours</u> at the pool every day.

   C Kira spends at least <u>to ours</u> at the pool every day.

   D Kira spends at least <u>two ours</u> at the pool every day.

2 **A** Her teammates practice with <u>their</u> team, <u>to</u>.

   B Her teammates practice with <u>their</u> team, <u>too</u>.

   C Her teammates practice with <u>there</u> team, <u>too</u>.

   D Her teammates practice with <u>they're</u> team, <u>two</u>.

3 **A** <u>Its</u> not easy to be <u>there</u> each day after school.

   B <u>Its</u> not easy to be <u>their</u> each day after school.

   C <u>It's</u> not easy to be <u>they're</u> each day after school.

   D <u>It's</u> not easy to be <u>there</u> each day after school.

4 **A** Kira <u>new</u> she <u>would</u> have less time for writing.

   B Kira <u>knew</u> she <u>would</u> have less time for writing.

   C Kira <u>knew</u> she <u>wood</u> have less time for writing.

   D Kira <u>new</u> she <u>wood</u> have less time for writing.

5 **A** "I <u>know</u> I will <u>right</u> about my swimming someday," she says.

   B "I <u>no</u> I will <u>write</u> about my swimming someday," she says.

   C "I <u>know</u> I will <u>write</u> about my swimming someday," she says.

   D "I <u>no</u> I will <u>right</u> about my swimming someday," she says.

Capitalizing Names of People

LAFS.4.L.1.2a: Use correct capitalization.

Introduction
A noun that names *any* person, place, or thing is a **common noun**. A noun that names a *particular* person, place, or thing is a **proper noun**. When you write, capitalize proper nouns.

- The names of people are proper nouns.
- Some names include a title or initials. Capitalize them also.

People	
Mr. Gomez	Ms. Eileen M. Bryant
President Lincoln	Dr. Kuri Suzuki
P. F. Ling	Martin Luther King, Jr.

- Family titles such as *mom*, *dad*, *grandma*, *grandpa*, *aunt*, and *uncle* are capitalized only when they are used as a person's name. When they are used as common nouns, do not capitalize them.

I like visiting my **aunt**. Her name is **Aunt Shana**.

Guided Practice

Write each sentence correctly. Add capital letters where they are needed.

HINT Some titles used with names are abbreviations. They end with a period. For example, the title *Mr.* is an abbreviation for *Mister*, and *Jr.* is an abbreviation for *Junior*.

1 Our uncle, dr. castillo, told us about a civil rights leader.

_____

_____

2 Rev. dr. martin luther king, jr., was born on January 15, 1929.

_____

_____

3 His parents were rev. michael king, sr., and alberta williams king.

_____

_____

Independent Practice

For numbers 1–4, in which sentence are capital letters used correctly?

1 **A** King studied about the famous civil rights leader, mahatma gandhi.

   B King studied about the famous civil rights leader, Mahatma gandhi.

   C King studied about the famous civil rights leader, mahatma Gandhi.

   D King studied about the famous civil rights leader, Mahatma Gandhi.

2 **A** King's Father asked his son to become a pastor with him in Atlanta.

   B King's father asked his son to become a Pastor with him in Atlanta.

   C King's father asked his son to become a pastor with him in Atlanta.

   D King's Father asked his son to become a Pastor with him in Atlanta.

3 **A** Many people admired King, including President John F. Kennedy.

   B Many people admired King, including president John f. Kennedy.

   C Many people admired King, including President John f. kennedy.

   D Many people admired king, including president John F. kennedy.

4 **A** Both King and his wife, Coretta scott king, worked hard for civil rights.

   B Both King and his Wife, Coretta Scott King, worked hard for civil rights.

   C Both King and his wife, Coretta Scott King, worked hard for civil rights.

   D Both King and his Wife, Coretta scott King, worked hard for civil rights.

Lesson 10
Capitalizing Names of Places and Things

LAFS.4.L.1.2a: Use correct capitalization.

Introduction You know that a **common noun** names *any* person, place, or thing. A **proper noun** names a *particular* person, place, or thing. Remember to capitalize proper nouns. When a proper noun contains more than one word, begin each important word with a capital letter.

Places	Things
West Park Avenue	Veterans Day
Durham	Pen and Pencil Company, Inc.
Hanging Rock State Park	Green Bay Packers
United States of America	Saturday
Asia	February

Guided Practice Write each sentence correctly. Add capital letters where they are needed.

HINT When you write the name of a place or thing, do not capitalize small words, such as *a*, *and*, or *of*.

1 We have a big party in our town on the fourth of july.

_____

_____

2 Before the holiday, people put up flags along kinsman drive.

_____

_____

3 This july, the event will begin on monday afternoon.

_____

_____

4 There will be fireworks that night in eagle creek park.

_____

_____

Independent Practice

For numbers 1–5, in which sentence are capital letters used correctly?

1
A In the United States, Thanksgiving is celebrated in November.

B In the united states, Thanksgiving is celebrated in november.

C In the United States, Thanksgiving is celebrated in november.

D In the united states, thanksgiving is celebrated in November.

2
A A similar holiday is celebrated in Canada on the second monday of october.

B A similar holiday is celebrated in Canada on the second Monday of october.

C A similar holiday is celebrated in Canada on the second Monday of October.

D A similar holiday is celebrated in Canada on the second monday of October.

3
A In north america, families give thanks as their ancestors from Europe did.

B In North america, families give thanks as their ancestors from europe did.

C In north America, families give thanks as their ancestors from Europe did.

D In North America, families give thanks as their ancestors from Europe did.

4
A Last year we went to my aunt's house on scudder st. in Amarillo.

B Last year we went to my aunt's house on Scudder St. in Amarillo.

C Last year we went to my aunt's house on scudder St. in Amarillo.

D Last year we went to my aunt's house on Scudder st. in amarillo.

5
A My aunt served pie from Albert And Sons Baking company.

B My aunt served pie from Albert and Sons baking company.

C My aunt served pie from Albert and Sons Baking Company.

D My aunt served pie from Albert and sons Baking Company.

Punctuating Direct Quotations

LAFS.4.L.1.2b: Use commas and quotation marks to mark direct speech and quotations from a text.

Introduction Using a **direct quotation**, or a person's exact words, can help make your writing come alive. You can write the exact words of a character in a story, or you can write what someone in real life has said or written. Use **quotation marks** (" ") before and after the exact words of a speaker or author.

- A direct quotation can come at the beginning of a sentence.

  "I can't wait to see the Washington Monument!" said Elena.

- A direct quotation can also come at the end of a sentence. Use a **comma** (,) to separate the beginning of the sentence from the quotation.

  Author Rachel White wrote, "The Washington Monument is one of the most popular tourist attractions in the United States."

- Use quotation marks only when you are showing a person's exact words, not when you are explaining what the person said.

  Nathan said, "I look forward to the trip to Washington."

  Nathan said that he looks forward to the trip to Washington.

Guided Practice Add the correct punctuation where it is needed in each sentence.

HINT Be sure the end punctuation after a speaker's words is inside the quotation marks.

Example:
Len asked, "Where have you been?"
"I've been right here!" I shouted.

1 I'm almost ready to go! exclaimed Kris.

2 Mr. Mendez said Before we go, we need to learn about the Washington Monument.

3 Why did they build the monument? Alva asked.

4 Kris replied It was built to honor George Washington.

5 The monument is a symbol of his leadership wrote author Rachel White.

Independent Practice

For numbers 1–4, which sentence in each group uses the correct punctuation?

1 **A** The Washington Monument is huge!" Anna exclaimed.

   B "The Washington Monument is huge! Anna exclaimed.

   C "The Washington Monument is huge"! Anna exclaimed.

   D "The Washington Monument is huge!" Anna exclaimed.

2 **A** The tour guide said, "The monument is more than 555 feet tall."

   B The tour guide said "The monument is more than 555 feet tall."

   C The tour guide said, The monument is more than 555 feet tall.

   D The tour guide, said "The monument is more than 555 feet tall."

3 **A** Author Carter Bailey wrote, More than 500,000 visitors go to the top of the monument in most years."

   B Author Carter Bailey wrote, "More than 500,000 visitors go to the top of the monument in most years."

   C Author Carter Bailey wrote "More than 500,000 visitors go to the top of the monument in most years."

   D Author Carter Bailey wrote More than 500,000 visitors go to the top of the monument in most years.

4 **A** The monument is temporarily closed for repairs, the officer said.

   B "The monument is temporarily closed for repairs, the officer said.

   C "The monument is temporarily closed for repairs," the officer said.

   D The monument is temporarily closed for repairs," the officer said.

Using Commas with Coordinating Conjunctions

LAFS.4.L.1.2c: Use a comma before a coordinating conjunction in a compound sentence.

👥 **Introduction** Sometimes you can make your writing sound less choppy by combining two sentences into a **compound sentence**. A compound sentence is two sentences joined together by the **coordinating conjunction** *and*, *but*, *or*, or *so*. There is usually a comma before the conjunction.

The United States has many national parks. Yosemite is one of the oldest.

The United States has many national parks**, and** Yosemite is one of the oldest.

It is home to many animals. It also has unusual plant life.

It is home to many animals**, but** it also has unusual plant life.

You can camp at Yosemite. You can stay in a hotel.

You can camp at Yosemite**, or** you can stay in a hotel.

I love seeing wildlife. I want to visit Yosemite.

I love seeing wildlife**, so** I want to visit Yosemite.

👥 **Guided Practice**

Combine each pair of sentences to make a compound sentence. Choose the correct coordinating conjunction in parentheses ( ).

HINT Use *and* when you mean "also." Use *but* when you want to show a difference. Use *or* when you want to show a choice. Use *so* when you want to give a reason or show a result.

1 You may bring your dog to Yosemite. Dogs are only allowed on paved trails. (or, but) _____

_____

2 There are wild animals in the park. You need to be careful as you hike. (so, but) _____

_____

3 You should never leave food out in the open. You must remove your garbage. (but, and) _____

_____

_____

Independent Practice

For numbers 1–4, what is the correct way to write the underlined part of each sentence?

1 Yosemite became a national park <u>in 1890 and today millions</u> of people explore it.

   A in 1890 but today millions

   B in 1890 and, today millions

   C in 1890, and today millions

   D in 1890 so, today millions

2 At Yosemite's museum you can read <u>books so you can look at</u> photographs on the walls.

   A books, or you can look at

   B books, so you can look at

   C books or, you can look at

   D books but, you can look at

3 The park is open <u>all year round but some</u> of the roads close in winter.

   A all year round or some

   B all year round, but some

   C all year round, or some

   D all year round but, some

4 Yosemite is filled with <u>natural wonders, or enjoy</u> it when you visit!

   A natural wonders, but, enjoy

   B natural wonders so enjoy

   C natural wonders, so enjoy

   D natural wonders, and enjoy

Lesson 13
Precise Words and Phrases

LAFS.4.L.2.3a: Choose words and phrases to convey ideas precisely.

👥 **Introduction** What is the difference between a dog and a puppy? Maybe 10 years! If you just used the term *dog*, a reader would never know you meant *a brown bulldog puppy*. It is important to choose words and phrases that tell **precisely** the meaning you wish to convey.

- Using precise words helps to convey your ideas exactly as you intended.

Vague: Parts of Hawaii have been disappearing.	**Precise: Wetlands** of Hawaii have been disappearing.

- Using precise phrases will help readers picture and understand what you mean.

Vague: Many fruits grow in Hawaii.	**Precise: Tropical pineapples, mangos, and bananas** grow in Hawaii.

👥 **Guided Practice** Read each sentence. Circle the word or phrase that conveys a more precise meaning for the vague underlined words. Tell a partner what additional information each phrase adds to the original sentence.

HINT Ask yourself which word or phrase best helps you to picture or understand what is being described.

1 Hawaii has <u>a lot</u> of the coral reefs in the world.

     a majority   **a large number**

2 Oahu is filled with tourists who want to enjoy the island's <u>beautiful</u> beaches.

     white-sand   **pretty**

3 The North Shore is the ideal location to watch big-wave surfing, as waves <u>go</u> up more than 30 feet high.

     move   **stretch**

4 Hanauma Bay, with its <u>nice</u> waters, is popular for snorkeling.

     clear blue   **pleasant**

5 <u>Tall</u> mountains can be found on the "Big Island" in Hawaii.

     High   **Towering**

Independent Practice

For numbers 1–3, read each sentence. Which word or phrase best replaces the underlined text in the sentence?

1 Maui has <u>good</u> rainforests.

A nice

B special

C wide and large

D lush and fertile

2 The <u>big</u> cliffs on the island of Kauai were in the movie *Jurassic Park 3*.

A full

B great

C steep

D large

3 One waterfall on the "Big Island" <u>goes down</u> into a large bowl-shaped gulch.

A falls

B jumps

C moves

D plunges

For numbers 4 and 5, read the paragraph and choose the correct answer.

An inactive volcano, Diamond Head, is the most famous <u>place</u> on the island of Oahu. Most volcanoes, like Diamond Head, rarely erupt. But when they do, <u>hot</u> lava can blaze wildly.

4 Choose a word to replace <u>place</u> that better describes what Diamond Head is.

A area

B spot

C section

D landmark

5 Choose a word to replace <u>hot</u> that better describes volcanic lava.

A fiery

B grand

C warm

D heavy

Lesson 14
Punctuation for Effect

LAFS.4.L.2.3b: Choose punctuation for effect.

Introduction You know that a sentence is a group of words that expresses a complete thought. Sentences can end with a period (**.**), a question mark (**?**), or an exclamation point (**!**). Using a variety of sentence types will make your writing more interesting to read.

Sentence Type	Example
Statement	Summer is my favorite time of year**.**
Question	What season do you like best**?**
Exclamation	This summer, I went white-water rafting**!**
Command	Tell me when you get my photos**.**

- Instead of beginning a report with a statement, try beginning with a question.
  Statement: At the end of the summer, we went kayaking**.**
  Question: Have you ever tried kayaking on a hot summer day**?**

- If you want to express strong emotion, consider writing an exclamation instead of a statement.
  Statement: Kayaking is an exciting sport**.**
  Exclamation: What an exciting sport kayaking is**!**

Guided Practice Rewrite each sentence as either a question or an exclamation. Tell a partner how the change in punctuation changes the meaning of the sentence.

HINT Think about how the end punctuation you choose will affect the way the reader "hears" your sentences and understands your meaning.

1 You all must wear lifejackets. (question)

_____

2 Kayaking is easy to learn. (question)

_____

3 There are rocks ahead. (exclamation)

_____

4 I enjoy kayaking. (exclamation)

_____

490 **Language Handbook Lesson 14** Punctuation for Effect ©Curriculum Associates, LLC Copying is not permitted.

Independent Practice

Read the passage on kayaking. For numbers 1–4, choose the most effective way to rewrite the sentences.

(1) I like nature and adventure. (2) Kayaking is a great way to experience both. (3) We set out on a sunny clear day. (4) It was easy paddling, and we were having a good time. (5) Someone shouted, "Rocks ahead." (6) Then I shouted back. (7) "Can you move to the left of them now?" (8) We were lucky to escape the rocks. (9) Suddenly, I saw lightning and heard a huge clap of thunder. (10) "Oh no, we're going to be struck by lightning."

1 Which rewrite of sentence 1 makes the most engaging opening?

 A   You like nature, and you like adventure.

 B   Do you like nature and adventure?

 C   You should like nature and adventure.

 D   What about nature and adventure?

2 Which rewrite of sentence 5 shows strong emotion?

 A   Someone shouted, "Rocks Ahead."

 B   Someone shouted, "Rocks ahead?"

 C   Someone shouted, "Rocks ahead!"

 D   Someone shouted that rocks were ahead.

3 Which rewrite of sentence 7 best gives the effect of a command, or orders?

 A   "You could now move to the left of them."

 B   "Move to the left of them now."

 C   "Why not move to the left of them now?"

 D   "You would now move to the left of them."

4 What rewrite of sentence 10 best shows strong emotion?

 A   "Oh, no. We're going to be struck by lightning?"

 B   "Oh, no? We're going to be struck by lightning!"

 C   "Oh, no! We're going to be struck by lightning!"

 D   "Oh no? We're going to be struck by lightning?"

Lesson 15
Formal and Informal Language

LAFS.4.L.2.3c: Differentiate between contexts that call for formal English (e.g., presenting ideas) and situations where informal discourse is appropriate (e.g., small-group discussion).

Introduction You probably don't think much about the words you use or the way you speak when talking with friends. You probably take shortcuts, using contractions, one-word answers, and incomplete sentences. You might even use slang expressions, such as *hey*, *cool*, and *awesome*.

- **Informal language** is the language you use with friends in small-group discussions or in casual situations.

> *Two friends talking on the playground:*
>
> **Ben:** Hey, how was the field trip?
>
> **Sachi:** Pretty neat, dude. Like the museum's got all this totally cool old stuff.

- **Formal language** is the language you use in school or in other important situations. When you use formal language, you use words correctly and speak in complete sentences.

> *From Jacob's report about the class field trip:*
>
> On Monday, we visited the North Carolina Museum of History. We were able to visit many interesting exhibits about the history of our state.

Guided Practice Read each sentence. Label the sentence either *F* for *formal* or *I* for *informal*. Then talk with a partner about a situation or setting in which the language might be appropriate.

HINT More serious occasions and fancy settings require formal language. Formal language is also used to show respect for others, such as teachers or bosses.

1 At the museum, we saw a full-size model of the *1903 Wright Flyer*. _____

2 Man, I can't believe the model wasn't the real thing. _____

3 The first successful flight took place in Kitty Hawk, North Carolina. _____

4 What a short flight! Just twelve seconds, but so awesome. _____

5 Orville and Wilbur Wright had invented the first airplane, and now people could fly. _____

Independent Practice

For numbers 1 and 2, in which situation or setting would you use formal language?

1   **A**   at a family cookout

    B   speaking in front of the class

    C   making plans with friends

    D   at summer camp

2   **A**   at the beach

    B   at a soccer game

    C   speaking to a mayor or other official

    D   talking about a movie with a friend

For number 3, which sentence is the most formal request?

3   **A**   Can I go see the coolest movie ever with my friends?

    B   It would be super cool for me to see a movie with my friends, okay?

    C   May I please go to see a movie with my friends?

    D   Let me go to a movie with my friends, please?

For numbers 4 and 5, in which situation or setting would you use informal language?

4   **A**   sharing a project at a science fair

    B   sharing great news with your family

    C   presenting a report in your class

    D   asking a librarian to help find a book

5   **A**   at an event honoring your aunt or uncle

    B   asking a police officer for directions

    C   speaking with the school principal

    D   at baseball practice with your friends

Using Context Clues

LAFS.4.L.3.4a: Use context (e.g., definitions, examples, or restatements in text) as a clue to the meaning of a word or phrase.

👥 Introduction

Sometimes when you're reading a story or an article, you'll come across a word you don't know. When you don't know the meaning of a word, often you can figure it out by looking at the words and sentences around it. When you do this, you are using **context clues**.

Kinds of Context Clues	Examples
Look for a **definition** in the text.	In high school, Jim Lovell built his first rocket, a jet engine that could fly to great heights.
Find an **example** that will give you clues about the word's meaning.	Lovell's first attempt was a failure. His rocket flew into the air but then exploded and crashed.
Look for a **restatement**. A restatement happens when the word is discussed in a way that makes its meaning clear.	A rocket is pushed upward by materials that are combustible. These materials burn and release gases.

👥 Guided Practice

Read the paragraph below with a partner. Circle the context clues that help you understand the meaning of the underlined word. Write the meanings of the underlined words on the space provided.

HINT Sometimes context clues can be found in a sentence before or after the word you're trying to figure out.

Jim Lovell had always been fascinated by rockets. He was interested in learning everything about them and even built his own rocket. Lovell applied to the United States Naval Academy but was rejected. After failing to get into the Academy, Lovell did not give up. He persisted, or kept trying, and finally succeeded. After the Academy, he joined the NASA space program.

fascinated: _____

rejected: _____

persisted: _____

Independent Practice

For numbers 1–4, use context clues to figure out the meaning of each underlined word.

> NASA chose Lovell to <u>command</u> the *Apollo 13* space mission. Lovell was in charge of two men and of making all final decisions. After they were in space for a little more than two days, Lovell and his crew ran into trouble. One of the oxygen tanks blew up. The <u>explosion</u> caused a leak in another tank, and now there wouldn't be enough oxygen for a moon landing. Lovell and his crew had to return to Earth. Their safe return was due to Lovell's <u>capable</u> leadership.

1 What does the word <u>command</u> mean?

A to study

B to fly with others on

C to be at the head of

D to be part of

2 What words help you understand the meaning of <u>command</u>?

A "in charge of"

B "two men"

C "space mission"

D "chose Lovell"

3 What does the word <u>explosion</u> mean?

A a leak

B a bursting of something

C a lack of oxygen

D leaving outer space

4 What does the word <u>capable</u> suggest about Lovell as a leader?

A He is a gentle and patient leader.

B He is skillful at leading others.

C He is harsh to those he leads.

D He is weak when leading others.

Lesson 17
Greek and Latin Word Parts

LAFS.4.L.3.4b: *Use common, grade-appropriate Greek and Latin affixes and roots as clues to the meaning of a word (e.g., telegraph, photograph, autograph).*

Introduction English words come from many languages, including Greek and Latin.

- A **root** is a word part that usually can't stand alone as a word. Sometimes one root is added to another root to make a word, as in the word *photograph*.

Root	Meaning	Root	Meaning
graph	"write"	*act*	"do"
vis, vid	"see"	*photo*	"light"
phon, phono	"sound, voice"	*port*	"carry"

- **Affixes** are word parts, such as prefixes and suffixes, that are added to word roots to make words. You can add the root *vis* to *-ible* to make *visible*.

Prefix	Meaning	Suffix	Meaning
auto-	"self"	*-ist, -er, -or*	"someone who"
tele-	"distance"	*-able, -ible*	"able or capable"

- As you learn Greek and Latin roots and affixes, your vocabulary will grow.

Guided Practice | **Circle the roots in the underlined words. Write the meaning of each root. Then tell a partner the meaning of each underlined word.**

HINT Remember, words may have two roots or a root and an affix.

1 My favorite <u>actor</u> is Jesse B.

_____

2 I have five <u>photographs</u> of Jesse B. on my wall.

_____

3 One even has an <u>autograph</u> on it.

_____

4 I've asked my mom if I could <u>telephone</u> Jesse B.

_____

5 She said I could just watch Jesse B. on <u>television</u>.

_____

Independent Practice

For numbers 1–4, read each sentence. Then answer the question.

1 I decided to compose a letter to Jesse B.

The prefix *com-* means "with," and the root *poser* means "to put or set down." What is the meaning of compose as used in the sentence?

A to think

B to write

C to talk

D to mail

2 Dear Jesse B., I just read a biography about you.

The prefix *bio-* means "life," and the root *graph* means "write." What is the meaning of biography as used in the sentence?

A writing about the life of an actor

B writing about someone else's life

C writing about the beauty of life

D writing about how to live your life

3 Your life story inspires me and many other fans.

The prefix *in-* can mean "within," and the root *spir* means "breathe." What is the meaning of inspires as used in the sentence?

A causes people to become alive

B causes a heavy wind to blow

C causes people to faint

D causes strong lungs

4 I hear you are a very benevolent person, giving to many charities.

The prefix *bene-* means "well," and the root *velle* means "wish." What is the meaning of benevolent as used in the sentence?

A surrounded by good people

B showing good will to others

C liked by many good people

D hoping others are good

Lesson 18
Using a Dictionary or Glossary

LAFS.4.L.3.4c: Consult reference materials (e.g., dictionaries, glossaries . . .), both print and digital, to find the pronunciation and determine or clarify the precise meaning of key words and phrases.

Introduction

There are many places you can look to find information about words. A dictionary and a glossary are two kinds of references you can use.

- A **dictionary** lists words in alphabetical order. Each entry has an entry word, the pronunciation, the part of speech, and the meanings of the word.

> **break** (brāk) *v.* **1.** to smash **2.** to disobey **3.** to do better than: *Ina broke the record for the high jump.* *n.* **4.** time off **5.** luck   **break into** **1.** to disturb **2.** to start to do suddenly **3.** to start a new job: *He broke into acting.*

The pronunciation uses special symbols to show how to say the word.

The part of speech is abbreviated. Here it is *v.* for verb.

When there is more than one meaning, each definition is numbered.

- A **glossary** is a kind of dictionary often found at the back of a book. It lists important words from the book in alphabetical order. It gives the meaning of each word as it is used in that book.

Sometimes a sample sentence helps make the meaning of a word or phrase clearer.

> **carry** (kăr´ē) **1.** to move **2.** to hold   **carry on** **1.** to continue **2.** to act excitedly

Guided Practice

Read the paragraph. Use the entries above to find the meanings of the underlined words and phrases. Write the number of the correct meaning above each word or phrase.

HINT To find the right meaning of a word or phrase, read all the definitions first. Decide which meaning makes the most sense in the sentence.

Hank Aaron broke into major league baseball in the 1950s.

A big break came for him in 1954 when he replaced an injured

player. Aaron's talent helped him break Babe Ruth's record of

714 home runs. When Aaron hit his 715th home run, his fans

broke into cheers. Aaron carried on hitting home runs until he

retired in 1976.

🧍 Independent Practice

Use the dictionary entries to answer numbers 1–4.

---

material (mə tîr´ ē əl) *n.* **1.** fabric or cloth **2.** ideas and facts used in writing something *adj.* **3.** made of matter **4.** having great meaning or effect

---

1 Which definition matches how <u>material</u> is used in this sentence?

Hank Aaron had few material goods growing up, but his parents gave him love and encouragement.

- **A** Definition 1
- **B** Definition 2
- **C** Definition 3
- **D** Definition 4

---

hammer (hăm´ ər) *n.* **1.** a tool used for pounding objects, such as nails **2.** a part of a piano *v.* **3.** to hit hard **4.** to join with nails

---

2 Which definition matches how <u>hammer</u> is used in this sentence?

His skill at hammering baseballs helped Aaron become a successful baseball player.

- **A** Definition 1
- **B** Definition 2
- **C** Definition 3
- **D** Definition 4

---

stand (stănd) *n.* **1.** a display area **2.** an opinion or a position on an issue *v.* **3.** to be on one's feet **4.** to endure, put up with   **stand for** **1.** to represent, be a symbol of **2.** to allow **3.** to believe in and support: *He stands for equality.* **4.** an abbreviation for

---

3 Which definition matches how <u>stand</u> is used in this sentence?

Aaron could stand a lot of pressure, too.

- **A** Definition 1
- **B** Definition 2
- **C** Definition 3
- **D** Definition 4

---

4 Which definition matches how <u>stand for</u> is used in this sentence?

Hank Aaron stands for the talent, hard work, and courage that make an athlete great.

- **A** Definition 1
- **B** Definition 2
- **C** Definition 3
- **D** Definition 4

Similes and Metaphors

LAFS.4.L.3.5a: Explain the meaning of simple similes and metaphors (e.g., *as pretty as a picture*) in context.

Introduction
Authors sometimes help readers imagine what one thing is like by comparing it to something else. Comparisons can help readers picture what is being described by showing how two things are alike in some way.

- A **simile** makes a comparison using the word *like* or *as*. Look at these similes. The dog's paws are compared to dinner plates. His bark is compared to thunder.

Simile	What It Means
Alicia's dog, Ollie, has *paws* as big as *dinner plates*.	Ollie has very big paws.
His *bark* sounds like *thunder*.	Ollie has a loud bark.

- A **metaphor** makes a comparison without using the word *like* or *as*. In this metaphor, the dog's size is compared to a mountain.

Metaphor	What It Means
Ollie is a *mountain* of a dog.	Ollie is a very large dog.

Guided Practice
Find the simile or metaphor in each sentence. Underline the two things being compared. Then write the meaning of the simile or metaphor.

HINT After you find the two things being compared, ask yourself, *How are they the same?* Use your answer to figure out what each simile or metaphor means.

1 Ollie's mouth was a trap that held a giant stick.

_____

2 Ollie leapt toward Alicia like a clumsy ballerina.

_____

3 Ollie raced past Alicia like a strong wind.

_____

4 Suddenly, Ollie was a freight train racing into the house.

_____

Independent Practice

For numbers 1–5, read each sentence. Then choose the correct meaning of the underlined simile or metaphor.

1 The stick in Ollie's mouth <u>was a sword</u>, knocking over one object after another.

   A The stick was heavy.

   B The stick was dangerous.

   C Ollie was dangerous.

   D The stick was made of metal.

2 The plates on the table <u>became flying saucers</u> that Alicia had to dodge.

   A Flying saucers came from outer space.

   B Alicia had to play dodge ball.

   C Alicia had to fly across the kitchen.

   D Plates flew through the air.

3 Salad covered the floor <u>like a large blanket</u>.

   A The salad was warm.

   B The salad tasted awful.

   C There was a large blanket on the floor.

   D A layer of salad covered the floor.

4 The floor was <u>as sticky as glue</u>.

   A Glue covered the floor.

   B The floor was a glue stick.

   C The floor was very sticky.

   D Glue made the floor sticky.

5 Alicia <u>was a whirlwind</u> as she cleaned up the mess.

   A Alicia spun wildly.

   B Alicia worked quickly.

   C Alicia was getting tired.

   D Alicia was breathing hard.

Idioms

LAFS.4.L.3.5b: Recognize and explain the meaning of common idioms. . . .

Introduction

Have you ever been "in hot water"? When you hear these words, you might think about taking a hot bath. Or you might think about being in trouble. Phrases in English sometimes have more than one meaning.

- An **idiom** is an expression whose meaning is different from the meaning of its individual words. The idiom *up to my ears* means "very busy with."

  I was up to my ears in homework when my friend Mai called.

- The phrase *up to my ears* has a **literal** meaning, too. The meaning of the phrase is the same as the meaning of the individual words.

  I was chilly, so I pulled my sweater up to my ears.

Guided Practice

Read each sentence. Underline the idiom. Then circle the correct meaning of the idiom.

HINT If an idiom doesn't make sense, use context clues to help you understand it. Sometimes you can also find the meaning of idioms in a dictionary.

1 I knew Mai would talk my ear off if she had the chance.

   talk until my ear fell off   **talk a long time**   **talk loudly**

2 So I said, "My mom will fly off the handle if I'm on the phone and not studying."

   throw a pot   **get angry**   **take a trip**

3 I explained, "I'm in the doghouse because I didn't do well on my last spelling test."

   in trouble   **sitting in a doghouse**   **playing with the dog**

4 Mai said, "I don't want to rock the boat, so come over later."

   go boating   **throw rocks**   **cause problems**

5 It rained cats and dogs as I biked to Mai's house.

   was dark   **was foggy**   **rained heavily**

6 I knew I had to make tracks, or I'd soon be completely wet.

   slow down   **hurry**   **take a train**

Independent Practice

For numbers 1–5, read each sentence. Then choose the correct meaning of each underlined idiom.

1 I was <u>all ears</u> when Mai shared her news.

 A feeling my ears grow

 B getting a headache

 C listening carefully

 D unable to hear

2 Mai said, "I've just heard it <u>from the horse's mouth</u>. Our school is going to have an auction to raise money."

 A from a horse trainer

 B from an animal doctor

 C from the mouth of a horse

 D from a trustworthy person

3 I <u>held my tongue</u> even though I knew that Mai probably found out from her mom, our school principal.

 A kept quiet

 B grabbed my tongue

 C stuck out my tongue

 D made a funny face

4 Mai continued, "Let's <u>put our heads together</u> and think of something to contribute to the auction."

 A whisper quietly

 B sit next to one another

 C work together to make a plan

 D put our heads on the table

5 Mai is <u>head and shoulders above me</u> at cooking. I suggested that she bake a cake to sell at the auction.

 A much taller than I am

 B much better than I am

 C standing above me

 D faster than I am

Adages and Proverbs

LAFS.4.L.3.5b: Recognize and explain the meaning of common . . . adages, and proverbs.

Introduction Like idioms, **adages** and **proverbs** are also expressions that you cannot understand just by knowing the meanings of the individual words. Learning the meanings of these expressions can help you better understand what an author has written.

- An **adage** is a well-known saying that people have come to believe because it has been used for a long time.

Adage	Meaning
Variety is the spice of life.	Trying different things makes life interesting.

- A **proverb** is also an old, well-known saying. It sometimes gives advice about how to behave.

Proverb	Meaning
Look before you leap.	Think carefully about what you are going to do before you do it.

Guided Practice **Read the paragraph. Number and underline each adage and proverb. Then write the meaning of each on the lines provided.**

HINT If the meaning of a saying isn't clear, use context clues to help you understand what the words mean. You can also search online to find the meanings of many adages and proverbs.

My friend Omar is a great runner. He doesn't look like an athlete, but I never judge a book by its cover. Last week, we went running together. I thought I'd be able to keep up with him, but I couldn't. I told myself to keep going because there's no gain without pain. When I thought I would faint, I stopped to rest. After all, it's better to be safe than sorry.

1 _____

_____

2 _____

_____

3 _____

_____

Independent Practice

For numbers 1–4, read each sentence. Then choose the correct meaning of each underlined adage or proverb.

1 Omar said, "Remember, <u>slow and steady wins the race</u>. Run a little each day, and soon you'll become a good runner."

   A If you run slowly, you will win races.

   B It is better to run slowly than to win a race.

   C Slow workers have the most success.

   D Patience and hard work bring success.

2 I promised to run every day, but that was <u>easier said than done</u>.

   A easily said

   B easily done

   C easier to talk about than to do

   D easier to run than to promise

3 Then I thought, "If I want to be a good runner, I have to practice. I know that <u>practice makes perfect</u>!"

   A Being perfect is important.

   B You must practice perfectly.

   C You must practice something every day.

   D Practicing is the way to get good at something.

4 When I won my first race, <u>I gave credit where credit was due</u>, and I thanked Omar for helping me.

   A used a credit card to pay a bill

   B gave thanks to someone who deserved it

   C gave money that was owed to someone

   D had to give away the prize

Synonyms and Antonyms

LAFS.4.L.3.5c: Demonstrate understanding of words by relating them to their opposites (antonyms) and to words with similar but not identical meanings (synonyms).

Introduction
Words in English can have meanings that are similar or different. If you know how two words are related, you can sometimes use the meaning of a word you already know to understand the meaning of an unfamiliar word.

- A **synonym** is a word that has the same or almost the same meaning as another word. The words *select* and *choose* are synonyms.

  > I try to **select** foods from all five food groups.
  >
  > I often seem to **choose** the same foods, though.

- An **antonym** is a word that has the opposite meaning of another word. The words *forget* and *remember* are antonyms.

  > Sometimes I **forget** to eat different kinds of vegetables.
  >
  > I need to **remember** to vary my diet.

- If you find yourself using the same word again and again, replace the repeated word with a synonym. This will make your writing more interesting.

Guided Practice
Read each sentence. Write *S* next to the synonym for the underlined word. Write *A* next to the antonym.

HINT You can use a thesaurus to find synonyms and antonyms for many words. Sometimes a dictionary also lists synonyms and antonyms.

1   I made a <u>large</u> salad with many vegetables.

    enormous _____   **tiny** _____

2   A salad is a meal that is <u>easy</u> to make.

    challenging _____   **simple** _____

3   I used vegetables that are <u>commonly</u> grown in our area.

    unusually _____   **normally** _____

4   I bought them at our <u>local</u> farmer's market.

    distant _____   **nearby** _____

Independent Practice

For numbers 1–3, which word is a synonym for the underlined word as it is used in each sentence?

1 My doctor <u>asked</u> me about my diet.

   A answered

   B questioned

   C told

   D informed

2 She said that healthy food can also be <u>tasty</u>.

   A sweet

   B sour

   C enjoyable

   D delicious

3 She gave me a few <u>interesting</u> recipes.

   A dull

   B exciting

   C boring

   D tiring

For numbers 4 and 5, which word is an antonym for the underlined word as it is used in each sentence?

4 Is it <u>important</u> to eat foods that have protein?

   A unnecessary

   B required

   C needed

   D helpful

5 Can you <u>get</u> protein from meat, eggs, and fish?

   A gather

   B gain

   C lose

   D collect

Using a Thesaurus

LAFS.4.L.3.4c: Consult reference materials (e.g., . . . thesauruses), both print and digital, to . . . determine or clarify the precise meaning of key words . . . .

Introduction

A thesaurus, like a dictionary, is another kind of reference you can use to learn about words.

- A **thesaurus** lists words in alphabetical order. Each entry has an entry word, the part of speech, the word's meaning, and synonyms. Sometimes antonyms are listed at the end of the entry.

> **conceal** *v.* to hide someone or something: *Bushes conceal the entrance to the cave.* **camouflage, hide, shield** Antonyms: *reveal, uncover*
>
> **principal** *adj.* **1.** the main, or most important: *Drawing is my principal hobby.* **major, main, chief, prime** *Antonyms: lesser, minor* *n.* **2.** someone who is the head of a school: *The principal enforces our school rules.* **head, chief, leader**

A sample sentence helps make a word's meaning clearer.

Synonyms for the word follow the sample sentence.

When there is more than one meaning, each definition is numbered and includes the abbreviated part of speech.

- You can use a thesaurus to find precise words or to replace vague words. Learning synonyms for an unfamiliar word can also help you understand the word's meaning.

Guided Practice

Read the paragraph. Use the thesaurus entries above to answer the questions about the underlined words.

HINT Remember, synonyms are words that have the same or almost the same meaning. Antonyms have opposite meanings.

Cougars are powerful hunters. They often <u>conceal</u> themselves among rocks or in trees before attacking their prey. Deer are their <u>principal</u> prey, but cougars hunt other animals, too.

1 Which words are synonyms for the word *conceal* as used in the paragraph? _____

2 Which definition number helps you understand the meaning of the word *principal* as it is used in the paragraph? _____

_____

3 Which words are antonyms for the word *principal* as it is used in the paragraph? _____

Independent Practice

For numbers 1–4, read the sentence. Then use the thesaurus entry to answer the question.

---

uncertain *adj.* doubtful: *I'm uncertain if it will rain tomorrow.* **unsure, unclear, doubtful, unpredictable** *Antonyms: certain, predictable, sure*

---

1 The future of cougars is uncertain.

Which is a synonym for <u>uncertain</u> as it is used above?

A   sure

B   certain

C   clear

D   unclear

---

defend *v.* to keep safe from harm: *Dogs defend their puppies.* **protect, guard, shield** *Antonyms: attack, assault*

---

2 Ranchers defend their livestock against cougars.

Which is an antonym for <u>defend</u> as it is used above?

A   guard

B   protect

C   attack

D   shield

---

decrease *v.* **1.** to become smaller: *The size of the ice cube decreased as it melted.* **lessen, reduce, shrink** *Antonyms: increase, grow, rise*   *n.* **2.** the process of getting smaller **drop, decline, shrinking, reduction** *Antonyms: increase, growth*

---

3 Cougar populations decrease partly because of hunting.

Which is a synonym for <u>decrease</u> as it is used above?

A   rise

B   shrink

C   grow

D   increase

---

4 Destroying areas where cougars live also decreases the population.

Which is an antonym for <u>decreases</u> as it is used above?

A   grows

B   shrinks

C   drops

D   lessens

Precise Words for Actions and Feelings

LAFS.4.L.3.6: Acquire and use accurately grade appropriate . . . words and phrases, including those that signal precise actions, emotions, or states of being (e.g., *quizzed*, *whined*, *stammered*). . . .

👥 Introduction

Vague words, like *went*, *mad*, and *nice*, do not often paint a picture in a reader's mind. **Precise** words, like *stumbled*, *fuming*, and *gentle*, give more information. Often, you can use a thesaurus to find the precise word you need.

- Use precise action words and phrases to tell exactly what is happening.

Vague	Precise		
ask	inquire	question	quiz
cry	whine	weep	wail
stop	halt	pause	wrap up

- Use precise words and phrases to describe emotions and states of being.

Vague	Precise		
happy	content	thrilled	tickled pink
sad	grim	woeful	suffering
shy	afraid	modest	bashful

👥 Guided Practice

Read each sentence. Circle the precise word or phrase that best replaces the underlined text.

HINT Ask yourself which word or phrase creates the strongest image in your mind. Also, look for clues in the surrounding words to help you decide which words to choose.

1 Female sea turtles <u>go</u> ashore at night to lay eggs on sandy beaches.

    walk   **move**   **crawl**

2 <u>Confused</u> sea turtles will not lay eggs on brightly lit beaches.

    Shy   **Bewildered**   **Mysterious**

3 <u>Kind</u> people turn off their outdoor lights.

    Gentle   **Good**   **Caring**

4 After laying eggs, a sea turtle <u>goes away from</u> her nest of eggs and returns to the sea.

    rejects   **quits on**   **deserts**

5 Volunteers have to <u>put up</u> fences to protect nest sites.

    prepare   **construct**   **form**

Independent Practice

For numbers 1–5, read each sentence. Then choose the most precise word or phrase that best replaces the underlined text in the sentence.

1 Many people <u>see</u> sea turtles hatching from their nests.

  A spy

  B observe

  C note

  D eye

2 Volunteers protect the hatchlings by keeping overly <u>excited</u> visitors away from the hatchlings.

  A content

  B eager

  C pleased

  D cheerful

3 Newly hatched sea turtles <u>go quickly</u> to the sea.

  A scamper

  B take off

  C make their way

  D move on out

4 Many predators, such as crabs, <u>eat</u> hatchlings.

  A prey on

  B have

  C nibble

  D snack on

5 Pollution <u>causes problems for</u> sea turtles, too.

  A pains

  B questions

  C upsets

  D endangers

Glossary of Terms
Academic Talk Words and Phrases

academic vocabulary words that are commonly used in written texts but are not generally part of everyday speech

academic words see academic vocabulary

account a written or spoken report of an event or topic

act a main section, or part, of a play

alliteration repetition of initial consonant sounds in a piece of writing to create a special effect

allude to to mention something in an indirect way

analyze to closely and carefully examine a piece of text

beginning the start of something; the first part of a text, which introduces the characters and problem in a story or the topic and main idea in an informational text

bold print heavy, dark type; important words in a text are sometimes printed in bold print

caption a phrase or sentence set below a picture in a text that explains something about the picture

cast of characters a list of all the characters in a play, usually in order of appearance

cause something that brings about an effect or a result

cause and effect a relationship between things or events, in which one thing—the cause—brings about, or causes, something else—the effect

cause-and-effect text structure a text organization that tells about events and explains why they happen

central message a lesson about life the author of a story wants to share

challenge a problem or difficulty that needs to be solved

chapters sections, or parts, of stories or books

character person, animal, or made-up creature in a story or play

character traits special qualities of characters, such as shyness or honesty, that makes one character different from another

chronological text structure a text organization in which events are told in the order in which they happen

clues pieces of information that help you figure out something; hints

compare to describe how two or more things are similar

compare-contrast text structure a text organization that describes how two or more things are alike and different

comparison the process of showing how two or more things are alike and different

connected joined or linked together; when two or more things are connected, they are related in some way.

connection how the facts and ideas in a sentence or paragraph relate to each other, for example, some ideas have a cause-and-effect relationship, or connection; causal relations or sequence between two ideas

context clues words, phrases and sentences around an unknown word or phrase in a text that help to determine the word's meaning; context clues may be synonyms, antonyms, examples, or definitions.

contrast to describe how two or more things are different

contribute to add to something; to help bring about a result

describe to tell what something is like or to explain something

details facts, examples, and other pieces of information directly stated in a text

diagram a simple drawing that is used to explain something

dialogue the words the characters say in a story or play

digital source a text on a specific subject area or topic that is located on a computer website or provided in an electronic format

drama a story that is performed on a stage

effect something that happens as a result of something else

end the point at which something is completed; the last part of a text, in which the problem in a story is solved or the main idea in an informational text is summed up

events things that happen in stories and in the natural world

evidence facts, details, quotes, or other pieces of information used to support a claim, point, or an idea

Glossary of Terms

examples things that an author uses to represent an idea or a group of things

explain to describe or give details about something so it can be understood

figurative language writing that makes comparisons to describe familiar things and events in new and sometimes unusual ways

first before all others in time, order, or importance

firsthand account something written about an event by a person who witnessed the event or who took part in it

first person describes the narrator of a story who is a character in the story and actually experiences what happens; a first-person narrator uses the pronouns *I, me,* and *we*

focus a center of interest or attention

genre a type of writing characterized by a particular style, form, or subject area; narrative poems, mysteries, realistic fiction, historical texts, and technical texts are examples of genres

glossary a list at the back of a book of important words from the text and their meanings

graph a chart that is used to show the relationship between two sets of numbers

headings words or a phrase at the beginning of a section of a text that tell what the section is about

historical describes something based on history

historical events important things that happened in the past

historical text an informational piece of writing that tells about people, events, and ideas from the past

hyperlinks features in digital texts that allow you to quickly access additional information

idea a thought, an opinion, or a belief that exists in the mind about what something is like or should be like

illustrations pictures that accompany a text and that often provide additional details about the text

images the pictures, or illustrations and photographs, in a text

important points the most important details, facts, examples, and other pieces of information in a text

Glossary of Terms

index a list at the back of a book of all the topics in the book, in alphabetical order, and the page numbers where they can be found

infer to reach a reasonable conclusion about an idea or event not directly stated in a text based on text clues and background knowledge

inference the process of reaching a conclusion based on details in the text and your own background knowledge

influence to have an effect on something or someone

information facts and details about someone or something

integrate to put together or combine information on a topic from more than one source

interaction the way people or things affect each other

interpret to explain the meaning or significance of certain information

key detail an important fact, example, or other piece of information in a text that helps explain a main idea

key facts important ideas in a text that can be proven true

key point an important idea about a topic

key words words in bold print that call attention to something important in a text

knowledgeably in a manner that shows a clear understanding of something or, to speak or write about a topic like an expert

last at the end; after all others; finally

lesson something to be learned—for example, from a story or an experience—that imparts new knowledge

literal describes the usual or most basic meaning of a word

lyric poem a type of poem that uses language in unusual ways to express thoughts and feelings about something

main idea something important that an author wants readers to understand about a topic

main purpose what an author of a text wants to tell, describe, or explain to the reader

main topic what a selection is mostly about

maps drawings that show the cities, roads, rivers, and other details of an area

meaning the thoughts or ideas meant to be conveyed, especially by language

Glossary of Terms

Glossary of Terms

metaphor a kind of figurative language that compares two things that are not alike, without using the words *like* or *as*

meter the regular pattern of stressed and unstressed syllables in a verse, or line, of poetry

middle the central part of something; the part of a text after the beginning and before the end, in which the plot of a story or the main idea of an informational text is developed

mood a feeling a story creates in the reader; setting, word choice, and tone all contribute to mood

motivations the reasons why characters act, think, and feel as they do

mythology a collection of ancient stories belonging to a particular people that tell about their origin, history, gods, goddesses, and heroes

narrator the person who tells a story

nonliteral describes an unusual or unexpected meaning of a word

opposition strong disagreement or conflict; struggle

order the arrangement or sequence of things or events in time

paragraph a group of sentences about a particular idea or topic

personification a kind of figurative language that gives human qualities to animals or objects

persuade to cause someone to do something or to think a certain way about something, by giving them good reasons for it

phrase a short group of words that has meaning

play a story that is performed on stage by actors

plot the sequence of events in a story

points ideas that authors present to convince readers that something is true

point of view
Literary Text the perspective from which a piece of text is written
Informational Text the author's viewpoint that allows the reader to know how the author thinks and feels about a topic

primary source a description of an event from someone who experienced it, such as diaries, speeches, letters, or interviews

print source a text on a specific subject area or topic that is in print form, such as a book or magazine article

problem a challenge that the main character or characters face

problem-solution text structure a text organization that describes problems and solutions

procedures steps to follow to do something

prompt a writing assignment

prose any form of writing that is not poetry

qualitative measured by the quality of something rather than by quantity

quantitative describes information in the form of numbers or other data or, describes information in the form of quantities, or amounts, of things

quote a short passage, sentence, or phrase of exact wording from a text

reason an explanation for why an idea might be right or true

recount to retell events and details of a story in the order in which they happened using your own words

reflects thinks deeply or speaks seriously about something

regular beat the main rhythm in a piece of music; the main rhythm is created by having an equal amount of time between each occurrence of a beat

relationship the way in which two or more people, events, or things are connected

repetition the use of repeated words or ideas in a piece of writing for emphasis, or to show that something is important

respond to make a reply; to answer; to say or do something in reaction to something else

rhyme the repetition of the same or similar stressed sounds in words

rhythm the regular pattern of sounds in a poem or beats in a piece of music

scene a part of a play in which all the action takes place in the same setting

scientific text a piece of text that explains how or why something happens

script the written text of a drama, which is used by all people putting the drama on stage

Glossary of Terms

search tools Internet utilities that allow users to quickly find information on the Web

secondary source a description of an event based on research that includes key facts such as textbooks, biographies, and newspaper articles

secondhand account something written about an event by a person who did not experience it but rather heard or read about the event

sections smaller parts into which something is divided

setting when and where a story or play takes place

sequence the order in which events in a story or the steps in a procedure occur

sequence of events everything that happens in a story, in the order in which it happens

sidebars short, often boxed, articles included in longer texts that provide additional information related to the main text

significant large enough to be noticed or to have an effect

simile a kind of figurative language that uses the words *like* or *as* to compare two dissimilar things

solution the answer to a problem; or the way the main characters resolve the conflict at the center of a story

solved figured out; worked out a correct solution, or answer, to a problem

source a text on a specific subject area or topic; a source may be in printed or digital form

speaker the character whose "voice" you hear in a poem

stage directions instructions in a script that tell where a scene takes place, what the actors should do, and what should appear or happen on stage

stanza several verses, or lines, of a poem that are grouped together to describe an image, idea, or event

steps in a process a set of actions to do, or directions to make or do something

structural elements special features of texts; they vary from one form of written text to another

structure the particular way a writer organizes a text, such as acts for a drama or stanzas for a poem, that helps the reader understand the writer's meaning

subheading the title of a section, or part, of text; it tells what the section is about

subject a topic; something that is being talked or written about